CONSTITUTIONAL HEADS AND POLITICAL CRISES

CAMBRIDGE COMMONWEALTH SERIES

Published by Macmillan in association with the Managers of the Cambridge University Smuts Memorial Fund for the Advancement of Commonwealth Studies
General Editors: E. T. Stokes (1972–81); D. A. Low (1983–), both Smuts Professors of the History of the British Commonwealth, University of Cambridge

Roger Anstey
THE ATLANTIC SLAVE TRADE AND BRITISH ABOLITION, 1760–1810

John Darwin
BRITAIN, EGYPT AND THE MIDDLE EAST: Imperial Policy in the Aftermath of War, 1918–22

T. R. H. Davenport
SOUTH AFRICA: A MODERN HISTORY

B. H. Farmer (*editor*)
GREEN REVOLUTION? Technology and Change in Rice-Growing Areas of Tamil Nadu and Sri Lanka

Partha Sarathi Gupta
IMPERIALISM AND THE BRITISH LABOUR MOVEMENT, 1914–64

R. F. Holland
BRITAIN AND THE COMMONWEALTH ALLIANCE, 1918–39

Ronald Hyam and Ged Martin
REAPPRAISALS IN BRITISH IMPERIAL HISTORY

W. David McIntyre
THE RISE AND FALL OF THE SINGAPORE NAVAL BASE

D. A. Low (*editor*)
CONSTITUTIONAL HEADS AND POLITICAL CRISES: Commonwealth Episodes, 1945–85

A. N. Porter and A. J. Stockwell
BRITISH IMPERIAL POLICY AND DECOLONIZATION, 1938–64
Volume 1: 1938–51
Volume 2: 1951–64

Sumit Sarkar
MODERN INDIA, 1885–1947

T. E. Smith
COMMONWEALTH MIGRATION: Flows and Policies

B. R. Tomlinson
THE INDIAN NATIONAL CONGRESS AND THE RAJ, 1929–42
THE POLITICAL ECONOMY OF THE RAJ, 1914–47

John Manning Ward
COLONIAL SELF-GOVERNMENT: The British Experience, 1759–1865

Constitutional Heads and Political Crises

Commonwealth Episodes, 1945–85

Edited by
D. A. Low
President of Clare Hall
and Smuts Professor of the History of the British Commonwealth
University of Cambridge

M
MACMILLAN
PRESS

First published 1988

Published by
THE MACMILLAN PRESS LTD
Houndmills, Basingstoke, Hampshire RG21 2XS
and London
Companies and representatives
throughout the world

Filmsetting by Vantage Photosetting Co. Ltd
Eastleigh and London

Printed in Hong Kong

British Library Cataloguing in Publication Data
Constitutional heads and political crises:
Commonwealth episodes, 1945–85.—
(Cambridge commonwealth series).
1. Commonwealth countries. Political events,
1945–1985
I. Low, D. A. (Donald Anthony), *1927–*
II. Series
909′. 09171241
ISBN 0–333–46420–6

Contents

Preface

Since the publication of Eugene Forsey's *The Royal Power of Dissolution of Parliament in the Commonwealth* (Toronto 1943) there appears to have been no further compendium on the operations of constitutional headship in the countries of the Commonwealth. The present book is still not that. It nevertheless constitutes an overdue attempt to revive a comparative interest in an important – sometimes indeed vital – aspect of constitutional government in an important selection of the world's democracies. It seeks to do so by way of a series of studies principally of occasions since the Second World War when constitutional heads in a number of these countries became significantly involved in some constitutional and/or political crisis. Even apart from the large number of occasions when this has occurred in India, the Appendix illustrates that in the rest of the Commonwealth such occasions have all told been much more numerous than seems ordinarily to be appreciated. A subsequent volume which is under consideration will perhaps review the more regular operations of the office.

The present volume stems from a small conference at Churchill College, Cambridge, in June 1986 which was honoured by the attendance of Sir William Heseltine, the Private Secretary to Her Majesty the Queen, and Sir Zelman Cowen, Provost of Oriel College, Oxford, and formerly Governor-General of Australia. Dr David Butler, Dr Geoffrey Marshall, Mr Vernon Bogdanor, Professor David Fieldhouse and Dr David Cannadine were amongst those who also attended, and whose contributions were particularly welcomed. Financial support for the conference was generously provided by the Managers of the Smuts Memorial Fund in Cambridge, and by the Trustees of the Nuffield Foundation. The latter was especially appreciated since it enabled two of the North American contributors to this book, without whom it would have been substantially the poorer, to attend the conference. Thanks are due too to Churchill College, Cambridge, for the domestic and other facilities it provided; and not least to the ready co-operation which the authors of the papers have extended throughout to the editor.

D. A. LOW

Notes on the Contributors

Peter Fraser is Lecturer in Historical and Cultural Studies, Goldsmiths' College, University of London.

Ayesha Jalal is Professor of Political Science at the University of Wisconsin.

D. A. Low is President of Clare Hall and Smuts Professor of the History of the British Commonwealth at the University of Cambridge.

J. R. Mallory is Emeritus Professor of Political Science at McGill University.

James Manor is a Fellow of the Institute of Development Studies and Professorial Fellow of the University of Sussex.

D. J. Markwell is Fellow and Tutor in Politics at Merton College, Oxford.

David J. Murray is Professor of Politics and Pro-Vice-Chancellor (Academic: Courses and Research) at the Open University.

James O'Connell is Professor of Peace Studies at the University of Bradford.

J. B. Paul is Senior Lecturer in Political Science at the University of New South Wales.

A. J. Stockwell is Senior Lecturer in History, Royal Holloway and Bedford New College in the University of London.

Douglas V. Verney is Professor of Political Science at York University, Toronto.

1 Introduction: Buckingham Palace and the Westminster Model

D. A. Low

Constitutional monarchy was a long time in the making; two and a half centuries or so. Its principal evolution has been in Britain. But in various guises it has operated in a number of mainland European countries and in such eastern countries as Japan and Thailand. In an ostensibly modified form it underpins a good many 'presidential' systems of government, where the President is head of state but in no way head of government; and in a residual form it is even to be found in communist countries. In the style that is most commensurate with that which obtains in Britain, constitutional monarchy is chiefly to be encountered in the Commonwealth, not merely where governors-general are formally and explicitly representatives of the British sovereign within the local system of government, but in a number of cases where a local monarch or an elected monarch or a senior chief or an elected governor-general or an elected non-executive president or an appointed governor or an appointed lieutenant-governor is to be found. When to the list of independent states with heads of state of this kind one adds the Australian, Indian and Malaysian States and the Canadian Provinces, one finds that there are no less than 85 such polities in the Commonwealth all told,[1] each of which has a non-executive constitutional head that to a greater or lesser extent derives its constitutional precedents from the British model. Little systematic consideration has been given to this phenomenon. This collection is chiefly designed to draw attention to it by way of a number of studies of recent instances in which the actions of such constitutional heads have entailed important political consequences.

It is of the nature of constitutional monarchy that is has become combined with a number of other constitutional features. Of these the most important is parliamentary supremacy – the system in which not merely does an elected assembly have all the major legislative powers, but is the source from which the executive derives its composition and authority. Constitutional monarchy and parliamentary supremacy are then conjoined with cabinet government, in which executive power is exercised in the name of the constitutional monarch by those who collectively enjoy the political support of the key elected chamber of the legislature. Within cabinet government there are often many signs of prime ministerial government, since in many respects the head of government has a special position as chairman of the cabinet of ministers. The whole system is then subject to the doctrines of cabinet responsibility and responsible government. All ministers are collectively bound by the decisions taken in cabinet and are responsible in these and other respects for their actions to the key elected chamber of the legislature. Their decisions, however, are ordinarily carried out under the formal authority of the non-executive head of state – sometimes acting in council with a group of responsible ministers. With that goes the doctrine that 'the King can do no wrong', since in all but a residual minimum of instances a non-executive constitutional head of state in such a system cannot constitutionally take any action except upon the advice of a responsible minister.[2]

Overwhelmingly it would seem those who live in such a system of constitutional monarchy with its accompanying components – the Westminster model as it is conventionally called – believe it to be intrinsically superior as a system of government to the more centralised kind of fully executive presidential government – the Washington model – and its half-way house – the Gaullist model. As (like so many others) the great Canadian statesman, John A. Macdonald, put it in a Canadian Confederation debate in 1865: 'By adhering to the monarchical principle, we avoid one defect in the Constitution of the United States . . . [where the President] is at best the successful leader of a party . . . We . . . have a sovereign who is placed above the region of party . . . who is not elevated by the action of one party nor depressed by the action of another'.[3] Such encomia are regularly gilded. Thus the biographer of Britain's King George V, Sir Harold Nicolson wrote: 'The Monarchy is regarded . . . as the magnet of loyalty, the emblem of union, the symbol of continuity and the embodiment of national, as distinct from class or party, feeling'.[4] In the measured terms of the constitutional lawyer, S. A. de Smith, the monarchy stands as 'a symbol of national identity, a focal point of national loyalty, transcending partisan rivalry and strengthening social cohesion'.[5] While more recently, Britain's most articulate politician, Enoch Powell, rejoicing in the fact that in Britain 'the ultimate source of all lawful authority' was 'vested in a human individual', went on to say that it 'is an arrangement which imbues the exercise of government with characteristics – personality, symbolism and mystique – which, if not indispensable to the successful governance of a society, are highly valuable'.[6] The fact that the citizens of the United States are not greatly moved by the suggestion that their presidential constitution is based upon a misreading of the way constitutional democracy – to use the more embracing term – was moving in its homeland at the time it was adopted, and see ample, and not least countervailing advantages in it, is here quite beside the point. Most people revere their own traditions above all others.

For all that, given the extent to which Britain's 'Westminster' system of government has been exported to other – not least formerly British imperial – parts of the world, it is striking how frequently it is seen in terms of its more narrowly Westminster element only. The core of the model is clearly provided by the parliament that meets in the Palace of Westminster itself. Thus much attention is focussed on a two-party system (however often smaller third and fourth parties are to be found there and elsewhere), and upon the necessity for the head of government to have the support (or at least the acquiescence) of a majority there. There is, to be sure, often clear recognition that in the Westminster model 'No. 10 Downing Street' is also critical – the physical location of prime ministerial-cum-cabinet government which is so central to it. There is some awareness as well of what is meant by Whitehall, the non-political bureaucracy that is also characteristic of the Westminster system, where senior civil servants more especially retain their posts despite the changing complexion of governments. But Buckingham Palace is also to be found in London's postal district SW1, and a moment's thought will indicate that it is just as notable a part of the Westminster system as these others. Yet all too frequently, it is treated as of little practical account in the operations of the system, until it is suddenly lit up in the arclights of a political crisis to stand revealed as the imposing edifice it has been all along.

There are three parts to its functions as the model characteristically requires it to operate. In the public view there is first the role of what is unkindly called 'chief ribbon bestower and chief ribbon cutter'. As such it has been both lauded and periodically denigrated. The claim here to importance deserves consideration. As a former Governor-General of Australia, Sir Zelman Cowen, has put it:

> 'Let it be recognised that the bestowing of ribbons is a recognition of significant and diverse community service by individuals, and that is no poor thing. The many ceremonies and openings are associated with

a variety of activities in the country's national life, ranging from the broadly national to the local. . . . Through travel and participation in such activities, (a constitutional head) offers encouragement and recognition to many of those . . . who may not be very powerful or visible in the course of everyday life, and to the efforts of those individuals and groups who work constructively to improve life in the nation and the community'.[7]

Then there are the half-public half-hidden formalities that in such a system of government a non-executive head of state is obliged to perform: the opening of parliament, the assent to legislation, the swearing in of ministers, the receipt of ambassadors, the ceremonial inspection of armed forces, the hosting of foreign dignitaries, along (in many cases) with the generally little noticed task of perusing the papers thrown up by much government business, a miscellany of which – in addition to all parliamentary legislation – often needs the head of state's ratification, either personally or 'in council' with a small attendance of ministers.

The third function is the focus of this compendium – the distinct and personal role of the head of state in the ongoing working of the body politic. Here it is useful to distinguish between two rather different sub-sets of functions. One relates to the fundamental responsibility of a constitutional head of state to assist in as unobtrusive a manner as possible with the smooth functioning of government at its apex. The other concerns those highly charged occasions when the constitutional head of state is obliged to take – or decides to take – a public politico-constitutional decision of some, even considerable, moment, and acts (in the terms employed in many written versions of the model to be found in some of the newest Commonwealth constitutions) 'in his own deliberate judgment'.[8]

These are more ordinarily required when a change of government or a dissolution of parliament is called for. But there are more portentous occurrences as well. In the British case the most dramatic occasions concerned first the Reform Bill crisis in 1832 and then the Parliament Act crisis in 1911 (in both of which to a quite extraordinary degree the monarch supported the Prime Minister, even to the length of undertaking to restructure the British constitution to meet his government's wishes). But in the 20 years following the second of these there have been a number of further occasions when the monarch has played a very important role as well: in the Irish Home Rule crisis before the First World War; in the appointment of Baldwin as Prime Minister rather than Curzon in 1923; in the decision to grant MacDonald a dissolution in the following year; and in the formation of the National Government in 1931.[9]

When one looks to the experience of the Commonwealth, not least during its colonial years, it would not be difficult to compile a much longer list of occasions when this sub-function of its constitutional heads came into operation. There were two occasions, for example, when, as in the appointment of Baldwin, a critical role was played by the head of state in the appointment of the first Prime Minister of a new Dominion. In Australia in 1901 there occurred the so-called 'Hopetoun Blunder', when the first Governor-General, the Earl of Hopetoun, invited the Premier of New South Wales, Sir William Lyne, to form a government, but was then informed by Lyne that he could not do so, and so turned to Edmund Barton to become the first Prime Minister of Australia instead.[10] In South Africa in 1910, Viscount Gladstone, the first Governor-General of the Union of South Africa, was rather more circumspect, and correctly discerned that the politically appropriate course was to send for the Boer leader, General Botha, rather than the Premier of Cape Province, J. X. Merriman.[11]

Since 1707 no British monarch has refused assent to an act of parliament. Apart from an uncertain case in 1834 none has dismissed a government since 1783; and none has denied a British Prime Minister a dissolution of parliament either – though there is much conditional support for the view that this could still quite properly happen.[12] But, to take Canada alone, between 1867 and 1945 Lieutenant-Governors of Provinces refused assent to bills 28 times, and dismissed Premiers in Quebec in 1878 and 1891, and in British Columbia in 1898, 1900 and 1903. In the British Commonwealth taken as a whole, there were before 1943 nearly half as many refusals of a dissolution of parliament (in special circumstances) as there were grants – 51 to 110 – while in New Brunswick in 1856 a Governor actually forced a dissolution by dismissing his ministers so as to procure others who would advise this.[13]

The four most notable episodes occurred rather later than these. There was first in Canada the 'Byng–King–thing', as it has been inelegantly called, when in 1926 the Governor-General, Lord Byng, refused a dissolution to the Prime Minister, Mackenzie King, and replaced him by the Leader of the Opposition, Arthur Meighen, to whom he then granted a dissolution a few days later. King naturally attacked Byng bitterly in the ensuing elections – which King proceeded to win.[14] Then there was the case in New South Wales in Australia in 1932, when in the depths of the depression the Premier, Jack Lang, ordered his State Treasury officials not to pay some monies due to the Australian Commonwealth Treasury. The Governor, Air Vice-Marshal Sir Philip Game, thereupon warned Lang, not only that this was illegal, but that if he persisted with his instructions he would be dismissed. Lang did – and Lang was. Unlike King, Lang lost the election that followed, but the case became very controversial.[15] In that same year 1932, following upon a *contretemps* with a number of ministers, and then with Prime Minister de Valera himself, the Governor-General of Ireland was dismissed. Attempts to get the Chief Justice to assume the role failed; a *locum tenens* had to be appointed, and the office soon lost its standing totally.[16] The fourth episode occurred at the outbreak of the Second World War when Sir Patrick Duncan, the Governor-General of South Africa, refused General Hertzog, the Prime Minister, a dissolution when he lost a vote in favour of South African neutrality, whereupon Hertzog resigned and his erstwhile colleague, General Smuts, who had led the attack against him, was appointed Prime Minister in his place.[17]

It happens (as of this writing) that with at most five possible exceptions, there have been no such episodes in the operations of the Westminster model in its homeland since the Second World War. There are suggestions that George VI had to encourage Attlee to call a second general election in 1951.[18] It has been suggested too that the manner in which Macmillan succeeded Eden as Prime Minister in 1957 and Home succeeded Macmillan in 1963 might have been better handled.[19] There was the occasion in 1974 when Heath, who had lost his majority in the first election in that year, held on to office (not improperly) until he saw that the Liberals would not support him.[20] And there was then the *contretemps* in 1986 when it was alleged that the Queen stood at odds with her Prime Minister upon a number of matters, and not least over Mrs Thatcher's anti-sanctions policy towards South Africa.[21] None of these entailed, however, anything more than the Queen's own quite marginal involvement. It could well be different (as many commentators have noted) if in the 1980s or 1990s Britain were to have a 'hung' parliament; but there are many (unspoken) indications that the Queen would be well seized of the conventions that in the British case would then apply.

Since the Second World War the picture has in a number of respects been much more arresting in the Commonwealth taken as a whole. In many individual countries constitutional waters have been as undisturbed as in Britain itself. It warrants noting, for example, that in the ten Commonwealth countries in the South-west Pacific there have on a recent count been no less than 22 peaceful, constitutional changes of government, and (aside from the Fiji case in 1987) no military or other *coup* to mar the record either.[22] But even setting aside those developments, especially in Africa, which have led elsewhere, and not always via some military *coup*, to the supersession of the Westminster model – for example by a Gaullist one in Sri Lanka in 1978 – there have been a number of episodes within polities based on the Westminister model of a startling kind. The list of those considered in the chapters that follow is largely illustrative. Their implications, moreover, can only in part be considered since the principal concern here is to set down the course some of these took rather than to draw out any very extensive generalisations about them. That can perhaps be left to a later occasion.

Consideration is given in the first place to the occasion in Ceylon (now Sri Lanka) in 1952 when the Governor-General, Lord Soulbury, effectively secured the succession of Dudley Senanayake to the Prime Ministership in place of the governing party's preferred candidate, Sir John Kotelawala. Of several Australian episodes during these years which are then recounted, perhaps the most interesting, in the light of the 'Byng–King–thing' in Canada in 1926, occurred in Victoria in 1952 – albeit with a different *denouement*. Shortly afterwards there were two episodes in Pakistan. First, in 1953 the Governor-General dismissed a Prime Minister; the next year he dissolved the Constituent Assembly which had also served as its legislature. As it chanced, neither event caused very much public furore at the time. But each led to important actions in Pakistan's Supreme Court. In one of these the Court found, in strict accord with the Westminster model, that since the Governor-General had not given his formal assent to many of the Constituent Assembly's legislative acts, they were not the law of the land; while in a later 'reference' it opined not only that the Governor-General was entitled to dismiss the Constituent Assembly, but that on the basis of *salus populi suprema lex* he had reserve powers to call a new Constituent Assembly in its place. Clearly there was a great deal more to these events than a review of their formal aspects might suggest.[23] In 1962 there followed the major episode in the Western Region of Nigeria when the Governor, the Oni of Ife, dismissed the Premier, Akintola, after receiving a letter from a majority of Regional legislators expressing lack of confidence in him.

Of all the crises recounted here none has generated a larger literature than the dismissal of the Australian Labor Party Prime Minister, Gough Whitlam, by Sir John Kerr, the Governor-General of Australia, in 1975. Yet just two years later the Governor-General of Fiji, after first inviting the leader of the National Federation Party to form a government to replace that of the Alliance leader, Ratu Mara, who had been defeated at the polls, decided to reinstall Mara before his opponent had presented his list, and despite a motion in the legislature asking him not to grant Mara a further dissolution proceeded to do so. That was followed by a tangled episode in India in 1979 when the President appointed a Prime Minister who stayed in office for several months prior to an election without ever securing a vote of confidence in the lower house, the Lok Sabha.

In the early 1980s there were several further such episodes that are recounted here. In 1983 a Prime Minister was murdered in a *coup d'etat* in Grenada that was followed by a US invasion. Remarkably the Governor-General, Sir Paul Scoon, survived these *bouleversements* and emerged to become the peg upon which the restoration of constitutional government was hung. That year the refusal of the Premier of Queensland in Australia, Joh Bjelke-Petersen, to take into his coalition cabinet the new leader of its smaller partner led the latter to order its other cabinet ministers to resign, whereupon the Premier advised the Governor to refuse the proferred resignations. It was a short-lived affair, but upon the day the Governor felt obliged to accept the Premier's advice. By then a protracted dispute had begun to run in Malaysia. There the head of state is appointed for five years from amongst the hereditary sultans, and the reigning Yang Di Pertuan Agung, supported by his fellow sultans, and worried by the Prime Minister's amendments to emergency powers legislation, refused to sign any legislation, including the Budget, until eventually a compromise was worked out. During 1984 there were two somewhat unusual occurrences in India in Kashmir and Andhra Pradesh. We shall be noting in this chapter the very large number of times that India's distinctive provision for President's Rule has been brought into operation. But upon these two occasions that did not occur. Rather there were moves by the Indian Prime Minister to change two state Chief Ministers by using the reserve powers of centrally appointed state Governors. In the following year at the other end of the world there was one more of a succession of ripples on the Canadian constitutional surface when Ontario elected a hung parliament; but the Lieutenant-Governor seems to have handled this quite appropriately.[24]

The sequence thus far has no ending. Already a number of further episodes have occurred (for example in Western Samoa) which can only be noted in passing.[25] In 1984 the Governor-General of the Solomon Islands, Sir Baddeley Devisi, had to use his reserve powers to give retrospective legality to a caretaker government when it was tardily discovered by the opposition that under the constitution not only had the life of the legislature run out, but the term of the ministers with it.[26] Then in 1985 there was a considerable episode in the state of Sabah in Malaysia when the leaders of the defeated parties prevailed on the Governor, under threat and in the small hours of the morning, to swear in their candidate as Chief Minister, only to find that the acting Prime Minister of the federal government quickly came out against them – which led the Governor to swear in the leader of the majority party before the day was out instead.[27] In 1986 the Chief Minister of the Turks and Caicos Islands was dismissed.[28] In 1987 there was open controversy between India's President (its constitutional head) and its Prime Minister, Rajiv Gandhi, over a number of matters concerning the Prime Minister's alleged treatment of the President,[29] and in Fiji, the Governor-General, Sir Penaia Ganilau, moved to curb the full extent of the first military *coup* in the South-west Pacific, which following upon the installation for the first time in office of a party principally representing the Indian majority in the islands (which had just won a general election), had been mounted by the third ranking Fijian officer in the Fijian army. The 1977 antecedents to this affair are recounted at length in Chapter 7. One especially interesting feature of the 1987 sequel was the first open reference which can be recalled to the Queen's personal hopes for a resolution of a crisis.

Where next?

It cannot, however, be stressed enough that while the more dramatic of these episodes saw the extraordinary use of the personal discretion of the constitutional head, the Westminster model primarily calls overwhelmingly for the ordinary unobtrusive employment of the personal function of the head of state rather than the obtrusive intervention that such a catalogue might suggest. The starting point here has been endlessly expressed. Lord Esher for one put it authoritatively thus:

> In no case can the Sovereign take political action unless he is screened by a minister responsible to Parliament. This proposition is fundamental, and differentiates a constitutional monarchy based upon the principle of 1688 from all other forms of government.[30]

In reviewing his term as Governor-General of Australia Sir Zelman Cowen affirmed: 'I would raise questions and receive careful answers, but I respected the principle that I should finally act on ministerial advice'.[31]

In association with this there stand those three hallowed 'rights' that Bagehot set down in his oft-quoted dictum which warrants quoting again in full:

> To state the matter shortly [he wrote] the sovereign has, under a constitutional monarchy such as ours, three rights – the right to be consulted, the right to encourage, the right to warn. And a king of great sense and sagacity would want no others. He would find that his having no others would enable him to use these with singular effect. He would say to his Minister: 'The responsibility of these measures is upon you. Whatever you think best must be done. Whatever you think best shall have my full and effectual support. *But* you will observe that for this reason and that reason what you propose to do is bad; for this reason and that reason what you do not propose is better. I do not oppose, it is my duty not to oppose; but observe that I *warn*.' Supposing the king to be right, and to have what kings often have, the gift of effectual expression, he could not help moving his Minister. He might not always turn his course, but he would always trouble his mind.[32]

These three rights are frequently reaffirmed. In Canada, for example, they were explicitly endorsed by Prime Minister Bennett; and at the swearing in of Governor-General Jules Leger in January 1974 Prime Minister Trudeau went out of his way to invite him to exercise them.[33]

Yet one wonders how often they are quite as carefully followed. In Australia, for example, Bagehot's careful formulation of the 'warning' power was grievously misread by all parties to the dispute in 1975 (it did not call for the Governor-General to warn the Prime Minister that he might dismiss him; it did require that the Governor-General should have told the Prime Minister firmly – since this is what he believed – that what he 'proposed to do was bad').[34] More substantially it looks as if some constitutional heads, and it may be quite a number, are not properly assured of being able to enjoy them. Nehru's sister, Mrs Vijayalakshmi Pandit complained bitterly when she was Governor of Maharashtra in India in 1965 that (like her predecessor) she was 'kept out in the cold', not consulted and not permitted to see files; I 'soon found that I was isolated', she declared.[35] This was precisely the complaint of the President of India in 1987. Then we have the statement of Pauline McGibbon, Lieutenant-Governor of Ontario, expressing her pleasure at being assured that she would be briefed upon any controversial legislation by the minister responsible rather than hearing of it first from the media;[36] one would have hoped that she would have enjoyed that privilege as of right. Or again, there are the remarks of the Governor-General of one of the smaller Commonwealth countries, not only that he never sees a minister other than the Prime Minister except at a social function ('the only role that the Constitution gives me in relation to them is to appoint or dismiss them on the advice of the Prime Minister'), but that 'as to the function to "advise and warn", this is not enshrined in the Constitution and has not yet become a convention'.[37]

If the prototype precedents are to be followed wherever the Westminster model operates, three further aspects of the Buckingham Palace role need to be emphasised too. It is of considerable importance that relations of respect should be maintained between constitutional heads and their prime ministers. In Britain the personalities of twentieth century sovereigns have greatly assisted here. Attlee came to be much regarded by George VI. The ageing Churchill came to delight in Elizabeth II. But it had not always been so: Victoria, of course, never could abide her four terms' Prime Minister Gladstone. The need for good working arrangements in such a relationship[39] is the good reason why the nomination of an appointed head of state is usually the prerogative of the prime minister, but obviously this should not be to the exclusion of any alternative association for the former. There is in this connection notable testimony to the mutual regard in Australia in 1972–4 of Gough Whitlam and Sir Paul Hasluck, who were formerly political opponents, and the collapse of the relationship between Whitlam and Sir John Kerr by 1975.[39] There is witness too to the initial mutual regard in South Australia over the same period between the Premier, Don Dunstan, and the nuclear scientist he nominated as Governor, Sir Mark Oliphant, as well as its subsequent breakdown. Both polities bore the scars that resulted.[40]

In London the establishment of the necessary trust seems to turn principally upon the now well-established practice of weekly private meetings each Tuesday evening between the monarch and the Prime Minister in the Sovereign's private study at Buckingham Palace. Something of an agenda is previously arranged, but in no way meticulously followed. No others are present, and no notes are kept. Upon these occasions not only is the monarch informed of the Prime Minister's thoughts on any current or pending subject, but the Prime Minister, in the inevitably isolated, sometimes even lonely, position at the top, is enabled to canvas matters of concern with another person of consequence in an incontrovertibly confidential manner. A variety of British Prime Ministers have testified to the value of such meetings.[41] Prime Minister Trudeau has likewise spoken of the value of his own regular counterpart Wednesday evening meetings with the Governor-General of Canada in Canada's 'Buckingham Palace' at Rideau Hall.[42] There is some evidence too that this practice is broadly followed elsewhere. It is reported from Barbados, for example, that the Prime Minister generally lunches there with the Governor-General once a month, and this practice has lately been introduced in Victoria, Australia, as well. But there seems to be no such practice in New Zealand, and Sir Zelman Cowen has circumspectly regretted that no such regular meetings occur in Canberra either;[43] among other things that means that when the Prime Minister of Australia does call on the Governor-General there, the press inevitably senses that something unusual is up.

Beyond this there is then the well-attested fact that British monarchs from Queen Victoria to George V established a host of precedents for 'Buckingham Palace' playing a mediating role in any ongoing political conflict (as Jennings' *Cabinet Government*, which S. A. de Smith averred contained 'by far the best modern account' of the Crown and the royal prerogative,[44] and which has a whole section on 'The King as Mediator', illustrates).[45] It is worth noting the style that George V brought to this role. Nicolson recalls:

> The advice which he gave his Ministers (and it was persistent and could not be ignored) was invariably in favour of conciliation and accord. He would beg them not to make speeches which might arouse unneccessary antagonisms or commit the Government itself to irretrievable courses. On occasions he would urge them to discuss matters frankly and privately with their political opponents rather than to indulge in parliamentary polemics. He missed no opportunity to encourage such private conferences and his whole influence was exercised towards lowering rather than raising the temperature of party animosities.[46]

Easier no doubt said than done, and whilst one is reminded of Bagehot's reference to 'a king of great sense and sagacity', one must allow both for the advantages that an hereditary monarch enjoys and the peculiarities of differing political cultures. (It is striking, for example, how less smooth-running 'the usual channels' are between opposing parties in Australia than in Britain). All the same the precedents here are patent, and in no way detract, as George V demonstrated, from the overriding obligation to act constitutionally upon ministerial advice alone.

It is nevertheless important to remember that in a number of respects there is now a great deal less consistency between constitutions historically based upon the Westminster model than in earlier periods when they were directly dependent upon British control. Even in the oldest Dominions divergences have emerged. In Canada, for example, whilst there is provision for a privy council, and whilst it has occasionally been summoned to carry out ceremonial functions analagous to those of its British counterpart, as a formal instrument of government it fell into desuetude – to an extent that it has still not done in Britain – even before the end of the nineteenth century. The formal requirements of the Canadian constitution for acts to be done by the Governor-General in Council have thereafter been performed by a special committee of Cabinet usually consisting of four ministers – so that it has been paradoxically, but correctly, affirmed that in Canada, the Governor in council is a committee of cabinet and not a full cabinet'. Except as a recipient of minutes and of papers that require his signature, Canada's Governor-General plays no part at all in these proceedings.[47] By contrast in Australia the Executive Council, composed of a rotation of an even smaller number of ministers, deals with a great deal of formal business directly under the chairmanship of the Governor-General himself. Whilst here as elsewhere Governors-General ultimately abide by the advice of their ministers, it is abundantly clear that they do not hesitate to ask questions concerning the matters before them, refer them back for closer consideration, and are not afraid to exercise their responsibility to see that orderly government is maintained.[48]

But the specific divergencies from the pristine case go further than this. Not only have constitutions outside Britain come invariably to be written – and have thus become much more prone to judicial interpretation, but following the Canada Act of 1982 and the Australia Act of 1986 their formulation and amendment is now invariably in indigenous hands; while Governors-General have not infrequently been replaced by elected non-executive Presidents. In a number of instances there have been some quite deliberate deviations from the prototype too. For example, in several of the constitutions of the newer Commonwealth countries there are precise provisions for the formal election of the Prime Minister by the elected legislature,[49] where in the prototype case the decision would be left, formally at least, to the constitutional head. Or again, whereas Vernon Bogdanor has argued that were Britain to have a hung parliament, the Queen would not be able to invite the leader who might seem most able to form a workable coalition government to do so, but would have to leave the existing Prime Minister in office until either there was a voluntary resignation or a defeat in the House of Commons, and would then have to turn to the leader of the largest remaining party to try to form a government instead,[50] such matters can often be more expeditiously arranged in many of the newer Commonwealth countries where the head of state is explicitly authorised by the constitution 'acting in his own deliberate judgment' to appoint as Prime Minister the person 'likely' or 'best able' to command the support of a majority in the elected assembly.[51] Not infrequently, moreover, there are distinct political conditions that allow a constitutional head to act in one country in a way that could not possibly be used as a precedent in many others. It seems hardly conceivable, for example, that the Queen – or indeed many other heads of state – could now decline to sign into law legislation passed by Parliament as the Yang Di Pertuan Agung did in Malaysia in 1983–4.

Divergencies from the British case are most strikingly evident in India. In one respect the British precedent there seems to have been meticulously followed. Upon the promulgation of India's independence constitution in 1950, India's Governor-General was replaced by an indirectly elected non-executive President. The second of these was the longstanding Congress politician, Rajendra Prasad, a man of a distinctly conservative cast of mind who became much troubled by the reformist Hindu Code Bill of 1951, and thereupon suggested that when this came to him for signature he would be entitled to act solely upon his own judgment. He was firmly rebutted by the government's advisors. However, he returned to the fray in an address to the Indian Law Institute in 1960 in which he pointedly drew attention to the fact that there was 'no provision in the Constitution . . . that the President shall . . . act in accordance with the advice of his ministers', and suggested that since he was an elected President, India's constitutional position was in this recent 'not on a par with the British'. As he secured no public support for this stance, it has been suggested that he may actually 'have strengthened the Constitution by establishing the firm precedent that within the Executive the Cabinet is all powerful.[52] Yet in 1967 Mrs Gandhi went to the extraordinary length of campaigning against the nominee of her own party, and in support of an independent candidate for the Presidency, because she feared for her own position as Prime Minister if the former should win. She continued thereafter, moreover, to handle elections to the Presidency with especially close attention. The role played by a later President in the period prior to her return to office in 1980 (and the public controversy between India's President and Prime Minister in 1987) suggests that from her point of view that may well have been sensible.

The largest difference in the operations of the Westminster model in India are to be found, however, at state level, more particularly because there, following Section 93 of the Government of India Act of 1935, Sections 356 and 357 of the Indian constitution authorise the President of India, on the receipt of a certificate from the Governor of a state that the ordinary governmental processes have broken down, to dismiss the state government from office and establish in lieu what is called President's Rule. Whilst this has always led sooner or later to further elections and the re-establishment of an elected government, President's Rule was declared no less than 70 times in the years up to 1984. It clearly constitutes a major variation upon the Westminster model. So far as state governors are concerned, it means that while ordinarily they are required to act as constitutional heads, not infrequently they suddenly find themselves transformed into something closely akin to an executive President.[53]

One of the most notable aspects of Westminster models in the contemporary Commonwealth lies in the changing backgrounds of a number of their heads of state. Time was when Governors and Governor-Generals were not only constitutional heads and formal representatives of the British government, but very often either experienced British officials or British parliamentarians. Governor-Generals, moreover, were ordinarily known personally to the British sovereign, and thus were (or could become) familiar with British practice. But following the 'Byng – King – thing', and culminating in Sir Isaac Isaacs' appointment in Australia in 1931, even in the 'old' Dominions the break with the direct British connection gathered apace, until it is now virtually complete.[54] Interestingly the earlier model is most closely approximated in India where Governors and Presidents are ordinarily chosen from amongst former senior bureaucrats or leading politicians. Elsewhere there is some inclination to look to senior service officers (because, as a South Australian Premier was reported as saying, 'the most important organisations in the community were the Service Clubs').[55] But whilst former politicians are also much called upon, in Canada perhaps most strikingly, and whilst Australia has had three lawyers as Governor-Generals in succession, one notices that New Zealand has installed as its constitutional head its Anglican Archbishop, Barbados the former Secretary-General of a Commonwealth organisation, the Australian states an ex-Captain of HMY *Britannia*, a Fellow of the Royal Society, an aboriginal clergyman, a Methodist minister, a professor of political science, and a theologian, and that in Saskatchewan in Canada, apart from a former premier and a lawyer, the Lieutenant-Governors since 1945 have included a newspaperman, a physician and a publisher.[56] In many of these instances the constitutional head cannot have had much governmental experience before taking up the office.

It would thus seem permissible to make half a dozen more points, even if these are to a degree prescriptive. The first concerns the issue of the Private Secretary. British monarchs, despite some mid-nineteenth century uncertainties, have had their Private Secretaries for all but two centuries. There are dangers of course in the office. As a member of the British House of Commons put it in 1812: 'the office would be destructive of a fundamental principle of the constitution, which was that no one ought to use the name of the Sovereign, give him advice, or be the bearer of his commands, unless he be one of the responsible Ministers of the Crown.[57] One hears similar comments from distinguished officials even in the 'older' Commonwealth countries. But it is long since they would be made by any who have dealings with Buckingham Palace. Nor does the system depend upon any arcane social tradition; the Queen's Private Secretary in 1986 – the first to write to *The Times* on a royal matter over his own signature[58] – came from Australia. A principal remit of the office relates to the right that Palmerston affirmed to be the undoubted possession of a head of state in the Westminster system. 'A strict observance of the fundamental principles' of the constitution, so he told Sir Charles Phipps, one of Queen Victoria's Secretaries, that 'the Sovereign accepts and acts by the advice of . . . Ministers . . . does not, however, preclude the Sovereign from seeking from all quarters from whence it can be obtained the fullest and most accurate information regarding matters upon which the responsible Ministers may from time to time tender advice.[59]

Many constitutional heads seem to have an Official Secretary whose principal duties relate to the first two of the functions noted here at the outset. As regards the third, Sir Paul Hasluck noted of his time as Australia's Governor-General that 'neither in its membership nor in its functions is the staff at Government House designed to advise the Governor-General on the decisions he should take'. He would never, he said, 'discuss political questions with any of them'.[60] This has clearly not been the view of his successors, and with the 1984 amendments to the Governor-General Act of 1974, which converted the non-statutory office of Official Secretary to the Governor-General to a statutory one, the position there has in one further respect been changing too. The Official Secretary used always to be explicitly beholden to the Governor-General alone, but formerly he was still an official of the Department of the Prime Minister (and it is hardly any longer a secret that the Department was much put out that the Official Secretary did not alert them to what Sir John Kerr had in mind in November 1975). This anomaly has now been set right and the Official Secretary has become head of his own Office.[61] In the past Secretaries of the Department of the Prime Minister used to see themselves as principal advisors to the Governor-General. There is clear evidence, however, that some of them were at times ill-equipped to be this.

In Australia generally the situation varies in these matters quite extensively. In Tasmania there is a Governor of Tasmania Act – the prototype for the 1984 amendments to the Governor-General Act – which provides the Governor with an Official Secretary who has public service terms but is not a public servant. This, however, is not replicated elsewhere. In Queensland there have been written instructions from a Governor to his Official Secretary to:

> . . . furnish the Governor with information and advice, when required to do so, on any subject, or if he is not able to give it himself to get information and advice from the right quarter, and it is his special business to assist His Excellency in keeping in touch both with current events and current public opinion. He must also make himself thoroughly familiar with the constitutional position of the Governor, its duties and limitations.[62]

Broadly that would seem to be in line with the service provided in Buckingham Palace – and would certainly have been approved by Palmerston. Elsewhere in the Commonwealth one hears too of a Governor-General in one of the smaller Commonwealth countries who does have a Private Secretary who 'is my channel of communication in general, and with sources of advice in particular, including political and constitutional advice'. But even in Australia one hears of a state Governor with no Private Secretary and only an Official Secretary who 'is not equipped to provide constitutional and political information', and it is clear that this is much the case in other places too.

There certainly seems to be cause for doubt as to whether many new constitutional heads are at all adequately briefed on taking up office on the contingencies that may confront them. 'Jim', the widow of an Australian Governor relates, 'went to lunch with Dick Casey [the Governor-General] and that so far as I know was all'. A crash course [Sir Mark Oliphant's biographers recall of this distinguished scientist's appointment to South Australia] with a bibliography of required reading was administered by R. A Gollan, then a professorial research fellow at the Australian National University and by the Oliphants' son-in-law Ian Wilson, a lecturer in politics at the same University.[63]

Knowing both of those mentioned well, it would hardly be invidious to say that neither of them was a constitutional specialist. Even so that would seem to have been rather more guidance than most new heads of state receive. A Governor-General from elsewhere relates: 'There are no arrangements here to brief a new G.G. on his constitutional role'. Although there is a Canadian publication by J. M. Hendry, *Memorandum on the Office of Lieutenant Governor of a Province. Its Constitutional Character and Functions*,[64] it does not appear to have been regularly brought up to date, and with some marginal exceptions[65] there do not seem to be such handbooks elsewhere. In these respects it is no longer possible, of course, for the current holders of these offices to turn to the accumulated knowledge of the former British Colonial and Dominion Offices as their predecessors could, and did, in the colonial years, and little thought seems to have been given to making up the shortfall.

On a third point it may serve to repeat what I wrote elsewhere of Government House in Canberra during the Australian crisis in 1975. There:

> While as I understand it, on the largest issues the official secretary to the Governor-General . . . has ready to hand . . . copies of the Laws of Australia, of Quick and Garran's great commentary on the Australian constitution, Erskine May on parliamentary procedure, Evatt's book, and some of Dicey's, he nevertheless has no library, even a small one, containing those crucial additional authorities on constitutional monarchy . . . : Walter Bagehot's *The English Constitution*, Jennings' *Cabinet Government*, Nicolson's and Wheeler-Bennett's royal biographies, the key literature on the British Parliament Act crisis of 1909–11 and other things besides, not to mention the literature on all our own precedents here in Australia.[66]

If that was the position in the second oldest of the Dominions, one may wonder what may be the position in other places. Since then amends have been made there, and it should not indeed be too difficult to collect the not overlarge number of ready references to which a head of state can turn when considering the issues that may confront him. Faced late in 1986 with the possibility of a hung parliament – which in the event did not eventuate – the Governor of Queensland and his aides did precisely this, upon this one issue at all events.

In many instances it ought indeed to be possible to accumulate some rather more extensive and systematic guidance upon the procedures to be followed in many of the rather more likely situations to which a constitutional head's office is prone than is usually done. Whilst it would be foolish to expect all possible contingencies to be anticipated, at least it should be possible to provide something more like the kind of briefing we need not doubt Elizabeth II has secured against the possibility of a hung parliament in Britain. Some of this can be acquired from chief justices, attorneys-general and their like – and in their isolation in a crisis a number of heads of state have resorted to such legal advice at very short notice.[67] It may sometimes be necessary, however, to be cautious here, for situations can be cited where 'one or all is excluded for political, legal or constitutional reasons' from being an appropriate person to whom a head of state should turn. In this connection the former Australian Chief Justice, Sir Garfield Barwick, has argued forcefully 'that at least on non-justiciable matters advice may be given by the Chief Justice to the Crown's representative at his request with complete propriety'.[68] Yet since legal actions can quite readily arise over a head of state's decisions (as the Pakistani, Western Nigerian, Sarawak and Sabah cases all illustrate), it is doubtful whether the matter is quite as straightforward as that.[69] Certainly a former Governor-General of Canada has quite emphatically stated that it would have been quite wrong for him to turn to either the Chief Justice or the Minister of Justice for advice. Rather he undertook his own investigations in the parliamentary library, and kept his lines open to three or four academic specialists, not all of whom were lawyers (one knows the latter to be the case in at least one Australian state as well). Perhaps the way to proceed may be for successive constitutional heads with their Private Secretaries to put together for themselves and their successors, from one source or another, a compendium of authorities and references to which they can most readily turn when an important decision confronts them, as one has very little doubt has long since been done at Buckingham Palace.

There are probably three categories of circumstance that are especially important: the identification and installation of a new prime minister (following death, defeat in an election, or in a parliamentary vote); a prime ministerial request for a dissolution; and the final breakdown of the constitution where no readily available ordinary remedy seems to hand.

In respect of the appointment of prime ministers, the constitutional provisions, the political practices, and the prevailing circumstances now vary so much that it would be very difficult to generalise. In Congress-ruled Indian states, for example, it has been well understood that the choice of a state's Chief Minister may well lie with the Indian Prime Minister at the centre. In several of the South-west Pacific countries there is constitutional provision for the direct election of the Prime

Minister by the legislature (and provision too against no-confidence motions except at significant intervals). Here and elsewhere (as we have seen) constitutions provide, moreover, for heads of state 'in their own deliberate judgment' to appoint those who seem 'best able' or most 'likely' to command a majority, in a way that would apparently not be possible in Britain.[70] There are clearly divergencies of practice, moreover, as to what should occur upon the sudden death of a head of government. There are now several Australian and Indian precedents for the next most senior minister to be sworn in immediately for an interim period before the majority party has chosen its new leader[71] – as well as an Indian precedent (Rajiv Gandhi) for the President making a different choice. But elsewhere, in Quebec on three occasions, in Jamaica, and in South Africa, no such urgency has been displayed,[72] and a leading Canadian authority has remarked that 'usually on the death or resignation of a Premier whose party still commanded a majority, the Lieutenant-Governor has wisely waited until the party has spoken through cabinet or caucus'.[73] In the particular case of Australian Labour Party governments (to take another example), where the party elects the cabinet whilst the Prime Minister allocates the portfolios, there are now precedents both for the Prime Minister and his deputy initially sharing all the portfolios, and for the previous government being asked to stay on as a caretaker administration, until this has been done.[74] In all such matters it looks as if it is probably desirable (after full, but quiet, consideration) for local guidelines to be drawn up – as would now seem sometimes to be done.[75]

Beyond that the dissolution question can present some quite special difficulties, if only because, as the Canadian crisis in 1926 displayed, it may well not stand on its own. The starting point here in the prototype case would seem to be that no prime minister has a right to insist upon a dissolution when he wants one. He may ask for one; he cannot 'advise' that it should be granted. At the same time (as the Canadian case again illustrated) a refusal to grant a dissolution constitutes a major decision for a constitutional head to take, and it is clearly necessary to be very sure of the ground on which it is made. Sir Alan Lascelles' letter to *The Times* in 1950 (over the pseudonym of 'Senex'),[76] and a number of subsequent writings on the British view can be turned to.[77] But the particular circumstances of each country have to be allowed for. Australian Governors-General have to be ready, for example, to consider requests not merely for dissolutions but for 'double dissolutions' – of all of the Senate as well as the House of Representatives; Prime Ministers of Australia are expected upon these occasions to set out their reasons for such requests in writing (and they have sometimes been required to supply supplementary explanations too).[78] These matters can be very controversial as instances from as far apart as Sri Lanka, Newfoundland and Fiji serve to illustrate.[79] Again locally appropriate ground rules seem to be called for.

The occasions of real constitutional breakdown – except at the hands of a *coup d'etat* that destroys the Westminster system altogether and so creates a quite different situation from any of those considered here – should be rare. But Sir Paul Scoon faced this in Grenada; Ghulam Mohammed argued that he did so in Pakistan (and the Supreme Court thought so as well); and as recently as 1984 Sir Baddeley Devisi had to step into a breach in the Solomon Islands. As the Pakistan case illustrated, judicial decision may be rather more available on these occasions than too close a following of the unwritten British constitution might suggest. In this connection President's Rule in India makes much more provision than is usually elsewhere available.[80] But even in India no such regular procedure exists at the national level,[81] and a perusal of the reserve powers that may be available – and which back in 1936 Evatt in his *The King and His Dominion Governors* so regretted had not been formalised – may well seem called for much more generally.[82]

What is clear is that in all these instances a very fine judgment is required. It has been noted that in New South Wales in 1932 Game was completely open with Lang, who accepted his fate philosophically. It is one of the charges against Kerr in Australia in 1975 that he both misled and trapped Whitlam. Ghulam Mohammad, however, survived his dismissal of Pakistan's Constituent Assembly; the Oni of Ife his dismissal of Akintola; the Yang Di Pertuan Agung his months-long refusal to sign Malaysian legislation; and the Governor-General of Fiji his reinstallation of Mara. But Byng was never forgiven by his critics in Canada; Soulbury was the last British Governor-General of Ceylon (as it was then); Kerr, who had wanted a double term, found himself having to retire early; and in the interesting episode in Ireland in 1976 – in the one country which retained the Westminster system after it had left the Commonwealth – President Ó Dalaigh felt it necessary to resign after being denounced by a minister for submitting an Emergency Powers Bill to the scrutiny of the Supreme Court, which as the constitutionally authorised 'Guardian of the Constitution' he was fully entitled to do.[83] There have also been two occasions when Lieutenant-Governors of Canadian provinces have been dismissed by the Canadian federal government which makes their appointments; and there have been half a dozen and more occasions when constitutional heads in the West Indies have either been dismissed or have resigned early.[84] It can never be forgotten, that is, that the chief ribbon bestowers and chief ribbon cutters can all ultimately face the dire possibility of finding themselves becoming political footballs.[85] Thus while it may, therefore, be said that they are generally amply assisted to perform the first two of their functions as outlined in this chapter, in a number of instances it seems from the episodes recounted here that they could be rather more carefully aided to perform the third.

Notes

1. Even this number does not include either the remaining British colonies with 'responsible government', nor the islands of Jersey, Guernsey and Man.
2. W. I. Jennings, *Cabinet Government*, Cambridge 1936; P. Hennessy, *Cabinet: In Search of the Efficient Element*, Oxford 1986.
3. Quoted, J. Monet, *The Canadian Crown*, Toronto 1979, p. 20.
4. H. Nicolson, *King George V: His Life and Reign*, London 1952, p. 120.
5. S. A. de Smith, *Constitutional and Administrative Law*, London 1971, p. 99.
6. *The Times*, 20 March 1986.
7. Zelman Cowen, 'The Office of Governor-General', *Daedalus*, winter 1985, p. 143–4.
8. S. A. de Smith, *The New Commonwealth and its Constitutions*, London 1964, p. 93.
9. e.g. Jennings, *Cabinet Government*, passim.
10. J. A. La Nauze, *The Hopetoun Blunder*, Melbourne 1957.
11. N. G. Garson, *Louis Botha or John X. Merriman: The Choice of South Africa's First Prime Minister*, London 1969.
12. Jennings, *Cabinet Government*, passim.
13. E. A. Forsey, *The Royal Power of Dissolution of Parliament in the British Commonwealth*, Toronto 1943, Chs. I–IV, VIII and Appendix A; Monet, *Canadian Crown*, p. 63.
14. Forsey, chs. V–VI; R. M. Dawson, *Constitutional Issues in Canada 1900–1933*, Oxford 1933; R. Graham, *Arthur Meighen*, vol. II, Toronto 1963, chs. XIV–XVI; ibid., *The King–Byng Affair*, Toronto 1967; H. B. Neatby *William Lyon Mackenzie King*, vol. II, London 1963, Chs. 8–9.
15. H. V. Evatt, *The King and His Dominion Governors*, Oxford 1936, Chs. XIX; B. Foott, *Dismissal of a Premier. The Philip Game Papers*, Sydney 1968; J. M. Ward, 'The Dismissal', in H. Radi and P. Spearitt eds., *Jack Lang*, Sydney 1977.
16. Earl of Longford and T. P. O'Neill, *Eamon de Valera*, London 1970, ch. 23; D. McMahon, 'The Chief Justice and the Governor-General Controversy in 1932', *The Irish Jurist*, XVII (N.S.), 1982, pp. 145–167.

17. Forsey, op.cit., Ch. VII; P. N. S. Mansergh, *Survey of British Commonwealth Affairs. Problems of External Policy 1931–1939*, Oxford 1952, ch. X.
18. J. W. Wheeler-Bennett, *King George VI*, London 1958, pp. 791–4.
19. See the comments in A. Howard, *RAB. The Life of R. A. Butler*, London 1987, chs. 13, 15; and R. Churchill, *The Fight for the Tory Leadership*, London 1964.
20. See H. Wilson, *Final Term*, London 1979, p. 11.
21. *The Sunday Times*, 20, 27 July 1986.
22. G. Fry, 'Succession of Government in the Post-Colonial States of the South Pacific: New Support for Constitutionalism?', *Politics*, 18, 1, 1983, pp. 48–60.
23. W. I. Jennings, *Constitutional Problems in Pakistan*, Cambridge 1957.
24. J. R. Mallory, 'An Affair of Discretion', *Queen's Quarterly*, 92/4, winter 1985, pp. 758–64.
25. Y. Ghai, 'The Westminster Model in the South Pacific: the Case of Western Samoa', *Public Law*, winter 1986, pp. 597–621.
26. Australian Department of Foreign Affairs, *Backgrounder*, September 1984, pp. 2–3.
27. See *Tun Datu Haji Mustapha bin Datu Harun v. Tun Datuk Haji Mohammad Adnan Robert and Datuk Joseph Pairin Kitingan*, Malayasia High Court in Borneo, Suit K 467 of 1985; *Far Eastern Economic Review*, 24 April 1986.
28. *The Sunday Times*, 27 July 1986.
29. See many an Indian newspaper from March 1987 onwards. An extensive list of episodes is provided in the Appendix to this volume.
30. See his whole memorandum, M. V. Brett, ed., *Journals and Letters of Reginald, Viscount Esher*, vol. III, London 1937, pp. 126–9.
31. Sir Zelman Cowen's Commonwealth Lectures, Cambridge 1984, lecture 4.
32. W. Bagehot, *The English Constitution*, London 1967 edition, p. 111.
33. Monet, *Canadian Crown*, p. 67.
34. see D. A. Low, 'Wearing the Crown: New reflections on the Dismissal 1975', *Politics*, 19, 1, May 1984, pp. 18–24.
35. *Tribune* (Punjab), 21 November 1965.
36. Monet, *Canadian Crown*, p. 68.
37. This and subsequent unattributed quotations are from personal communications or interviews.
38. See P. Hasluck, *The Office of Governor-General*, Melbourne 1979, p. 33; for an illuminating account of an earlier relationship see J. Adam Smith, *John Buchan*, London 1965, pp. 395–9, 437–41.
39. Hasluck, *Governor-General*, Melbourne 1979, p. 33; J. Kerr, *Matters for Judgment*, Melbourne 1978.
40. S. Cockburn and D. Ellyard, *Oliphant*, Adelaide 1981, chs. 20–22.
41. e.g. *The Sunday Times Magazine*, 13 April 1986.
42. Monet, *Canadian Crown*, p. 69.
43. Hasluck, *Governor-General*, pp. 32; Cowen, 'Governor-General', pp. 140–1.
44. de Smith, *Constitutional and Administrative Law*, p. 99.
45. Jennings, *Cabinet Government*, ch. XII, 6.
46. Nicolson, *George V*, p. 121.

47. J. R. Mallory, *The Structure of Canadian Government*, Toronto 1971, pp. 65–8. See also J. T. Saywell, *The Office of Lieutenant-Governor*, Toronto 1957.
48. Hasluck, *Governor-General*, pp. 18–21, 35–42; Cowen, 'Governor-General', pp. 141–2.
49. see generally de Smith, *New Commonwealth*, pp. 90–9.
50. V. Bogdanor, *No Overall Majority*, London 1986; see also V. Bogdanor, *Multi Party Politics and the Constitution*, Cambridge 1983; D. Butler, *Governing without a Majority: Dilemmas for Hung Parliaments in Britain*, London 1983, and R. Brazier, 'Government Formation from a Hung Parliament', *Public Law*, autumn 1986, pp. 387–406.
51. de Smith, *New Commonwealth*, p. 95–6.
52. G. Austin, *The Indian Constitution*, Oxford 1966, pp. 135–43.
53. P. Singh, *Governor's Office in Independent India*, Deoghar 1968; J. R. Siwach, *The Office of Governor*, Delhi 1977; ibid. *Politics of President's Rule in India*, Simla 1979; R. Maheswari, *President's Rule in India*, Delhi 1977; B. D. Dua, *Presidential Rule in India 1950–1974*, Delhi 1979; M. S. Dahiya, *Office of the Governor in India*, Delhi 1979.
54. C. Cuneen, *The King's Men*, Sydney 1983.
55. Cockburn and Ellyard, *Oliphant*, p. 282.
56. E. Eager, *Saskatchewan Government*, Saskatoon 1980.
57. Wheeler-Bennett, *George VI*, Appendix B. See more generally P. H. Emden, *Behind the Throne*, London 1934; H. J. Laski, 'The King's Secretary', *Fortnightly Review*, 158, July–December 1942; R. Churchill, *They Serve the Queen*, London 1953; D. Morrah, *The Work of the Queen*, London 1958.
58. *The Times*, 28 July 1986.
59. quoted Emden, *Behind the Throne*, p. 15.
60. Hasluck, *Governor-General*, p. 21.
61. see Office of the Official Secretary to the Governor-General, *Annual Report 1985–86* etc., Canberra 1986–
62. The Queensland Constitution Act had been amended in 1977 to provide, Section 14(2), that in the exercise of his power to appoint and dismiss ministers the Governor 'shall not be subject to any direction by any person whatsoever nor be limited as to his sources of advice'.
63. Cockburn and Ellyard, *Oliphant*, p. 284.
64. Ottawa: Ministry of Justice 1955.
65. e.g. L. J. Rose, *The Framework of Government in New South Wales*, Sydney 1972, chs. II, III. (Mr Rose was at the time Official Secretary to the Governor of New South Wales).
66. Low, 'Wearing the Crown', p. 22.
67. D. Markwell, 'On Advice from the Chief Justice', *Quadrant*, July 1985, pp. 38–42.
68. G. Barwick, *Sir John Did His Duty*, Wahroonga 1983, p. 94.
69. The Pakistan and Western Nigerian cases are reviewed later in this volume. On the Sarawak case see *Ningkan's Case*, 2 Malay Law Journal, 187, 1966, and 238, 1968. On the Sabah case see fn. 27 on previous page.
70. de Smith, *New Commonwealth*, pp. 95–6; see also Y. Ghai 'The Making of the Independence Constitution', in P. Larmour, ed., *Solomon Islands Politics*, Suva 1984, Ch. 2. For the Irish precedent for the election of the

head of government see P. N. S. Mansergh, *The Irish Free State*, London 1934, p. 152.

71. Following the deaths of Lyons (1939), Curtin (1945), Holt (1967), Nehru (1964) and Sastri (1966). (The decision following Holt's death has been strongly criticised in J. Killen, *Inside Australian Politics*, North Ryde 1985, pp. 121–2). The Australian High Commissioner in India in 1964 has mentioned in a personal communication that President Radhakhrishnan told him that upon Nehru's death he had consciously followed the Australian precedent. (There was a further Australian episode of this kind when in Queensland upon Pizzey's death in 1968, Chalk became Premier for a week before being superseded by Bjelke-Petersen).
72. Following the deaths of Duplessis (1959), Sauve (1960), Johnson (1968), Sangster (1967), Strijdom (1958), and Verwoerd (1966).
73. J. T. Saywell, 'The Lieutenant-Governors', in D. J. Bellamy, J. H. Pammett, D. C. Rowat, *The Provincial Political Systems*, Toronto 1976, p. 302.
74. Cf. the new Prime Minister Whitlam's actions in 1972 and the new Prime Minister Hawke's actions in 1982.
75. For some comparisons see V. Bogdanor, 'The Government Formation Process in the Constitutional Monarchies of North-West Europe', in D. Kavanagh and G. Peale, *Comparative Government and Politics*, London 1984, ch. 3.
76. *The Times*, 2 May 1950 (the text is most easily provided by Wheeler-Bennett, *George VI*, p. 775).
77. e.g. B. S. Markesinis, *The Theory and Practice of Dissolution of Parliament*, Cambridge 1972.
78. e.g. 'Dissolving Both Houses of Parliament', in Sir Robert Menzies, *The Measure of the Years*, Melbourne 1970, ch. 5.
79. A. J. Wilson, 'The Governor-General and the Two Dissolutions of Parliament, December 5 1959 and April 23 1960', *Ceylon Journal of Historical and Social Studies*, 3, 2, July–December 1960, pp. 187–207; P. Neary, 'Changing Government: The 1971–72 Newfoundland Example', *Dalhousie Law Review*, V, 3, November 1979, pp. 631–57; D. J. Murray, 'The Governor-General in Fiji's constitutional crisis', *Politics*, XII (2), November 1978, pp. 230–8.
80. For one similarity in Malaysia see *Ningkan's Case*, fn. 69 above.
81. D. A. Low, 'Emergencies and Elections in India', in G. Martel ed., *Studies in British Imperial History*, London 1986, ch. 6.
82. The Australian Constitutional Commission established in 1985 is looking into this possibility.
83. D. G. Morgan, *Constitutional Laws of Ireland*, Blackrock, Co. Dublin, 1985, pp. 14, 74–5.
84. See Appendix A.
85. See, for example, 'The Occupational Hazards of Present-Day Heads of State in the Commonwealth Caribbean', in Sir Fred Phillips, *West Indian Constitutions: Post-Independence Reform*, New York 1985, ch. X. For some unusual counter examples see Azlan Shah, 'The Role of Constitutional Rulers in Malayasia' in F. A. Trindade and H. P. Lee, *The Constitution of Malaysia*, Singapore 1986, pp. 80–2.

2 Setting a Precedent by Breaking a Precedent: Lord Soulbury in Ceylon, 1952[1]

James Manor

This chapter and chapter 8, which deals with an episode in India, are partly meant to stand on their own as case studies. But they are also intended to suggest that the Westminster model when exported contains a flaw which is absent in the system as it operates within Britain. The flaw seldom manifests itself, but when it does it raises serious questions of fairness that can undermine public confidence in the impartiality of political institutions.

We need to pay close attention to the manner in which heads of state in the Commonwealth obtain their offices. Only the British monarch succeeds to his or her position by heredity. All other heads of state in Westminster systems are selected, and many of them are in effect chosen by a single person – the Prime Minister – after little or no bipartisan consultation, or consultation with anyone at all.[2] It is in this that the flaw resides. The scrupulously non-partisan behaviour of British monarchs follows logically both from constitutional precedents and from the process by which they obtain their high office. Heads of state in the Commonwealth no doubt feel constrained to behave in an even-handed manner by the example of British monarchs, by British and Commonwealth precedents and by their own role as figures expressing national unity. But those who have been selected by a prime minister who stands in the thick of the partisan political conflict, may also feel countervailing pressures either to prove helpful to their benefactor or to go further than even-handedness would require to demonstrate that they are not bound by any such obligation. Most Commonwealth heads of state have not behaved in a partisan manner, but a few have and we need to come to terms with this.

It must of course be emphasised that the considerations which motivate Commonwealth Prime Ministers in choosing heads of state vary enormously. The nadir was probably reached in 1982, when the Indian Prime Minister, Mrs Indira Gandhi, selected as President (head of state) a man who had disgraced himself by commending the memory of Adolf Hitler to the Indian Parliament. He qualified in her eyes precisely because he *had* disgraced himself and would therefore owe his elevation to the Presidency entirely to her, so that if she needed his assistance – in, for example, a hung parliament – he would be very likely to provide it. Mrs Gandhi's grotesque criteria were radically different from those used by most other Commonwealth Prime Ministers, including her father, Jawaharlal Nehru. But the case discussed in this chapter set a much less objectionable precedent for partisan transactional relationships between prime ministers and heads of state in Ceylon (Sri Lanka) – a precedent that was faithfully adhered to at every subsequent opportunity. And when when *no* transactional element is intended, a head of state who owes his office to the leader of the ruling party may feel – as a British monarch never does – at least a modest impulse in a crisis to respond to, or to kick against that fact.

Anyone with more than a superficial understanding of the recent political history of Sri Lanka will know that the conventions, precedents and norms associated with Westminster (or with any liberal order) have undergone erosion there. This has occurred, to some extent, under all of the island's eight post-independence governments and it has been particularly noticeable under the last two. For example, during Mrs Bandaranaike's most recent Prime Ministership (1970–1977), a new constitution was introduced during the second of the five years which she was elected to serve. But since it gave her government a five-year term in office beginning from the constitution's enactment, it had the effect of prolonging the lifetime of her government without any further reference to the electorate. When asked whether this conformed to the proprieties of politics as they have been practised at Westminster, one of Mrs Bandaranaike's close advisors said 'not in the least – it was just power'.[3]

After her government was defeated at the election of 1977, its successor was similarly cavalier in its ways. Retrospective legislation was passed and then used to strip Mrs Bandaranaike of her civic rights – barring her from public life – for seven years as a result of her 'abuse of power' during her prime ministership. This was after she had been tricked into participating in the drafting of a new constitution by false promises from the government of J. R. Jayewardene that the process was only intended to amend the old one. This was hardly likely to win the bipartisan support which in liberal systems is usually sought when fundamental consitutional change is proposed. And since its passage in 1978 the constitution has often been used and hastily amended to serve the partisan needs of the ruling party. In late 1982, an amendment was passed prolonging the life of the Parliament elected in 1977 by a further six years without a general election. This was put to the people in a referendum, but government supporters engaged in so many illegalities and so much intimidation in the run-up to the referendum that the 'yes' vote which was obtained must be regarded with some scepticism.[4]

Lest these comments be seen as yet another example of Anglo-Saxon tut-tutting at the failure of brethren in the non-Western Commonwealth to 'maintain standards', three pertinent points should be added. First, these events deserve attention precisely because Sri Lanka remains a potentially vibrant democracy. Second, the voices that have complained most bitterly about the flouting of democratic norms are Sri Lankan.[5] Finally – to come directly to the subject of this chapter – the first major violation of the conventions of Westminster to occur in the island was the work of an Englishman, none other than its second Governor-General, Lord Soulbury.[6]

After a distinguished career at Oxford and in the First World War, Herwald Ramsbotham (as Lord Soulbury was then known) was elected a Conservative Member of Parliament for Lancaster at the third attempt in 1929. After spells as a parliamentary secretary at the Ministry of Education and then at Agriculture and Fisheries, he was made Minister of Pensions in 1936. After three years in that job, he was appointed a Privy Councillor and First Commissioner of Works. In 1940, he became President of the Board of Education (that is, Minister of Education) until 1941 when, at the age of 54, he was eased out of ministerial office and into the House of Lords. Thereafter, he served as Chairman of the Assistance Board and of the Burnham Committees, but these posts were of such minor importance as to be a bitter anti-climax after a brief period as a senior minister. Then in 1944, he was invited to head the Commission being sent to Ceylon (as it was then known) to recommend constitutional advances to be granted to the island after the war.

At first glance this may not have seemed a particularly inspiring appointment, but the goodwill which developed between Soulbury and key members of the Ceylonese political elite appeared to hold out some promise for the future. This point will be examined in more detail in due course, since it has a direct bearing on the present discussion. But for now, it is enough to say that when Ceylon was granted her independence on 4 February 1948, the last Governor, Sir Henry Monck-Mason Moore – who had supported the appeals of the first Prime Minister, D. S.

Senanayake, for a rapid grant of full independence – was invited by the island's new government to stay on as the first Governor-General. This was the most exalted office in the island, a role in the political system akin to that of the monarch in Britain, and Moore was pleased with the invitation as a sign of the new government's regard for him. But after a long career in which he had exercised considerable autocratic powers in various colonies, he was also rather bored,[7] and he remained in Ceylon for just over a year. In 1949, Lord Soulbury accepted the invitation of the island's government to succeed him.

The new Governor-General found the atmosphere in Ceylon quite congenial. The tiny westernised elite which dominated the island's politics in those days took great delight in the notion that Ceylon represented 'a little bit of England'[8] at the extremities of Asia. Nearly all of them spoke and thought in English most of the time, wore western clothes, and indulged anglicised tastes. The first Prime Minister, D. S. Senanayake, was far more inclined to operate in the manner of the Prime Ministers of the older Dominions – a Menzies or a Mackenzie King – than to adopt the new mode which was being established by his neighbour Jawaharlal Nehru. Senanayake's Ceylon (unlike India) retained its ties to the British Crown and was very much an ally of Britain, part of the chain of imperial defence providing naval and air bases linking Suez with Singapore and the Antipodes beyond. Perhaps the most telling – and, from the perspective of today, astonishing – indication of their attitudes was the continued use after independence in 1948 (as a matter of routine until 1951 and optionally thereafter) of the Union Jack alongside the Lion Flag of Lanka on public buildings and occasions, and frequent playing of 'God Save the Queen'.

Lord Soulbury suited the tastes of the island's political elite splendidly. With his monocle and rather old-fashioned sartorial elegance, he seemed the quintessential English gentleman of the old school. His first two and a half years in the island passed off uneventfully but in 1952 things changed. On 21 March, Prime Minister D. S. Senanayake suffered a stroke and fell from his horse during his early morning ride and was rushed to hospital, unconscious. He died the following afternoon.[9] Lord Soulbury had only recently reached Britain where he planned a holiday. Ceylon's Chief Justice, Sir Alan Rose, who was standing in for him had strict instructions from the Governor-General that if the prime ministership fell vacant, no action was to be taken until he returned to the island. It took him five days to do so and in that time, a great deal of discussion occurred in political circles and in the Ceylon press about a possible successor.

There were two candidates: Sir John Kotelawala and Dudley Senanayake. Of these, Sir John – the nephew of the late Prime Minister – seemed at first glance the more likely choice. He had held ministerial rank since 1936, whereas his much younger rival had less than five years in the Cabinet. He was deputy leader of the ruling party, its chief organiser and the manager of its funds. He also held the post of Leader of the House which was regarded as the *de facto* deputy Prime Ministership and he had presided over the government's affairs during D. S. Senanayake's absences from Ceylon. Dudley Senanayake, the son of the late Prime Minister, had the closest family tie, but he had displayed an odd diffidence as Minister of Agriculture and Lands which on occasion had seemed to be a melancholy aversion to politics. His appointment to that hugely important post had caused a sensation, partly because of his inexperience and partly because it smacked of nepotism.

In the days between D. S. Senanayake's fall and the return of the Governor-General, a clear view had formed – in Parliament and in the ruling party – that Sir John Kotelawala would be called to lead the government. Amid frantic manoeuvrings, he obtained the support of the majority of MPs from the ruling party.[10] Sir John was in no doubt of this himself since he went to the trouble of writing his acceptance speech which he intended to broadcast to the nation.

Lord Soulbury's plane landed at 12.35 pm on 26 March and he drove straight to Queen's House, his official residence, half an hour or so away in the Fort in central Colombo. He held no consultation of any substance with any Member of Parliament, and at 1.55 pm, less than an hour after the Governor-General had reached the residence, Dudley Senanayake arrived. After a 45-minute interview, the latter proceeded to the Cabinet room nearby where he met for ten minutes with ministerial colleagues. He then returned to Queen's House to accept formally the summons to be Prime Minister.[11] This was the most important act that Lord Soulbury would perform in his five years in office. By calling a man other than the one who could command the majority of the ruling party's MPs, he had breached one of the most fundamental conventions of Westminster.

How could this happen? The answer has to be traced back to the mid-1940s when the Soulbury Commission visited Ceylon to consider changes in the island's constitutional status. The elected Ceylonese Ministers, who were led by D. S. Senanayake and who had produced their own draft scheme for self-determination, refused for complicated reasons to appear formally before the Commission which was taking evidence from a wide array of groups. But there was abundant informal contact as Lord Soulbury himself indicated when he wrote that D. S. Senanayake 'made extensive arrangements for the Commissioners to see the island' and 'accompanied us on many occasions'.[12] The contact was maintained later while the Commission was drawing up its report in London where Sir Oliver Goonetilleke, D. S. Senanayake's representative, was an assiduous lobbyist. At times the lobbying took the form of rather heavy-handed hints that a grateful island nation might seek to show its appreciation to generous Commissioners. Indeed one Commissioner has remarked rather wryly on this.[13] It must be emphasised that none of the Commissioners appears to have taken these supposed enticements very seriously. And they appear to have regarded Goonetilleke – who was widely seen in Ceylon as a shady intriguer who was later convicted, after his spell as Governor-General, of currency offences – as an overenthusiastic and rather unreliable negotiator.

Therefore the decision of the Soulbury Commission to adopt, very substantially, the Ceylonese Ministers' plan should in no way be seen as a response to hints of future *largesse*. It made perfect political sense on its own terms. But it is possible that some Ceylonese leaders believed that their enticements *had* played a part and that, as a result, they owed the Commissioners something. It is not clear whether this was in their minds in early 1948 when D. S. Senanayake offered Lord Soulbury the Governor-Generalship. What is clear is that the offer was very welcome to a man who had resumed his uninspiring committee work back in Britain and whose prospects, under a Labour government, were quite bleak. Senanayake was a very canny operator and would not have been unaware of this. His experiences with the British during the negotiations over post-war constitutional reform had confirmed him in his tendency to perceive institutions and constitutional processes in rather personalised, transactional terms. The imperial power had, after all, granted independence as much to one man – D. S. Senanayake – as to the nation that he represented. This process – unlike the transfer of power in India where the British were not in control of the situation – was very substantially a private transaction where Senanayake quite rightly gained the credit for winning self-rule while the British strengthened the man who would pay the greatest heed to their military, naval, financial and foreign policy interests.[14]

With this experience vividly in mind Senanayake knew that by appointing Lord Soulbury Governor-General, he would be getting a man who shared his own deeply conservative view of Ceylonese society[15] and a man who would work co-operatively with him. He knew that

Soulbury would do so partly because he quite genuinely admired D. S. Senanayake but more especially because the invitation to become Governor-General was seen by both men in transactional terms to bond Soulbury to Senanayake. The Prime Minister believed that if he faced a crisis in which his Governor-General could assist him, then Soulbury – a man with whom you could do business – could be relied upon. One such eventuality might be a hung parliament after a general election, which was not at all unlikely given that Senanayake's ramshackle party had failed to win a majority in the 1947 election. Another, which Senanayake discussed quite plainly with the Englishman, was his desire to see his son Dudley called to lead the government in the event of his death.[16] In inviting Dudley to do so in March 1952, Lord Soulbury was completing his great transaction with D. S. Senanayake. That he did so in the knowledge that most of the ruling party's MPs preferred another leader is clear from the extraordinary haste in which he acted and from his failure to hold consultations of any substance with a single legislator.[17]

It must be emphasised that this discussion is in no way intended as a partisan case in favour of Sir John Kotelawala. When he eventually became Prime Minister, he was in my view the most destructive failure ever to hold that office.[18] Instead, I am arguing first that the Governor-General should have called on Sir John because he clearly had the most support within the ruling party in the House. Second, and more importantly, he should – as he well knew – have taken soundings among MPs of that party before summoning anyone. Even to have summoned Sir John without at least some consultations would have represented a breach of convention. To call a man with less support than Sir John without taking soundings was doubly objectionable.

Lest there be any doubt that the conventions of Westminster were applicable to Ceylon in 1951, it should be noted that Section 4 of the Ceylon (Independence) Order-in-Council, 1947 explicitly stated that

> All powers, authorities and functions vested in . . . the Governor-General shall . . . be exercised as far as may be in accordance with the constitutional conventions, applicable to the exercise of similar powers, authorities and functions in the United Kingdom by His Majesty.[19]

Among these powers and functions was that of 'appointing Ministers', especially the Prime Minister.[20] Indeed, the Order-in-Council and certain provisions of the Constitution of Ceylon went further than the statutes of Britain and embodied these conventions *in law* to make doubly sure that they would be adhered to. As two distinguished authorities wrote:

> It gave greater sanctity to the rules because they were laws and not conventions; and in a country which had never known conventions there was much to be said for giving the additional moral authority of legal enactment.[21]

However, this anchoring of convention in law was not done so that the conventions 'might be "enforced" by legal remedies'. Section 4 of the Order-in-Council also 'provided that no act or omission on the part of the Governor-General shall be called in question in any court of law or otherwise'.[22]

So when Lord Soulbury summoned Dudley Senanayake to be Prime Minister, he was violating not only the conventions of Westminster but the laws of Ceylon which supposedly 'compelled the Governor-General to act as constitutional monarch' in a country where, until then, 'not only British constitutional practices but even British constitutional forms are followed with remarkable fidelity'.[23] And yet the law offered injured parties – in this case, Sir John Kotelawala – no legal means of challenging this action. His only recourse would have been to force the new Prime Minister to demonstrate his support by a vote in Parliament. But since Lord Soulbury enjoyed very considerable deference from MPs of the ruling party, and since the summons to the Prime Ministership had clearly given Dudley Senanayake the initiative, Sir John knew that any such action would have proved a damaging failure.

For several days he sulked and raged on his estate, threatened to resign and leave the country, and refused to attend Cabinet meetings. He eventually relented but he sometimes behaved contemptuously in Cabinet and literally turned his back on the proceedings. He drafted (anonymously) a provocative account of the events surrounding the succession which eventually found its way into the hands of a great many people. While Sir John was visiting the USA, the Prime Minister – reportedly at Soulbury's urging – demanded his resignation. Sir John rushed home and, by his own account salvaged his position by gently blackmailing Soulbury, albeit at the cost of some humiliation.[24] When in October 1953, Dudley Senanayake proved himself unequal to the strain of office and suffered an emotional breakdown, the Governor-General had no option but to summon Sir John to lead the government.[25]

This soon opened the way to an unseemly incident which reminded the nation very forcefully of the breach of convention which had occurred in

1952. During Sir John's first month in office, the Cabinet ordered an end to the optional playing of 'God Save the Queen' and the display of the Union Jack on official occasions. Or to be more precise, they decided that the anthem would be played and the flag flown when the monarch was present but not when the Governor-General was. Soulbury then wrote to the Prime Minister[26] saying that he was 'very much peeved' about this.[27] Sir John responded with a stinging letter saying that there were

> . . . three points that the people of Ceylon are unable to understand. First, why in this free land should there be a foreign Governor-General? Second and third: why should there be an English flag and an English national anthem in free Ceylon?
>
> The second and third have been suitably dealt with, which may kindly be taken note of.[28]

After this exchange appeared in the newspapers of both Britain and Ceylon,[29] it is hardly surprising that in June 1954, Lord Soulbury ended his term of office.[30]

Notes

1. An earlier version of this chapter appeared in *The Round Table*, 292 (1984) pp. 424–31.
2. This has usually been true in India, especially but not only since the death of Nehru in 1964. It was always true in Sri Lanka (Ceylon) until the Westminster model was abandoned in 1978 in favour of a Gaullist constitution. This has also often been the case in, for example, Canada. See J. C. Courtney, 'The Defeat of the Clark Government: The Dissolution of Parliament, Leadership Conventions and the Calling of Elections in Canada', *Journal of Canadian Studies*, xvii, 2 (Summer, 1982) pp. 82–4.
3. Interview, Colombo, 4 September 1978.
4. For fuller discussions of these events, see J. Manor (ed.) *Sri Lanka in Change and Crisis* (London, 1984).
5. See for example, the work of the Civil Rights Movement in Sri Lanka and the essays by 'Priya Samarakone' and Gananath Obeyesekere in Manor.
6. It should be noted that a different interpretation of these events will appear in K. M. de Silva's forthcoming biography of J. R. Jayewardene.
7. This emerges from the letters of Lady Moore to Jan Smuts between 1947 and 1949, Smuts Papers, University Library, Cambridge.
8. There are numerous references to this, but see for example, *Times of Ceylon*, 18 November 1953.

9. *Times of Ceylon*, 21–22 March 1952 and *Ceylon Daily News*, 23 March 1952.
10. This like one other key point in this discussion (see note 16), has been wilfully obscured by people seeking to conceal this breach of convention. One example is J. L. Fernando *Three Prime Ministers of Ceylon – An 'Inside Story'* (Colombo, 1963) pp. 39–51. He seeks to reinforce the false impression created by Lake House newspapers, for which he was political correspondent, that Dudley Senanayake's support outweighed Sir John's. My view that Sir John was supported by most MPs is based on numerous interviews with journalists, civil servants, scholars and MPs of that time, mainly in Colombo in 1978 and 1980. See also, Sir John Kotelawala, *An Asian Prime Minister's Story* (London, 1956) especially chs. 9 and 10.
11. *Times of Ceylon*, 26 March 1952 and *Ceylon Daily News*, 27 March 1952.
12. Lord Soulbury, 'D. S. Senanayake the Man', *Ceylon Historical Journal* (1955–6) p. 63.
13. J. F. Rees, 'The Soulbury Commission', *Ceylon Historical Journal* (1955–6) pp. 23–48.
14. The most authoritative accounts of the transition to independence are by K. M. de Silva in his *A History of Sri Lanka* (Delhi, 1982) chs 31 and 32, and in his 'The History and Politics of the Transfer of Power' in K. M. de Silva (ed.) *The University of Ceylon History of Ceylon*, III (Peradeniya, 1973) pp. 489–533. My point on the transactional character of the transfer of power is reinforced by the fact that it was *written into the Constitution* that the Prime Minister (who for some years was going to be D. S. Senanayake) would have control of the defence and external affairs portfolios. For an elaboration of this discussion, see J. Manor, *The Expedient Utopian: Bandaranaike and Ceylon*, forthcoming, chs. 5 and 6.
15. See, for example, Lord Soulbury's rather naive and less than warm response to testimony about the difficulties of depressed Sinhalese castes, during the Soulbury Commission hearings, *Ceylon Daily News*, 14 February 1945.
16. This is true despite Soulbury's predictable denials. My conclusion is based on discussions with four persons who were close to D. S. Senanayake in the last years of his life in Colombo, September 1980. See also J. R. Jayewardene's comments reported in Fernando, *Three Prime Ministers* pp. 39–40.
17. This is also confirmed by the recollections of the same persons mentioned in the previous note. There is no evidence to indicate that Soulbury had had extensive communications with people in Ceylon during his return journey. The reported comments of the man who had temporarily taken charge in his absence (Fernando, *Three Prime Ministers*, p. 40) strongly suggest that he had not been in more than perfunctory contact.
18. This case is made more fully in ch. 7 of Manor, *The Expedient Utopian* . . .
19. As quoted in I. Jennings and H. W. Tambiah, *The Dominion of Ceylon: The Development of its Laws and Constitution* (London, 1952) p. 68. For further material, see A. J. Wilson, 'The Role of the Governor-General in Ceylon', *Modern Asian Studies* (1968) pp. 193–220.
20. Jennings and Tambiah, *The Dominion of Ceylon*, p. 69.

21. Ibid., p. 71. It ought to be said that the earlier disfranchisement of Indian Tamil voters was a violation of the *spirit* of the Westminister system.
22. Ibid., pp. 68 and 70.
23. Ibid., pp. 71–2. Jennings and Tambiah completed their manuscript in January 1952 (see p. x) before the death of D. S. Senanayake.
24. The account which he wrote was called 'The Premier's stakes, or how I was led down the garden path'. Sir John told me that he had written it in an interview at Kandawela, 9 September 1978, at which he also explained his 'blackmailing' of Lord Soulbury.
25. This is much more fully discussed in Manor, *Sri Lanka in Change and Crisis*.
26. *The Times*, London, 7 November 1953.
27. *Times of Ceylon*, 31 October 1953.
28. *The Times*, London, 11 November 1953. Sir John later denied that he had written these things (*Times of Ceylon*, 13 November 1953), but the point had been clearly made.
29. *Times of Ceylon*, 12 November 1953.
30. Lord Soulbury's wife was tragically killed when struck by a bus in London in February 1954.

3 Governors and Politicians: the Australian States principally in the 1940s and 1950s

J. B. Paul

This chapter concentrates on events in the Australian State of Victoria, with one reference to Tasmania.

The two principal Victorian crises (1947 and 1952) and the Tasmanian crisis (1948) involved the denial of supply by the upper house, or Legislative Council, to an administration secure in its control of the lower house: they therefore have in common one important characteristic with the 1975 crisis in Australia to be addressed by Professor D. A. Low in Chapter 6.

This chapter is a drastic abridgement of a conference paper in which I demonstrated that two nineteenth century crises in Victoria involving inter-House disputes (1865–6 and 1877–8) were of such a character as to present no ready comparison with the later crises of 1947 and 1952. I also denied that the 'toughing it out' strategy without gubernatorial interference undertaken by ministries in the 1860s and 1870s had a parallel with that attempted by the Australian Prime Minister, Gough Whitlam, in 1975. I maintained that vice-regal intervention to obtain a dissolution in either of those nineteenth century crises could have seemed a compelling option if the circumstances attending the denial of supply had been different.

VICTORIA: THE DEFEAT OF THE DUNSTAN GOVERNMENT 1945

Mr (later Sir) Albert Dunstan first led a government confined to Country Party members and supported by the Labor Party from 1935 until 1942. From then until the 1943 election Dunstan's Ministry remained in office with United Australia Party support. That election, like almost all elections in that period in Victoria, resulted in a Legislative Assembly in which no one party commanded a majority but in which the combined numbers of the Country Party and the UAP exceeded the Labor Party, the largest party. Defeated in the Assembly, Dunstan resigned to be succeeded by a Labor ministry led by John Cain, but, on patching up a coalition deal with the UAP, Dunstan was able to marshal the two parties to defeat Cain's Labor Ministry within a matter of days. Refused a dissolution by the Governor, Sir Winston Dugan, Cain resigned and Dunstan was commissioned to lead a Country Party–United Australia Party coalition. The UAP emerged as the new Liberal Party in 1945.

A note on a Dominions Office file recorded that a 'full account of the political crisis in Victoria last October has not come to hand from the Governor.'[1] Perhaps in view of the Governor's actions, this was not surprising, but Dominions Office officials were able to set out the course of events after a fashion from other available reports. This note stated *inter alia*:

> At the end of September last, the Government was defeated in the Legislative Assembly, when the House refused Supply. Five Liberals, two Country Party members and one Independent voted with the Labor Opposition, on the grounds of dissatisfaction with the Government's legislative programme and opposition to Mr Dunstan's leadership.
>
> Mr Dunstan asked the Governor for a Dissolution which was granted on the understanding, in accordance with the usual practice, that he would first obtain from the House a grant of Supply.

This suggests wrongly that the dissolution was granted conditionally upon the grant of supply being made by the Assembly.

The Governor's letter to Mr Dunstan of 27 September 1945 was read by him the same day to the Assembly:

> In accordance with the advice contained in the memorandum which you tendered to me last night, I have decided to grant a dissolution of Parliament.
>
> The dissolution will be as from Wednesday, the third day of October next.
>
> I have selected this date for the dissolution in order that in the meantime, the House may have an opportunity to consider the desirability of granting Supply during the interval between the dissolution and the elections and thus obviating the illegality of

payments due to public services or possibly the withholding of such payments during that period.[2]

This letter, as the Premier used it, amounted to an instruction to the Legislative Assembly to grant supply to a ministry which had already been refused it and to no other ministry. One seasoned politician of the time remarked to me years ago that it said much for Albert Dunstan's capacity to cajole that Sir Winston Dugan could have been persuaded to accept advice in those terms.[3] The Legislative Assembly within minutes of Dunstan's reading of this letter voted down his Supply Bill a second time.

Later that evening the Leader of the Opposition, John Cain, attempted to move by leave for the presentation of an address to the Governor in the following terms:

> We, the Legislative Assembly of Victoria, in Parliament assembled, beg to respectfully direct Your Excellency's attention to the fact that this House is of opinion that, in order to obviate the illegality contemplated by the Government between the dissolution and the elections of making payments due to public services or of withholding such payments, an administration can be formed to which Supply can be granted.

When Dunstan refused leave for this address to be moved and told the Assembly that notice would need to be given, Cain retorted that he was giving notice that he would submit his motion at the next sitting of the House, and then stole a march on Dunstan by moving an amendment to the latter's motion that remaining business be postponed until the following Tuesday. Cain's amendment, ultimately carried by the Assembly, was to keep the Assembly sitting that day and included such terms, as Dunstan petulantly remarked, as to be almost identical with the motion he had earlier moved unsuccessfully. The Speaker accepted his amendment.

A suitable conclusion to this sorry chapter, which does not, because it cannot, recapture the acrimony of the ensuing Parliamentary debate, is set out in the Dominions Office note already quoted:

> After a few days' delay, during which he sustained two more defeats, Mr Dunstan resigned, and the Governor sent for the Leader of the Opposition. The latter asked for time to consider the matter, since the Labor Party, under its Constitution, was not entitled to form a Government unless it possessed a majority in the Assembly or to enter into a Coalition with another Party. Subsequently he informed the

> Governor that he could not obtain sufficient support to form a Government, and the Leader of the Liberal Party, who also was consulted by the Governor, was in a similar position.
>
> The Governor accordingly commissioned as Premier, Mr (Ian) Macfarlan, the Deputy Leader of the Liberal Party, who had been Attorney-General in Mr Dunstan's Government, on the production of written assurances of support from the Labour Opposition and from members of the Liberal Party, the Country Party and the Independents whose revolt had led to Mr Dunstan's defeat. Mr Macfarlan formed a Government, both Houses passed Votes of Supply, and the dissolution took immediate effect.
>
> At the subsequent General Election in November, the Labor Party obtained a majority (with the support of two Independents) and formed a Government. The position of Parties was Labor 32, United Country Party 18, Liberals 13, Independents 2. Mr Macfarlan was one of the defeated candidates.[4]

A fitting postscript to this statement is to record that when Dunstan first took office as Premier, he did so after he had played a not insignificant role in breaking up a non-Labor coalition for which he had campaigned in the 1935 election as a minister. The Governor, Lord Huntingfield, required written assurances of support from the then Labour leader, Thomas Tunnecliffe, just as Sir Winston Dugan had required the same before commissioning Mr Ian Macfarlan as Premier.

THE 1947 CRISIS

The Legislative Council's denial of supply to the Cain Government in 1947 was a politically inspired manoeuvre to force a State election to test the electorate's reaction to the bank nationalisation proposals of the Federal Labor Government led by J. B. Chifley.

The curtain-raiser to this crisis was the Governor's Speech at the Opening of Parliament on 30 September 1947 which contained the seemingly innocuous statement, 'A Supply Bill for the month of October will be submitted to you today.'[5] The Premier's announcement in the Legislative Assembly that same day put the matter in more stark terms:

> The period for which Supply has been granted by Parliament expires today, and it is essential, pending the passing of the Appropriation Act, that further provision should be made. The amount included in the Supply Bill is £2,717,903 and is sufficient for one month's

requirements. The Budget statement will be submitted to the House within two or three weeks . . .[6]

The issue was then joined by the Leader of the Opposition (and of the Country Party), Mr J. G. B. McDonald:

> I inform the Committee that members of the Opposition are not prepared at this stage to grant Supply to the Government . . . In refusing Supply we intend to create a crisis whereby the Government will be compelled to consult its masters, the people, and when the people have spoken, we are prepared to accept their verdict, as all democrats should. We have the courage and the determination to go to the people and we hope that the Government will also accept the people's decision.[7]

As was expected, the Assembly passed supply in a pattern which was to be repeated in that House: Committee vote, Ayes 32, Noes 29: majority three; with the Speaker in the Chair, Ayes 33, Noes 29, majority four. On 1 October, the Legislative Council, still at that time elected on a property franchise which gave it a constituency with roughly half the number of electors enrolled for the Assembly, refused supply. Not all Legislative Councillors customarily taking the Opposition whip were prepared to vote in conformity with the party line on this Bill, but this defection was still not sufficient to give the Government a majority. The figures were Ayes 13, Noes 19 – majority for refusal six.

The Leader of the Opposition, Mr J. G. B. McDonald, had the following to say in the Assembly later that day:

> A Supply Bill has already been passed by this House, but information has been received to the effect that the Council has dealt with that measure in no uncertain manner. As a unit of the Victorian Parliament the Council obviously acted within its constitutional rights . . . It is clear that the Government has been defeated not necessarily in the Assembly but certainly by the Parliament of Victoria . . . If the Government, in view of the decision of Parliament, will go to the people as it should, I can guarantee that Supply will be passed without any debate. That statement is conditional upon a dissolution being obtained from the Governor. I know that members of another place are prepared to grant Supply on that condition. From assurances I have received, I can say with the utmost confidence that Supply will be passed by the Council to enable Public Service salaries to be paid for a period covering an election and a reasonable time thereafter.[8]

The following day the Premier, John Cain, denounced the Legislative Council's rejection of the Supply Bill in a fighting speech. In two sentences, however, he acknowledged one obstacle which for him was to prove insurmountable:

> The strict legal position is clear enough. The Council, under Section 56 of the Victorian Constitution, has the legal power to reject Bills for appropriating the Revenue, and by section 36 of the Constitution Act Amendment Act (1903) has the power of suggesting to this House amendments to money Bills, but not of amending those Bills.[9]

All Cain's fulminations in the name of 'constitutional practice', which were to find their echoes in many of the inter-party slanging matches of 1975, could not get him around the legal position. In his acknowledgement of this legal position he also implicitly acknowledged that, if the Legislative Councillors remained intransigent and uncompromising, the logic of events would require him to accept the conditions which they and McDonald had imposed. Cain nonetheless attempted to break the Council's determination. He concluded his speech:

> I ask this Parliament . . . to pass a fresh Supply Bill providing for two months' Supply instead of for one month . . . I wish to say very frankly that we feel the Upper House must be given the opportunity to reconsider its attitude.[10]

As a further test to the Council's resolution, Cain introduced on 3 October (a Friday) a Legislative Council (Referendum) Bill which like his second Supply Bill passed easily through the Assembly. The Legislative Council disposed of the Referendum Bill with an even greater negative majority than it did the first and second Supply Bills. On 7 October (Tuesday of the following week) Cain presented to the Assembly a third Supply Bill 'substantially different from those brought forward last week'. The Legislative Council threw it out shortly before it rose for dinner at 6.22 pm that same day. At 10.28 pm the Premier announced that he had obtained a dissolution of the Assembly from the Governor (Major-General Sir Winston Dugan). In conformity with previous undertakings, the Legislative Council passed supply before the Parliament rose for the election.

Sir Clifden Eager, the then President of the Legislative Council, told me many years ago that Cain, on returning from Government House, had confided to him the advice the Governor had accepted. Eager, commiserating with him on his political fortunes, commended him for taking the right course: Cain agreed it was the right course.

A TASMANIAN DIVERSION 1948

In the case of the refusal of supply to the Cosgrove Labor Government by the Tasmanian Legislative Council in 1948, I have been able to consult one interesting report held in the Public Records Office which was sent by the Governor some time before the Legislative Council's action but none reporting the episode itself.

A letter to the Permanent Under-Secretary of State for Commonwealth Relations, Sir Eric Machtig, from the Governor of Tasmania (Admiral Sir Hugh Binney, KCB, DSO) highlighted the problems associated with vice-regal advice to a Premier on a question of propriety when political party interests were engaged. When in the course of a Royal Commission's investigations, allegations of bribery were made against the Premier of Tasmania, Mr (later Sir) Robert Cosgrove, the Royal Commissioner decided that it was not his proper function to enquire into them, but advised that criminal proceedings should be instituted against Mr Cosgrove. After discussing the political position Sir Hugh Binney reported further:

> It appears therefore that the Government is safe for the present but they will be very vulnerable to attacks by the Opposition both inside and outside of Parliament. As Supply has been voted up to the end of the present financial year (30 June) it is generally expected that they will survive the present short session and that the test will come in July. Many people talk of the Legislative Council following the lead of Victoria by refusing Supply and forcing an election, but whether they follow this doubtful expedient or not, it looks as if an appeal must be made to the country in the not too distant future.
>
> From the point of view of the problems of a Governor perhaps the most interesting events occurred immediately the Royal Commissioner decided that Mr Cosgrove's case should be decided by a jury in the Criminal Court.
>
> Mr Cosgrove's wish was immediately to resign but his party fearful of their majority and basing their claim on the fact that every man is innocent till he is proved.guilty tried hard to persuade him to remain in office and face his trial as Premier. I believe there would have been no precedent for this and at any rate it would have been repugnant to everyone's sense of dignity to see the Premier of a State as such in the dock. My job was therefore to persuade the Premier where his duty lay without actually calling for his resignation which in the party's view was their affair. In his endeavour to get out of the difficulty the

Premier asked me in writing what I would do if he did not resign. I had of course to tell him that I could not give a decision on a hypothetical case. There followed an unpleasant 48 hours of consultation between the Premier and his party but I am glad to say that better counsels prevailed and that Mr Cosgrove resigned nine days after the Royal Commissioner's decision.[11]

The upshot of all this was that Mr Cosgrove stood trial and was acquitted by a Supreme Court jury, whereupon he was recommissioned as Premier. But, as the Governor had foreshadowed, the Legislative Council at the first opportunity denied supply to the Cosgrove Government. What passed as a result of this between the Governor and the Premier has to my knowledge never been revealed and, apart from this, the Tasmanian Parliament was notorious for not having a Hansard or official record of its debates. I have never seen it suggested that the Government, however loath it was to face the electors, challenged the Legislative Council's constitutional power to deny supply or resisted the idea of seeking a dissolution, on which supply was made contingent by the upper house. The Governor granted a dissolution on the Premier's advice, supply was obtained, and the subsequent election resulted in a narrow victory for the Government.

VICTORIA AGAIN – 1952

The following brief outline of political events takes us from the time of the Cain Government's defeat at the polls in 1947 up to the 1952 crisis.

After the election in November 1947, a Liberal–Country Party composite ministry was formed with the Liberal leader, T. T. Hollway, as Premier and the Country Party leader, J. G. B. McDonald, as deputy Premier. Tom Hollway was brought around by McDonald to the very grudging acceptance of Albert Dunstan as a cabinet minister and allotted him the Health portfolio. This coalition fell apart in December 1948, with Hollway claiming that Dunstan with his compulsive intriguing was the principal disrupter.[12] Hollway reconstructed his Ministry from among his own Liberal supporters while the Country Party, though excluding itself from office, undertook to continue supporting that Ministry from the corner benches. Some Country Party members, sickened by the previous inter-party brawling and by Dunstan in particular whom they saw as its instigator, joined the Liberal Party, which then to confuse matters called itself the Liberal and Country Party. This party made a bold attempt at the May 1950 election, and in the time leading up to it, to destroy the Country Party as an electoral force. The results were disappointing. The Liberal and Country Party emerged from the poll as the largest party in the Legislative Assembly with 26 seats, the Australian Labor Party held 24 seats, and the Country Party 13 seats.

The Premier, Mr Hollway, still determined if he could to strike another blow against the Country Party, attempted to obtain Labor support by an offer of an electoral redistribution. (The last redistribution, passed by the Dunstan–Hollway Government in 1944, which reduced to some degree the pro-rural, anti-urban bias, had been reluctantly conceded by Dunstan as the price of Hollway's co-operation in keeping Labour in opposition.) When the Labor Party turned down Hollway's offer, he sought a dissolution which was refused by the Governor, General Sir Dallas Brooks, who had in 1949 succeeded Lord (the former Sir Winston) Dugan who had in not dissimilar circumstances in 1943 refused a dissolution to the Labour leader, John Cain. The Labor Party, still prevented by its own platform from entering a coalition or forming a minority government dependent on another party, undertook to support a Country Party ministry committed at Labour's bidding to a specified programme of reform. Sir Albert Dunstan was no longer available. He had died the previous month. A letter, dated 9 March 1951, to Sir Dallas Brooks from the Permanent Under-Secretary of State for Commonwealth Relations, Sir Percivale Liesching, spoke of 'some very interesting reports on your Premier's request for a dissolution' forwarded the previous year. I have not been able to turn up these reports, I regret to say, and have had to compile this summary from other sources.

The Labor Party withdrew its support from the McDonald Government on 22 July 1952 chiefly because of its reluctance to implement the Labor Party's demands for a redistribution of electorates and for the reintroduction of the Greater Melbourne Bill. An election which seemed imminent was averted when the Liberal and Country Party under new leadership (Hollway had been deposed in December 1951 and replaced by L. G. Norman) undertook to support the McDonald Government in place of the Labor Party. Hollway's obsession with redistribution had cost him his party's leadership and it was to be the issue dominating the 1952 crisis. Once again he approached the Labor Party with the offer they had rejected in 1950 of a redistribution if they would join him and six other Liberal rebels in defeating the McDonald government's combined support of Country Party and Liberal and Country Party members.

On this occasion the Labor Party agreed to support Mr Hollway and in September 1952 he challenged the Government with a motion of no-confidence based on the question of electoral reform. The voting was 32 for the Government and 31 against (comprising Hollway and his six supporters and the Labor Party). Hollway was then expelled from the Liberal Party. Allegations were made that he had attempted to bribe members and a Royal Commission comprising the Chief Justice and two puisne justices of the Victorian Supreme Court was appointed to enquire into them. The Royal Commission decided to adjourn *sine die* when notified that two of the witnesses before them including Hollway had taken out defamation suits in both Victoria and New South Wales. As the Commissioners explained themselves on 5 November 1952:

> If this Commission proceeds, there will in all probability be things spoken both in the witness box and at the bar table, and perhaps written in the Commission's report that will prejudice or will be calculated to prejudice one or both of the parties to the pending actions.

This Royal Commission never reconvened.

The Royal Commission's decision was announced six days after the crisis I shall now describe had been resolved; it is safe to say that political animosities throughout that crisis must have been exacerbated by the pervasive atmosphere of suspicion which accusations of political bribery must encourage.

Fortunately I have been able to peruse a Dominions Office file[13] on which Sir Dallas Brooks's numerous letters and telegrams concerning this crisis have been placed, together with intra-office memoranda and notes and also correspondence with the then Private Secretary to Her Majesty the Queen, Sir Alan 'Tommy' Lascelles. In a note entitled 'Political Parties in Victoria' issued on 1 November 1952 from the Commonwealth Relations Office's Political Affairs Department, there is a suggestion of Gulliver's lofty contemplation of the antics of Lilliputians:

> In the State's 96 years of responsible government there have been a considerable number of political crises, strange alliances and party somersaults, in the course of which the State has had 58 ministries, 17 of them in the past 30 years.

In a letter dated 16 October 1952, Sir Dallas Brooks informed Sir Percivale Liesching of the events which led to the appointment of the above mentioned Royal Commission. He then warned of the crisis which was to exercise him until the end of the month:

> In the meantime, the position of the present Government has become increasingly precarious as a result of the publication of an agreement between the Labour Party and the Honourable T. T. Hollway, supported by his six 'followers'. It appears that the Labor Party have undertaken to vote for Supply only to Mr Hollway; and then only on condition that he immediately forms a Care-Taker Government with the sole purpose of bringing down legislation to set up a commission to delineate the new boundaries of the electorates within the present 33 Federal boundaries. On completion of this task Parliament would be dissolved and an election held on the 'two for one boundaries'.

Brooks went on to explain that supply would run out on 31 October and that, although the Supply Bill had been passed by the Assembly by 32 votes to 31, the combined Labor and Hollway Liberal forces which enjoyed a two-vote majority in the Legislative Council would agree to give supply only to Mr Hollway on the above stated conditions. Brooks concluded:

> If this forecast of what may happen proves to be correct, then I think it is inevitable that the Honourable the Premier will call upon me to seek a dissolution.

On 21 October, the Legislative Council acted in the way Brooks had expected. The Legislative Council by legislation in 1950 had had its property qualification abolished and adult suffrage established in its place. In the elections in June 1952, Labour gained seven seats, the Liberals lost eight seats.

On 17 November 1952, Sir Dallas Brooks addressed a letter marked 'Personal and Confidential' to the Secretary of State for Commonwealth Relations (the Most Honourable the Marquess of Salisbury, KG) referring to his telegrams dated 23 and 31 October and to his other 'Personal and Confidential' letter to Sir Percivale Liesching, mentioned earlier. This letter gave a full outline of the way the crisis had developed and his justification of the way he had discharged his responsibilities in relation to it.

After giving details of the adjournment of the Royal Commission Sir Dallas Brooks addressed himself to the Legislative Council's vote on the Supply Bill which had already been passed by the Legislative Assembly:

> This action would mean that so far as Mr McDonald's Government was concerned, there would be no Supply after the 31st day of October, 1952, to provide for the continuance of the ordinary services of the State.

As the Governor had forecast, the Premier sought a dissolution and submitted a supporting memorandum which Brooks annexed to his letter to Lord Salisbury. Sir Dallas continued:

> I informed Mr McDonald that before I gave a decision regarding his advice that I should dissolve Parliament, I should need time to inform myself of the general political situation which had developed in the House and that I intended at once to send for the Leaders of the other Parties.

Sir Dallas then sent for Messrs Cain, Norman and Hollway, the first two being the Labour leader and LCP leader respectively. These consultations took place while supply was still being withheld. As Brooks put it:

> I was, to say the least of it, very concerned indeed about the little time that remained for Supply to be obtained before the 31st October.

McDonald's problem was that, unlike Cain in 1947, he could not ensure the passage of supply through the Legislative Council simply by obtaining a dissolution of the Legislative Assembly from the Governor. And it was for this reason that Sir Dallas Brooks, having satisfied himself of this after consulting all the party leaders, refused McDonald's request for a dissolution. McDonald thereupon resigned.

These consultations and the cautious approach Sir Dallas Brooks adopted to them at all times demonstrate that he was much more sensitive politically than his predecessor Lord Dugan had been in dealing with Albert Dunstan over the refusal of supply to his Government by the Legislative Assembly in 1945. Mr McDonald's inability to obtain supply pending an election, which his advice for a dissolution, if accepted, would have pre-ordained, made his resignation necessary, and it is to McDonald's credit that he ultimately conceded this and thereby relieved the Governor of any necessity to revoke his commission unilaterally.

The Governor then commissioned Hollway to lead a minority administration which comprised himself and his seven rebel Liberals, who could count on the support of the Labour Party, on the understanding that 'he could and would obtain Supply in the Legislative Council by the end of October.' Sir Dallas, in his letter, continued:

> I, however, took pains to inform Mr Hollway that even if he succeeded in obtaining Supply and then was defeated on the floor of the Legislative Assembly and advised me to dissolve Parliament, I could by no means give him any assurance that I would do so at his particular request.

The fortunes of this Government were described by Sir Dallas in his despatch to Lord Salisbury:

> At noon on Tuesday, the 28th October, the new Hollway Government was sworn in, and that Government, with the support of the Labor Party, succeeded in getting the Supply Bill through the Legislative Council late that evening. Immediately that had been achieved, the Hollway Goverment was defeated on a Motion of Procedure in the Legislative Assembly by 33 votes to 31. And on Wednesday, the 29th October, a vote of no-confidence was moved by the Leader of the Country Party, and after an eight-hour debate, the Hollway Government was again defeated by 33 votes to 31 at about 3.00 am on the 30th October.

Brooks's despatch chronicled that later that same morning Hollway called to seek a dissolution of the Parliament, leaving a memorandum supporting his case which emphasised that he had been commissioned as Premier to ensure supply. Brooks, describing the situation as 'very unusual', reported that he had decided to see the leaders of the other parties. They all 'appeared to agree that Parliament should be dissolved, as seemingly no other course was practicable'. McDonald pressed his case to lead an interim government pending an election and Brooks asked him for a memorandum supporting this viewpoint. Copies of Hollway's and McDonald's memoranda were annexed by Brooks to his despatch to Lord Salisbury, dated 17 November, 1952.

Hollway's memorandum, in its first one and a half closely typed pages, stressed the unworkability of Parliament and the need for a dissolution. It argued against an interim commission to McDonald as being 'contrary to constitutional theory and, as far as can be ascertained, without precedent in the history of responsible government in the Empire'. Hollway based his case for retaining the Premiership on having been selected to break the deadlock over supply, which he had done. He reminded the Governor that his Ministry commanded the support of a majority in the Legislative Council, although defeated in the Assembly. McDonald had not been able to do this and, Hollway maintained, consequently 'had no constitutional claim to be entrusted with the responsibility of carrying on the government of the State'.

The memorandum went on to say that the purpose of commissioning another government merely to obtain a dissolution would cause public confusion. Brooks was reminded that he was supposed to act on the recommendation of 'his responsible Ministers' and any departure from this principle 'would be attended with a grave danger of conveying to the electorate an impression of political partisanship'. The only constitutional justification for refusing to act on the Hollway Cabinet's advice was where an alternative government with the support of both Houses could be formed. 'Those circumstances', the memorandum claimed truthfully enough, 'do not now exist'.

McDonald's memorandum, on the other hand, said it would be constitutionally valid for Brooks to commission him to form a government to obtain a dissolution of Parliament. He said, 'the Leader of the present Government' (Hollway) should 'resign his position and thereby relieve Your Excellency from embarrassment'. Brooks could then commission McDonald. The memorandum continued:

> I do not feel it necessary at the present stage to tender any advice to Your Excellency as to the exercising of the extreme if undoubted power to withdraw the present commission and dismiss the Government as a prelude to commissioning myself.

Turning to 'principle and precedent', McDonald argued that there were only limited grounds for the action of the Legislative Council to refuse supply. He said such action could be justified if the upper house wanted to test whether the majority in the lower house still had the support of the electorate or as a legitimate step towards testing whether some other ministry more acceptable to the lower house than the existing government could be installed without an appeal to the electorate. Any move by an upper house in other circumstances would 'destroy the effective balance of parliamentary institutions and defeat the democratic rights of the electorate'.

In the particular instance with which the Governor was dealing, McDonald claimed that the subsequent history showed that he retained the numbers in the Assembly after supply had been granted. The alternative government had not been able to control the business of the House. McDonald said that in these circumstances the constitutional reason for the Legislative Council's action was 'open to extreme doubt'. He continued:

The alternative justification for the action of the Council is, I think, indicated above and is that the Upper House may legitimately act as an instrument for restoring to the electorate a decision as to the exercise of Government Authority.

I would recognise the propriety of this course and I have at all times indicated to Your Excellency my readiness to accept the action of the Legislative Council as an appropriate step towards seeking recourse to an election.

I am still prepared to render legitimate the course pursued by the Legislative Council by myself advising a dissolution and in consequence, if commissioned, I would advise Your Excellency that the true course is to dissolve Parliament within the shortest time practicable.

The memorandum continued with a discussion of the Byng case in Canada, reviewing such sources as Evatt and Berriedale Keith, who disapproved the course pursued by Lord Byng, and, for the purpose of giving him short shrift, Dr Eugene Forsey, who had defended Lord Byng's decision.

Hollway, in the preparation of his memorandum, was able to rely on advice from the State's law officers – including the Solicitor-General, Mr H.A. (later Sir Henry) Winneke, QC, to be in time Chief Justice of the Supreme Court of Victoria and then Governor of that State. McDonald, being on the Opposition benches, had no such recourse but his memorandum has all the marks of sophisticated counsel in its drafting.

Brooks's despatch to Lord Salisbury of 17 November continued the story from the time he received the memoranda from Hollway and McDonald:

At the same time, I felt it advisable to seek the advice of the Chief Justice of the Supreme Court of Victoria, Lieutenant-General the Honourable Sir Edmund Herring. After discussing the matter with Sir Edmund Herring and hearing his views, I felt it wise also to seek the advice of the Chief Justice of the High Court of Australia, the Right Honourable Sir Owen Dixon. Having informed Sir Owen Dixon of what passed between myself and the four Leaders of the respective Parties, I had the advantage of hearing the view of Sir Owen Dixon expressed independently of that of Sir Edmund Herring. Both Chief Justices expressed the same view, namely that I ought not to grant a dissolution to Mr Hollway.

After conferring with Mr Cain and confirming that he was not prepared to accept a commission, Sir Dallas then itemised and elaborated on five specific factors and completed his despatch as follows:

> In the light of all these factors and of the advice I had received from both the Chief Justices, I ultimately came to the firm conclusion that ordinary British justice and convenience demanded that I should refuse a dissolution to Mr Hollway and grant one to Mr McDonald. And so, on Friday morning, the 31st October, I sent for Mr Hollway and informed him of the advice I had received, *and from whom* (my emphasis), and that I had decided to refuse his request for a dissolution of Parliament. With the knowledge that feelings were running high and with the object of making it as easy as possible for Mr Hollway, I gave him the alternative either of voluntarily tendering his resignation or of doing so at my request. Unhappily, he chose the latter course and that was for me a disappointment. He then requested that I should permit him to make public his memorandum which he submitted to me in support of his case for a dissolution. This I refused on the grounds that it was a privileged document which could not be published. I might add that I think it would have been most unfortunate if any documents concerned with this political crisis had been made public at this time.
>
> Subsequently, on the same day, I invited Mr McDonald to call upon me and offered to recommission him for the Election. Mr McDonald at once accepted this Commission and his Ministry was sworn in on the 31st October. The General Election will take place on the 6th December.

The Labor Party won that election, gaining its first ever majority over all other parties, and then legislated for the electoral redistribution, the demand for which had precipitated both the denial of supply by the Legislative Council and the subsequent election for the Legislative Assembly.

Hollway's resignation at the Governor's request was similar to Lord Melbourne's in 1834 at the request of King William IV. Although not technically a dismissal as was the dismissal of Lord North by King George III in 1783, of J.T. Lang, the New South Wales Premier, by Air Vice-Marshal Sir Philip Game in 1932, and of Gough Whitlam by Sir John Kerr in 1975, it was effectively a dismissal. It must have been as clear to Hollway, as it had been to Lord Melbourne, that his refusal to resign would have resulted in his dismissal in the full technical sense, the necessity for which in this extreme case had already been acknowledged by Mr McDonald in his memorandum. And the two Chief Justices, whom, it is clear, the Governor consulted without Mr Hollway's permission, in advising Brooks to refuse Mr Hollway a dissolution, must themselves have been mindful of the necessity of his dismissal in the last resort.

Sir Dallas Brooks's conduct was not questioned within the Commonwealth Relations Office. In an unsigned note on the political situation in Victoria, initialled in an earlier draft by Sir Charles Dixon, Advisor for the Commonwealth Relations Office, which was forwarded to Buckingham Palace with other documentation and with a covering letter dated 10 November, 1952, from the Permanent Under-Secretary, the following statement appears:

> The Governor's action seems to have been throughout in accordance with established constitutional principles. It is generally accepted that a dissolution need not be granted if there is a reasonable prospect of an alternative Government and that the voting of Supply is a pre-requisite of a dissolution. The Governor was therefore justified in not granting Mr McDonald's original request until it was clear that there was no possibility of an alternative Government and until Supply had been voted. His action in refusing Mr Hollway's request, recalling Mr McDonald and granting him the dissolution is the course which eminent authorities consider should have been followed by Lord Byng when, as Governor-General of Canada, he was faced with a somewhat similar situation in 1926. Lord Byng's action was in fact different since, after refusing a dissolution to Mr Mackenzie King, he granted one to Mr Meighen a few days later. For this, he was much criticised, and although some authorities have argued that he acted correctly, the contrary view was expressed by Dr Evatt in his book *The King and his Dominion Governors* and in subsequent private conversation by Mr Churchill and Mr Mackenzie King, all of whom held that the proper course would have been to refuse Mr Meighen's request, when he would have resigned and the Governor-General would have sent for Mr Mackenzie King again and granted him the dissolution.

On 18 November 1952, the Queen's Private Secretary, Sir Alan Lascelles, who at that stage had not had the benefit of reading Brooks's despatch of 17 November, was still able to write confidently to Sir Percivale Liesching:

> The whole thing is an excellent example of what poor Byng ought to have done in Ottawa in 1926, but did not do largely owing to the bad advice of the then Secretary to the Governor-General who, as you will remember, was more of a rascal than most of them.

Against this Liesching initialled the following pencilled marginal comment: 'Yes. Poor Sladen'. Dr Eugene Forsey, a defender of Lord Byng, has, in private correspondence I have seen, questioned the justice of Sir Alan Lascelles's assessment of poor Sladen.[14]

SOME CONCLUSIONS

There are some obvious similarities and dissimilarities in contrasting the Victorian crises of 1947 and 1952 with the Australian crisis of 1975. The Victorian Legislative Council, with powers respecting money Bills similar to those of the Senate, has twice denied supply to a government and all parties have accepted the logic of this: such a government cannot ignore the conditions the upper house attaches to the granting of supply.

In 1947 the Legislative Council in refusing supply forced an election for the Legislative Assembly. In 1952, the Legislative Council, again in refusing supply but this time with the Labor Party's full support, went even further by forcing one government to give way to another. In 1947 John Cain, unlike Gough Whitlam, conceded the need for a dissolution little more than a week after his first Supply Bill had been thrown out. In 1952, McDonald, again unlike Whitlam, sought a dissolution on the very day the Legislative Council denied supply to his Government. But the Governor felt obliged to find other ministers capable of obtaining supply even though their prospects of obtaining majorities in the Legislative Assembly were slight. With the voting of supply to that Ministry and its subsequent defeats in the Legislative Assembly, all parties conceded the need for a dissolution; but such unanimity was lacking at all times in 1975.

Unlike the situation confronting Sir John Kerr when he sought Sir Garfield Barwick's advice in 1975, all that Sir Dallas Brooks required from Sir Edmund Herring and Sir Owen Dixon in 1952 was advice as to whether or not Mr Hollway should be granted a dissolution and not whether a dissolution was necessary. Yet strangely enough, in advising Sir Dallas Brooks against granting a dissolution to Mr Hollway, the two Chief Justices intervened more directly in the political process than Sir John Kerr had invited Sir Garfield Barwick to do when he sought from him an opinion on his constitutional rights and duties. McDonald was re-commissioned on the clearest possible understanding that he would renew the request for the dissolution which the Governor had earlier felt obliged to refuse him. Mr Whitlam, with the passing of supply, could not have been recommissioned on that understanding after the Fraser Government's defeats in the House of Representatives on 11 November, 1975, because at no stage after the Senate had denied supply to his government had Whitlam conceded the need for a dissolution. In fact his tactics in the House on that day had as their object the obviating of any such dissolution.

Sir Dallas Brooks conducted himself impeccably in 1952 but controversy was minimised by the circumspect conduct of the party leaders. I would maintain that Sir John Kerr, in much more difficult circumstances, conducted himself impeccably in 1975, but his difficulties and the lingering controversy concerning his conduct respectively were and are due to Gough Whitlam's unpardonable lack of circumspection.

There remains the question of Sir Dallas Brooks's consultations with the two Chief Justices. Consultations with State Chief Justices have taken place regularly and are now well documented. More than one consultation has been revealed between Governor-Generals and Chief Justices of the High Court, and my fellow contributor, Don Markwell, has proved pertinacious in bringing them to light. Sir Owen Dixon's conduct in 1952 constitutes a precedent (though not the only one) for Sir Garfield Barwick's action in 1975, which cannot be distinguished simply because it was a State Governor Dixon advised, and not the Governor-General. Dixon, by common consent the most eminent lawyer Australia has produced, also advised a West Australian State Governor, Sir Charles Gairdner. Since I first made this point, this transposition between the State and Commonwealth spheres has been questioned but the supporting arguments have impressed me as being facile and unpersuasive.[15]

Notes

1. DO 35 1120 G584/4, Public Records Office.
2. *Victorian Parliamentary Debates*, 27 September 1945, p. 4330.
3. The late Sir Clifden Eager, President of the Legislative Council for many years said this in a private conversation.
4. DO 35 1120 G584/4, Public Records Office.

5. *Victorian Parliamentary Debates*, 30 September 1947, p. 2.
6. *Op.cit.* pp. 32–3.
7. *Op.cit.* p. 34.
8. *Op.cit.* p. 163.
9. *Op.cit.* pp. 224–5.
10. *Ibid.*
11. DO 35/3197, Public Records Office.
12. The concluding paragraph to my entry on Sir Albert Dunstan in the *Australian Dictionary of Biography* reads: Whether he was in the leadership of the Country Party or out of it Dunstan seemed to hold the key to its fortunes. Moreover, he seems to have been pivotal to the chances and changes of Victorian politics over thirty years. He might well be judged to have lacked statesmanship, but statesmanship was not the key to survival in Victorian politics, and Dunstan was without peer in his ability to survive. *Australian Dictionary of Biography* Vol. 8 1891–1939 p. 376 at p. 379.
13. DO 35/3195, Public Records Office.
14. SLADEN, Arthur French, CMG. 1911; CVO 1916; b. 30 Apr. 1866; e.s. of late Col. Joseph Sladen, m. 1891 . 3s. *Educ* Haileybury Coll.; Royal Naval Coll. Greenwich. Entered the Gov. General's Office, Ottawa, 1890; Private Secretary to Lord Minto 1899–1904; to Lord Grey, 1904–11, to the Duke of Connaught 1911–16; to the Duke of Devonshire 1916–21; to Lord Byng of Vimy, 1921–26. [Died 7 March 1944]. From *Who Was Who*, 1941–1950.
15. I first drew attention to this in an article 'History Justifies Barwick's Advice', *The Bulletin* (Sydney) March 1, 1983 pp. 50–59. But see the following: Geoffrey Sawer, 'Parallels between State and Federal crises not really relevant', *The Canberra Times*, 23 March, 1983, p. 2; J. B. Paul, 'Constitutional consultations', *The Canberra Times*, 14 April, 1983, p. 2 (letters).

4 The Politics of a Constitutional Crisis: Pakistan, April 1953–May 1955

Ayesha Jalal

Pakistan is no longer a member of the Commonwealth. Its state structure, however, is as much a legacy of the connection with the British Crown as it is a product of the clashing particularisms of its constituent units. Indeed, without the wanton use of the Commonwealth connection and the powers Dominion status bestowed upon the Governor-General – the head of state – Pakistan's fledgling political process might not have crumbled quite as easily as it did. This is borne out by Pakistan's very first constitutional crisis which marked a decisive shift in the institutional balance of power within the incipient state structure. In April 1953, when a Bengali Prime Minister enjoying the confidence of the Constituent Assembly was summarily dismissed by a Punjabi Governor-General there were no major ripples on the unstable sea of Pakistani politics. Yet on 24 October 1954 when a similar fate greeted the Bengali-dominated Constituent Assembly which had after some seven years of tortuous debate agreed on the principles of its future constitutional framework, the legality of the Governor-General's action did not go unchallenged. The Sind High Court's ruling on the Federation of Pakistan *vs.* Tamizuddin Khan case went against the Governor-General, but was overturned on technical grounds and precedents in British common law practice by the mainly Punjabi judges of the Supreme Court.

It was a momentous ruling, one from which Pakistan has never wholly recovered. Half a dozen constitutions later – a remarkable feat even by the exacting standards of political instability and constitutional breakdowns in newly independent countries – and after the breakaway of its eastern wing, Pakistan continues to grapple with fundamental questions about the powers of the head of state and the national Parliament. With a political horizon charred by extended periods of rule by a predominantly Punjabi military and bureaucracy, and persisting tensions between the Punjab and the non-Punjabi provinces, it is doubtful whether a seventh attempt at constitution-making can resolve an issue that to begin with was never purely a constitutional one but which now calls into question the nature of the state itself.

Given the very large impact which the constitutional crisis during April 1953 and May 1955 has had on the Pakistani state structure, it would be a mistake to see it as just another variant in disputes between Governor-Generals and cabinets or Governor-Generals and parliaments even if, according to Sir Ivor Jennings, it raised 'fundamental principles of constitutional law of interest throughout the Commonwealth'.[1] From the outset, the Pakistani experiment with the Westminster model diverged rather than converged with similar attempts in the Commonwealth. When the British transferred power in 1947, Pakistan joined the Commonwealth as an independent Dominion and its Governor-Generals took oaths of loyalty, though not of allegiance, to the British Crown. The Government of India Act of 1935 – that ultimate instrument of imperial control – was modified to serve as the interim constitution. Consequently, despite the elements of the structure, the spirit of Westminster was conspicuous by its absence.

So instead of inserting another interpretative footnote in an already lengthy legal debate on the constitutional propriety of decisions taken by the Governor-General, Ghulam Mohammad, it might be more sensible to focus on how the powers of the head of state were exploited for personal or partisan ends and why ambiguities in relations between the Crown and an independent Dominion made it possible for the Governor-General to secure judicial sanction for his actions. Such an approach has the added advantage of showing how the methods adopted to resolve the constitutional crisis helped not only to establish the supremacy of the executive over the legislative arms of the state but also that of the civil bureaucracy and the military over parties and politicians with popular bases of support.

The root of the problem has to be traced to the period immediately preceding the creation of the Pakistani state. At the helm of a movement which was least well-organised in the areas that became part of Pakistan, Mohammad Ali Jinnah – the leader of the All-India Muslim League – opted for the office of Governor-General rather than Prime Minister. A constitutional lawyer of considerable perspicacity, Jinnah had seen the advantages in exercising the wide-ranging powers which the Indian Independence Bill conferred upon the Governor-General.[2] Under

Section 9(1) of the Bill, the Governor-General had virtual dictatorial powers over the entire sphere of government (including the judiciary). The Constituent Assembly, which was to also serve as the national legislature until the framing of the constitution, could curb the powers of the Governor-General, but rule by executive decree was entirely within the realm of the possible. It was indeed an irresistible temptation for a leader uncertain of controlling his contumacious followers or countering the manoeuvres of his rivals in the Indian National Congress, while at the same time establishing real central authority over riot-torn territories separated by over a thousand miles.

As it turned out, Jinnah's role as Governor-General proved to be indispensable in confirming the presence of a central authority over the Pakistani provinces. The more so since those who set about creating the new central government apparatus in Karachi were soon at odds with the provincial leaders on matters to do with the allocation of power and financial resources, most of which had to be diverted to bolster the state's internal and external defences.[3] Issuing ordinances and Governor-General's orders from Karachi was one way of taking the sting out of provincial demands before they managed, jointly or severally, to make nonsense of the new central government's authority. During the heady first months of Pakistan's existence there was, in the words of a constitutional historian who might have read Jinnah's mind, simply 'no room for a weak Centre'.[4] This imperative combined with a personal prestige untarnished by the unseemly exploits of other League leaders, saw Jinnah securing the Pakistan cabinet's approval to overrule their decisions and assuming similar levers of power *vis-à-vis* the Legislative Assembly.

The appropriation of such enormous powers by Jinnah might seem to have set the example for subsequent Governor-Generals, but to adhere to such a view would be an oversimplification of the complex historical processes that enabled Ghulam Mohammad, a civil bureaucrat, to take over as head of state and begin dismantling the fragile facade of 'democratic government'. In any case, after Jinnah's death in September 1948 the most important figure in the emerging configuration of forces was the Prime Minister, Liaquat Ali Khan, not the Governor-General. But with growing tensions between the centre and the constituent units, fuelled by the increasing extraction of resources from the provinces to finance the war with India in Kashmir, Liaquat Ali Khan was unable to stem the erosion of the Muslim League. Without some sort of a popularly-based institutional support, Liaquat could not establish the supremacy of the prime ministerial office, much less prevent an alliance of largely Punjabi civil and defence officials from manipulating their international connections to tip the balance of power against the political leadership.[5] His assassination in 1951 removed the one remaining obstacle to the ascendancy of the civil bureaucracy and the military over parties and politicians. So far from being an inevitable consequence of the all-powerful role played by Jinnah as Governor-General, that of Ghulam Mohammad was facilitated by the changes wrought by the interplay of domestic, regional and international factors on the institutional balance of power within the emerging structure of the Pakistani state.

Clearly then, long before the Governor-General's unceremonious dismissal of Pakistan's second Prime Minister, Khwaja Nazimuddin, the pendulum of power had been gravitating away from the political leadership towards the bureaucracy and the Army High Command. Sprung on an unsuspecting people on 17 April 1953, the dismissal of Nazimuddin was explicitly demanded by the defence establishment, backed by senior bureaucrats and members of certain influential Punjabi families – all anxious to hitch Pakistan's wagons to the United States' star in return for a military aid package and a wheat loan. It came at a convenient moment. Pakistan was facing a serious food crisis; and the Punjab, under martial law, was facing the combined challenge of the non-Punjabi provinces on major constitutional issues. It was not a mere coincidence that Nazimuddin, a scion of the Nawab of Dacca's family, was sacked within weeks of the adoption by the Legislative Assembly (which despite the Muslim League's absolute majority was overwhelmingly Bengali)[6] of a budget slashing allocations to the defence and the administrative services.

The timing of the decision, however, was determined by a more pressing consideration – the Prime Minister was apparently planning to recommend that London recall the ailing but incorrigibly heavy-handed Punjabi Governor-General. Ghulam Mohammad in collusion with General Ayub Khan, the Commander-in-Chief of the Pakistan Army and Iskander Mirza, the Secretary of Defence, had little difficulty pre-empting the Bengali move.

Under the umbrella of the royal prerogative the Governor-General had carried out something very near a military *coup d'etat*. This was a typically Pakistani twist to the Westminster system. It took another year and worse political disasters before anyone realised that Pakistan was in the throes of a constitutional crisis. In early 1954 the Muslim League met its nemesis in East Bengal; it was routed by the United Front and reduced to a mere ten seats in an assembly of 309. There were immediate calls for the dissolution of the Constituent Assembly on the grounds that its Muslim League majority no longer reflected, let alone represented, the interests of the eastern wing. The central government was unmoved. The new Prime Minister, Mohammad Ali Bogra, a political nonentity from East Bengal who was unequivocally pro-US, argued that the Constituent Assembly was immune from electoral swings in the provinces – which was incorrect since its members were indirectly elected by the provincial assemblies – and could be dissolved only after it had completed drafting a constitution, which was a stickier issue.

The central government was to soon change its tack in the name of the people's democratic freedoms. A couple of points on this are here in order. After reluctantly granting a 59-day grace period to Fazlul Huq's United Front ministry, the first non-League ministry in post-independence Pakistan, Governor's Rule was slapped on East Bengal and the United Front ministry was dismissed. Huq was charged with pro-Indian and pro-communist leanings and, worse still, secessionism. The real reason, however, was that the United Front's populist posture and unflagging opposition to the central government's pro-US foreign policy threatened the position of the bureaucratic-military clique. Hardly surprisingly, the new Governor of East Bengal was none other than Iskander Mirza, the rising star who was to soon outshine Ghulam Mohammad in the art of political intrigue. Having quashed the siren calls for democracy in East Bengal, the central government seemed content to let an unrepresentative Constituent Assembly proceed with the framing of the constitution.

Bogra actually cobbled together a compromise formula which in principle, if not in fact, was accepted by the self-styled representatives of Bengal and Punjab in the Constituent Assembly. But contrary to the plans of the bureaucratic-military axis and some of its allies in the Punjab, it made no provision for lumping the smaller provinces of West Pakistan into a single administrative unit and so foreclosing the possibility of their negotiating jointly with East Bengal. Instead, the most notable features of Bogra's formula were to give Bengali the status of a national language, parity of representation between eastern and western Pakistan, and the stipulation against the office of Prime Minister and Governor-General being held by individuals belonging to the same wing. The latter provision was consistent with the principle of parity which had been the main reason for the acceptance of Bogra's formula by the Punjabi members of the assembly. Yet it raised a knotty question: who was to be more powerful, the Prime Minister or the Governor-General? Since Bogra and Nazimuddin were both from the eastern wing, the Bengali contingent, aided and abetted by non-Punjabi allies for whom the bureaucratic-military combine's plans to abolish provincial boundaries in West Pakistan were pure anathema, ingeniously amended the interim constitution in order to restrict the Governor-General's powers. The amendments effectively prevented the Governor-General from dismissing the central cabinet which was now to be directly responsible to Parliament.

On 20 September 1954 everyone was stunned by the news of the amendments. Here at last was a revolt by politicians against constitutional autocracy. There was reason to welcome a move to uphold the supremacy of Parliament, but sadly for Pakistan, it had been taken by an unrepresentative Constituent Assembly whose partisan interests were patently obvious. Spurred by their own daring, the members of the Constituent Assembly had also scrapped the Public and Representative Offices (Disqualification) Act or PRODA, that Damocles' sword hanging over the head of all politicians, whether straight or crooked. Since its introduction in 1949, a number of politicians had been convicted of malpractices and debarred from the political arena. So those expecting to be felled by its provisions wanted its repeal. To make this as well as the other amendments palatable to public opinion, the Constituent Assembly announced that its seven-year-long constitution-making ordeal would soon be over; the constitution bill was finally 'ready' to be enacted into law.

Before that happened, the Governor-General dealt the fatal blow. On 24 October 1954, he declared a state of emergency, axed the Constituent Assembly, and promised fresh elections. The naive, and there were many, believed that the Governor-General had released them from the clutches of an unrepresentative oligarchy bent upon perpetuating itself indefinitely. The more astute could see that the Governor-General's decision to include in his so-called 'cabinet of talents' men who had never contested public office – the Commander-in-Chief of the Army and Iskander Mirza for instance – was a potential death-knell for representative government in Pakistan. They were right; although Pakistan was without a legislature, the Governor-General had no qualms about publicising that the country would be presented with an officially approved constitution on the eighth birthday of its independence.

These were issues of vital importance. The Bengali President of the Constituent Assembly, Maulvi Tamizuddin Khan, took up the cudgels against the Governor-General and his military and bureaucratic associates. On 2 February 1955, a full bench of the Sind High Court unanimously decided that the Governor-General had no 'power of any kind to dissolve the Constituent Assembly'.[7] This was a reassuring sign of the independence of the judiciary, but bitter disappointments were on the way.

The Governor-General consulted the Punjabi Chief Justice of Pakistan, Muhammad Munir, who in sympathy with the centre was ready to over rule the Sind High Court's judgement.[8] With the highest judical authority swinging behind it, the Pakistan government appealed to the federal court which decided by a vote of four to one that the Sind Court had no jurisdiction to issue a writ in Tamizuddin's favour. The federal court did not consider whether the Governor-General had rightly dissolved the Constituent Assembly; it merely overruled the lower court's decision on technical grounds, namely that Section 223A under which the Sind Court had heard the appeal did not have the Governor-General's assent and therefore was not part of the law.[9]

It was an amazing verdict. To their consternation, the people of Pakistan now discovered that the Constituent Assembly was not a fully sovereign body. Since it was also the federal legislature it operated under the restrictions specified in Section 6(3) of the Independence Bill. A close reading of the section makes it amply clear that the provision for the Governor-General's 'full power of assent' was not tantamount to a power of veto on constitutional provisions. If anything it aimed at underscoring the degree of autonomy an independent Dominion had from the British Crown and Parliament. Yet it suited the four federal court judges to interpret the clause otherwise. And this despite the fact that for the past seven years, the rules of procedure for the Constituent Assembly – formulated while Jinnah was alive – specifically stated that the Governor-General's assent was not necessary for a Bill to be placed on the statute book.[10]

The exercise of personal discretion by the four honourable judges fitted in splendidly with the central government's plans to scotch Bengali demands for autonomy by merging the West Pakistani provinces into one unit – a necessary condition for strengthening the executive at the expense of the legislature and, implicitly if not explicitly, the judicial arms of the state. After the federal court's decision in March 1955, Pakistan was not only without a legislature but as many as 46 acts on the statute books had suddenly lost their legal sanction. At least three major court cases had been decided on the basis that laws passed by the Constituent Assembly did not need the Governor-General's assent. Pakistan was well and truly in the depths of a constitutional crisis with serious political and legal ramifications.

Undeterred by the implications of the federal court's ruling, the Governor-General and his 'cabinet of talents' decided to concentrate on foisting a constitution by executive decrees. So Ghulam Mohammad issued the Emergency Powers Ordinance XI, declaring a 'state of grave emergency' throughout Pakistan, and placing a blanket prohibition on all proceedings against the central government dealing with the dismissal of the Constituent Assembly.[11] The Ordinance gave him powers to frame a constitution by nominating the members of a 'Constitution Convention', to convert West Pakistan into a single administrative unit, to validate 35 of the 46 laws which had become void due to the federal court's ruling, to pass the central budget and finally, to rename the eastern wing as 'East Pakistan'.[12]

The assumption of draconian powers by the Governor-General forced the federal court to alter its tune. On 13 April 1955, a full bench of the federal court, with Justice Munir in the chair, gave its final decision on Usif Patel's case against the Crown. It now ruled that while the Governor-General could 'give or withhold assent' to Bills passed by the Constituent Assembly, actual constitution-making could only be carried out by the elected representatives of the people.[13] Maintaining that the central government had 'grievously misunderstood' the federal court's ruling on the Tamizuddin case, the Chief Justice castigated the Governor-General for issuing an Ordinance which made 'no reference to elections'; the 'first concern' of the central government should have been to 'bring into existence another representative body to exercise the powers of the Constituent Assembly'.[14] The Chief Justice also confessed that he did 'not know whether the Constituent Assembly was dissolved legally or not'.[15]

This threw the Governor-General and his cabinet into momentary disarray. The federal court now declared that unless the central government formally asked for its opinion on the thorny question of whether the Constituent Assembly was dissolved legally or not, the honourable judges could not establish the legality of any alternative constitution-making body. Ghulam Mohammad and his team relented and made a special reference to the federal court. Although the Independence Bill had not given the Governor-General any power to dissolve the Constituent Assembly, four out of the five federal court judges upheld the legality of his action by drawing upon the laws of natural necessity and two famous maxims in British common law doctrine: *salus populi superma lex* (safety of the people is the supreme law) and *salus republicae est suprema lex* (safety of the state is the supreme law).[16] By declaring necessity as the legal basis for all that was unlawful, the federal court had handed the Governor-General and his bureaucratic and military associates a face-saving device manufactured not in Pakistan but, ironically enough, in Britain.

Legal niceties aside, the outcome of the constitutional crisis had laid the basis for the future state structure: the supremacy of the head of state over the national cabinet and the legislature, and a judiciary whose independence was at best extremely equivocal. Personal, partisan and particularistic interests had triumphed, making a mockery of the Westminster model, and weakening the political process irreparably. General Ayub's take-over in October 1958 merely put the coping stone on a long-drawn-out but largely successful struggle waged by the bureaucratic-military axis to control, if not altogether do away with, the political process in Pakistan. The 'constitutional' abortion of the political process had helped gear the state apparatus more effectively behind such US-inspired strategies of economic growth that were better suited to the institutional interests of the military and the bureaucracy and, naturally, of their allies among Karachi-based industrialists as well as certain landed and business families of the Punjab.

Notes

1. Sir Ivor Jennings, *The Constitutional Problems in Pakistan*, Cambridge 1957, preface, cited in G. W. Choudhury, *Constitutional Development in Pakistan*, second edition, Lahore 1969, p. 89.
2. For a detailed analysis of Jinnah's decision, see my article 'Inheriting the Raj: Jinnah and the Governor-Generalship Issue', *Modern Asian Studies*, Volume 19, Part 1, February 1985, pp. 29–53.
3. See my article 'The Partition of India and the Defence of Pakistan: an Historical Perspective', *Journal of Imperial and Commonwealth History*, Volume XV, May 1987, Number 3, pp. 269–310.
4. Choudhury, *Constitutional Development in Pakistan*, p. 28.
5. This is a theme developed in my forthcoming work on post-independence Pakistan, *The State of Martial Rule: Pakistan's Political Economy of Defence*. For an overview see my paper, 'Constructing a State: the interplay of Domestic, Regional and International Factors in Post-Colonial Pakistan', presented at the Woodrow Wilson International Center for Scholars, Washington, D.C. April 1986.
6. The provincial breakdown in the first Constituent Assembly was as follows:

East Bengal	44	Baluchistan	1
Punjab	22	Baluchistan States	1
NWFP	3	Khairpur State	1
Sind	5	Bahawalpur State	1
NWFP States	1	TOTAL	79

7. Cited in Choudhury, *Constitutional Development in Pakistan*, p. 86.
8. A recent article has alleged that Munir had 'assured the Government in advance that he would upset . . . [the Sind High Court's] judgement when it went before him . . . (see *Dawn*, 9 August 1986).
9. Federation of Pakistan *vs*. Tamizuddin Khan, in *Federal Court Reports, 1955*, Karachi 1955.
10. Ibid.
11. *Dawn*, 28 March 1955.
12. Choudhury, *Constitutional Development in Pakistan*, pp. 87–88.
13. See Usif Patel vs. the Crown, *Federal Court Reports*, 1955, p. 366.
14. Ibid., p. 372.
15. *Dawn*, 14 April 1955, cited in Inamur Rahman, *Public Opinion and Political Development in Pakistan, 1947–1958*, Oxford 1982, p. 166 and Choudhury, *Constitutional Development in Pakistan*, p. 88.
16. Special Reference no. 1 of 1955, *Federal Court Reports*, p. 495.

5 Politics, Law and Constitutionalism: The 1962 Western Region Crisis in Nigeria.

James O'Connell

At independence in 1960 both Nigerian leaders and the British officials from whom they had formally taken over power believed that the country's main political and constitutional arrangements had been dealt with and agreed on during the protracted negotiations that had taken place between the colonial government and the Nigerian party leaders during the 1950s.

The constitution had been fashioned under British supervision and with British technical help. Its main features had however been worked out, and agreed to, by Nigerians. The commonly made charge that colonial constitutions were imposed, and that foreign institutions were not suitable to the non-Western developing world could not easily be sustained. The constitution was not imposed; it was not foreign made, even if it did bear foreign influence; and in any case, population concentrations so large, so spread out geographically, and so much in need of adequate administration and leadership needed the kind of institutional devices that were being taken over from the Western world but had nothing peculiarly Western about them. Some shrewd observers thought that the constitution was too complex, but it was also possible to say that the complexity was more apparent than real. The Nigerian constitution simply spelt out arrangements that in Britain were left to unwritten conventions; and it seemed sensible to write in legally to the constitution conventions that were crucial to its working and that in a new and multi-ethnic country were better not left to the evolution of a political culture in which these conventions had not grown up originally.

Nigeria in 1960 was seen from outside the country as the most stable and mature of the new African states. In a federal system that had central institutions (and territory) and three regions or states (Eastern, Northern and Western Regions), the Nigerian leaders had possessed effective self-government for most of the 1950s. Formal independence in 1960 seemed more important in external than in internal relations. The civil service functioned efficiently, and except for the Northern Region and to a lesser extent the federal centre, it was almost completely Nigerianised in its administrative cadres. The opposition in the federal parliament had settled into the role of a British-type loyal and constitutional opposition. Each of the three federal regions was governed by a party that was based on the support of the main ethnic group in that region; and, not least, the economy, though not buoyant, was continuing to grow. Moroever, the federal political alignment had not followed completely certain natural lines of cleavage. In the ruling federal coalition government the Northern People's Congress (NPC), which represented a conservative ruling class and peoples in the less well-developed economy of the savanna country, was allied with the National Council of Nigeria and the Cameroons (NCNC), which represented the economically dynamic Ibo groups of the Eastern Region as well as many Yoruba and non-Yoruba groups of the Western Region (the Eastern and Western Regions were also commonly referred to as the South as opposed to the North). It was also committed to more socialist and populist policies than its Northern allies who were the major group in the coalition. Obafemi Awolowo, the dominant Yoruba politician and the leader of the opposition Action Group, had in 1959 paid the great tribute to the federal system of leaving the premiership of the Western Region to contest power at the federal level. When he failed to achieve a majority in the 1959 federal election on the eve of independence, he settled for the attrition of opposition and continued campaigning against the ruling coalition.

On leaving his regional premiership Awolowo accepted, albeit reluctantly, that his deputy Premier, S. L. A. Akintola, should take over the post. Awolowo however believed that the power he held as party leader would ensure his continuing authority within the region which was his political base and that in spite of Akintola's formal powers as Premier the main decisions within the region would still be controlled by him. Rivalry between the two men – and their respective groups of followers – was not going to be easily set aside however. It was to come to a head in the 1962 crisis that revealed how unresolved could be the relations between constitutional norms and conventions and the play of power politics in a new federation. Much of the emphasis of this chapter will be on the political interplay between politicians with differing power bases and constitutional roles. The constitutional issue that came to be posed – namely, under what conditions could a regional governor remove a premier from office – arose initially out of a political split in the ruling party of their region; it continued to pose a problem for the federal government which supported one faction in the split, and it was finally set aside rather than resolved when the possession of political power overrode a Privy Council decision. But in the process what was called into question was less the issue of respect for the letter of constitutional law than constitutionalism itself.

On the surface, the Action Group in 1962 looked solidly established within its own Western Region, unlike the other Southern party, the NCNC, which ruled the Eastern Region and which seemed to be under pressure from the ambitions of individual leaders, from the fissiparous tendencies of segmentary Ibo clans and lineages, and from the strains of coping with the diversity of its ethnic support. The Action Group had ranged behind it, within a coherent and disciplined party organisation, the strength of majority Yoruba sentiment; it had the nearly unanimous support of Yoruba chiefs as well as most of the mid-Western chiefs (the mid-West area contained the non-Yoruba groups – Bini, Ishan, Urhobo, Itsekiri, Ijaw, Ibo and others who were a numerical minority within the region); it controlled regional economic patronage that attached both traditional notables and modernising middle level activists to its ranks; and it was able to raise party funds through using governmental institutions in the country's most prosperous region. These various strengths were – with the exception of the party's grip on Yoruba sentiment – to prove all too fragile once pressures were placed upon them.

BUILD-UP TO CONFLICT: TENSIONS OF POWER AND PATRONAGE

There were several different strands – constitutional tensions, ideological stances and personal bitternesses – in the conflict that, in 1962, tore the Action Group apart. The constitutional tensions hinged round the ambiguous relationship between the party leadership and the regional cabinet. The ideological stances raised issues of political tactics in campaigning for national power and in advocating socialist measures. The personal bitternesses emanated from temperamental and other conflicts among members of the top leadership, especially between Awolowo and Akintola. Whilst some of the factors in the dispute were more important than others, they converged to create a split that resisted all efforts to heal it.

The new Premier, Chief S. L. A. Akintola, and the majority of his cabinet resented Awolowo's assumption of continued control as party leader and resisted what they considered to be interference with their constitutional position. In this resistance they were supported by most of their upper civil servants who found it hard enough to cope with decisions made by ministers with whom they were in close contact without having to put up as well with decisions that were imposed from outside the region. Differences came to a head over two financial decisions that Western Region ministers reluctantly made on the advice of their civil servants: the raising of secondary school fees and the lowering of cocoa prices. In neither case was Awolowo consulted. He was not only personally affronted, but he considered that the decisions flouted the social welfare policies of the party. In the event he succeeded in having the regional cabinet go back on its decision to raise school fees. Inevitably the regional cabinet members felt humiliated and became embittered. The issue of governmental decision-making was further complicated by the question of the allocation of patronage within the region. Realising that the possibility of a confrontation was in the offing, Akintola set about using government powers of appointment to name men willing to support him to the boards of public corporations and similar institutions. In the process he ignored nominees whose merits were urged upon him by Awolowo. The latter, for his part, resented the attempt to erode his power base and became even more estranged from the deputy leader of his party and his successor as Premier. Gradually it became obvious in late 1961 to the Action Group leaders and to Western Region civil servants that the existing constitutionally ambiguous and politically tense relationship between the party leader and the Western cabinet could not continue for very much longer.

Apart from the personal power struggle, Awolowo and his supporters and Akintola and his differed on two crucial issues. The first concerned the scope of the party's campaigning: whether the party should continue to seek power on a national level or restrict its efforts to the Western Region. The second issue arose out of the ideology that Awolowo proposed for his policy of nationwide campaigning to gain federal power: he wanted the party to adopt what appeared to be a radical form of socialism that Akintola and the more conservative members of the party objected to, and that bitterly antagonised and frightened the ruling federal cabinet. Akintola and other senior leaders were opposed to political campaigning outside the Western Region for two main reasons. First, they feared retaliation by the federal government. They had had a foretaste of federal retaliatory power in an abortive federal attempt to investigate the affairs of the National Bank which was controlled by the regional government, and more seriously they feared that the federal government would find a pretext in some outbreak of local disorder to suspend the Western Region government and destroy the Action Group in its political base. They had been made nervous by the raising of this possibility by the NCNC during riots in 1961 in mid-Western minority areas. Second, they argued positively that the party should accept a policy of 'regional security' in which the main parties came to a gentleman's agreement to confine their activities to their home regions. They pointed out, moreover, that there were adequate pickings for the political class in a well-to-do region such as the West. The principal advocates of a policy of 'regional security', Akintola and another minister, Chief Ayo Rosiji, had worked with the Prime Minister, Abubakar Tafawa Balewa, and other federal ministers in the national coalition that preceded the 1959 federal election and were on excellent personal terms with them. They believed that once a policy of accommodation had been agreed to, it would only be a matter of time before their party was invited to join a national coalition government. The only obstacle they saw in the way of political compromise and a place in a national government was Awolowo's overweening ambition. They believed too that the majority of the well-to-do backers of the party wanted the struggle against the federal coalition to be discontinued and they disliked carrying the financial costs to the party of aiding the hopeless struggle of minority groups in the North and the East.

The socialist stand taken by Awolowo was geared to winning popular support on a national level. But it was more and more seen by leading members of his own party as well as by coalition opponents as a position that pandered to extreme levelling elements. Both Southern Region parties were self-declared socialist parties. However they much more stressed – and in this respect they were true heirs of a colonial autocratic tradition – the features of socialism that involved governmental intervention and public ownership rather than equality. The most radical turn that Awolowo gave to his socialist ideology was in advocating the nationalisation of foreign companies. He claimed that through such nationalisation, Nigerian businessmen would retain their own enterprises, would receive government help, and would be encouraged to take over certain fields of economic activity now monopolised by foreign investors. Federal and regional ministers who were trying to attract foreign investment to the country and its regions were fearful, however, that such investment would be frightened off by Awolowo's statements. Action Group ministers who were sensitive to pressure from Awolowo were more personally upset by another set of austerity measures that Awolowo propounded as part of his radical package: reductions in the salaries and emoluments of ministers. The ministers knew the popular appeal of this. Yet many were only barely able as it was to meet from their apparently substantial incomes the multiple demands on their purse that ministerial office brought. They resented Awolowo's advocacy of austerity all the more because they believed that he – not to mention his wife who was a substantial business women in her own right – had in one way or another put together a substantial personal fortune. Akintola and other leading cabinet members made no secret of their scorn for Awolowo's socialist conversion, which they saw as purely tactical. But there were older and wealthier party supporters who were afraid of its ideological implications and who believed Awolowo was being encouraged and advised by younger men who were communists. Essentially, however, Awolowo believed that discontent was growing among the less well-to-do classes. By capitalising on this discontent and by appealing to the idealism of young political activists, and their disgruntlement with ministerial performance and privilege, he believed that he could by-pass the obstacle that ethnic allegiances had offered to his search for national support in 1959.[1]

Within the Action Group support for Awolowo came from three groups. The first contained older Yoruba politicians like Daudu Adegbenro who stood by him out of personal loyalty and party solidarity. Among this group were also to be found senior mid-Western party members such as Tony Enahoro (Ishan) and Alfred Rewane (Itsekiri) who owed their political careers to support from Awolowo's attempt to extend the party beyond its Yoruba base. Generally the members of this group resembled Awolowo's party opponents in life style and political outlook. A second group contained most of the middle level party activists who cherished their own political ambitions, and who under existing conditions could not hope to dislodge the entrenched upper leadership. Included in this group were paid party organisers and other activists in the Eastern and Northern Regions who would be abandoned were a policy of regional security to be accepted. A third group overlapped in good measure with the second but was distinguished from it in that its members tended to be better educated – men like H. O. Oluwasanmi, S. O. Aluko and A. K. Mabogunje who were university teachers. This last group worked closely with Awolowo to produce the new documentation that expressed the party's change in ideology. In the course of the struggle that lay ahead most of Awolowo's early companions in the party and its senior members deserted him, although the middle level activists and the educated group mostly stayed with him. They also tended to possess jobs that were less open to pressure from the incumbent government. They provided Awolowo and the Action Group after the split with a hard core of activist supporters and organisers when almost the entire establishment of the Western Region had gone over to their opponents. Their backing proved strangely durable in the course of changing political fortunes.

Other differences between Awolowo and Akintola were exacerbated by personal antagonisms between the two men. Awolowo had not wanted Akintola to succeed him when he quit the premiership, but had been overruled by a party caucus. Akintola was genial and easy-going in personality in a way that the severe and humourless Awolowo was not. Akintola also came from the Oyo section of the party and seems to have shared some of the traditional Oyo contempt for the trading Ijebu from whom Awolowo came. Akintola and other senior party members distrusted Awolowo's political judgment after the electoral debacle of 1959. They disliked his stubbornness and arrogance, and saw these defects as being compounded by his tendency to surround himself with men they considered sycophants. Other senior members of the party shared Akintola's reactions to Awolowo; and by and large many came to believe with him that it was time to resist the ambitions and policies of a man whose character was at variance with the flexibility of the Yoruba tradition. They put the word around that Awolowo had become more and more difficult to deal with. Awolowo in turn reacted to their whispering campaign, and to the diminishing influence allowed his personal supporters in the Western Region, by building up his personal support among party activists. As differences between the two men accumulated, he decided to move against Akintola and his group at the party congress that was being held in February 1962 in Jos.

THE PARTY SPLIT: THE FAILURE OF CONCILIATION

To understand the pattern of events at the congress, a word is necessary on the formal structure of the Action Group in 1962. The annual congress had the power to lay down general policy and to make central appointments. Among those who had the right to attend were two representatives of the party from every federal constituency, all federal MPs, and two members from the Lagos Town Council. Between congresses the party was ruled by the Federal Executive Council, an unwieldy body of about a hundred members that included ministers, shadow ministers from opposition regions, and twelve representatives chosen by each regional conference. The latter conferences paralleled the national conference in each region, and laid down party regional policy. The leader and the deputy leader of the party were elected by a joint meeting of parliamentary councils (made up of all the party's Members of Parliament) and the Federal Executive Council. The body – much smaller than the representative groups mentioned so far – that planned electoral and other tactics and co-ordinated regional efforts was the Federal Working Committee.

Real power in the party lay in good measure outside the formal structures – with the President, Awolowo, and those closely associated with him, including his deputy, Akintola. Awolowo had not ruled as an autocrat – though he did have considerable personal initiative and influence – but on all main policy matters had consulted senior party members (ministers, financial backers, certain traditional rulers). Akintola's selection as deputy leader was a case where he had given way to advice and pressure. A public statement by S. G. Ikoku, one of Awolowo's followers and an activist from the Eastern Region, argued that Awolowo when he was in government never did anything without first consulting the deputy leader, then the Obas (paramount chiefs), then the party elders, and finally with what was described as an Ikenne (Awolowo's home town) meeting of party notables. All this was broadly true. It was the traditional Yoruba way for the ruler to consult with his senior chiefs, and to negotiate the policy worked out among them with his junior chiefs. In a remarkable way the decision-making structures of the Action Group conformed to traditional Yoruba patterns. So it was that when the Akintola group brought complaints against Awolowo in the period before the party split, one of their most serious charges was that he had ceased to consult effectively with the moderately minded party elders, and had been working out policy with doctrinaire and unrealistic young men. It does seem indeed to have been the case that after 1960 Awolowo had taken more party power into his own hands, and had worked principally with his own close associates, rather than with a wider spectrum of party elders. He also came more and more to control the party funds. Members of the party outside the top leadership, and Awolowo's business aides, were not let into the provenance of the party funds; and many, though they had their own suspicions, did not care to know. However, to ensure the continuity of contributions to the funds Awolowo needed the co-operation of the Western government. One of the ways in which Akintola had shown his hostility to Awolowo's interventions in the West and his socialist policy was to inhibit access to government controlled funds by Awolowo and his faction.

By appealing to a party congress Awolowo was using formal structures to outflank Akintola and his followers. Since the congress was in good part made up of representatives from outside the Western Region who depended for funds and for their political survival on the willingness of the party to maintain a national orientation, Awolowo could count on their support to obtain a majority vote for his policies. Moreover, the middle level activists, who had not grown rich in the service of the party, were also likely to support him against the well-to-do conservative party backers, who had considerable sympathy for Akintola's position. There were, however, dangers in this outflanking policy. Many senior party ministers, MPs and financial backers felt that the Yoruba formed the core of the party and wanted power kept solidly in Yoruba hands. They also felt they had a stake in the party which the younger activists did not have. Awolowo ran the risk of alienating them in appealing to formal structures for a majority that seemed to them to involve an artificial arithmetic that did not correspond with effective influence and support within the party.

In his presidential report to the congress, Awolowo restated his policies uncompromisingly.[2] He attacked his opponents, but avoided mentioning Akintola by name. He called attention to 'a growing disaffection between privileged and non-privileged classes (so-called) within the party', and elaborated on his socialist programme. He rejected calls to join the federal coalition to form a national government, and said that the party should continue its opposition in the North and the East. Part of his speech was calculated to rally those Yoruba representatives who were influenced by traditional hostility to the Hausa who controlled the NPC. The presidential report was approved. From the start of the congress men like Akintola and Rosiji (the latter in particular was one of the leading advocates of an alliance with the NPC) saw that they had little chance of carrying a majority of the congress with them. They were also so upset by what they felt was the deliberate loading of the votes against their views that they staged a virtual walk-out from the congress. Accompanied by several Western Region ministers and other delegates they departed, giving as their reason that they needed to return to Ibadan to receive Ahmadu Bello, the Northern Premier, who was coming on a visit.

Once the Akintola faction had left, Awolowo and his supporters took over the congress completely. The congress rejected Rosiji's report as party secretary which had drawn attention to the decline in the party's fortunes in the North and East. It also passed a series of amendments to the party constitution. Ministerial representation was removed from the Federal Executive Council – a move that was meant to weaken the Western Premier. The Federal President was empowered to nominate a majority of the Federal Working Committee, and preside over Regional conferences and Regional Executive Committees. A crucial amendment was then carried that stated: 'If in the opinion of the Federal Executive Council, the Leader of the Party, the Deputy Leader of the Party, or any of the Parliamentary Leaders in the Legislatures has lost the confidence of the Party, the President of the Party shall summon a meeting of the appropriate body which elected him and require the meeting either to reaffirm their confidence in the person confirmed or elect a successor.[3] That amendment opened the way for Akintola's removal. Finally, Awolowo's supporters took control of the party's offices. The most important change was that S. G. Ikoku, an Ibo from the Eastern Region and a man who was probably one of the few genuine social radicals in Nigeria, replaced Chief Rosiji as Federal Secretary, and so took over charge of the party's officials.

After the Congress, Awolowo called a meeting of the Western Parliamentary Executive Committee and the Parliamentary Council at his home in Ikenne. By summoning a meeting of the body that had elected Akintola, Awolowo evidently intended to invoke the recent amendment to the party constitution, and remove Akintola from his post of deputy leader. Older party members were horrified by the prospect of the conflict which was about to erupt. A group of leading party elders led by Dr Maja who held the honorary title 'Father of the Action Group' and Sir Adesoji Aderemi who was Governor of the Western Region and Oni (paramount chief) of Ife, prevailed on Awolowo to hold back from his contemplated action. It is probable that had Awolowo pressed on at this stage he would have been able to oust Akintola before the latter had had time enough to muster his forces. If Awolowo now drew back, it was mainly because to have flouted the Yoruba tradition of conciliation would have lost him much goodwill among the party elders. So in the event a peace of sorts was established, although it proved to be shortlived. Ikoku with Awolowo's backing asserted the supremacy of the party over other groups and institutions. Akintola for his part kept on excluding Awolowo supporters from patronage. Moreover he built up popular support in the Oshun areas from which he came – so effectively that Awolowo had to cancel a visit to Oshun lest it provoke violence. A peace committee was finally set up under Chief F. R. A. Williams, a distinguished lawyer and a former Western Region minister, who was respected by both sides. When Awolowo turned down the compromise proposals formulated by this committee, there was no alternative to open confrontation.

At a joint meeting of the Mid-West and West Executive Committee on 19 May Awolowo listed his charges against Akintola. He accused him of maladministration, anti-party activities and gross indiscipline. He also accused him of permitting improper spending by ministers, victimisation of loyal party members, taking decisions on cocoa prices and school fees without party consultation and opposing both democratic socialism and national campaigning. By 81 votes to 29 a motion was carried to request Chief Akintola 'to resign the premiership of the Region and his post in the party as deputy leader forthwith.[4] The decision was later approved by the Federal Executive by 59 votes to nil. But Akintola refused to resign. Few, however, at the time thought he could hold out against what seemed the overwhelming majority of the party.

CONSTITUTIONALITY, LAW AND POLITICS: THE POWER TO DISMISS A PREMIER

Akintola now wrote to the Western Governor to ask that the regional parliament be dissolved. It was a shrewd move, because his faction could hope to split the Action Group vote, and subsequently join with the NCNC which drew support from both Yoruba and non-Yoruba groups in the region, to form a majority government in the region. Prevailed upon by Awolowo and others the Governor refused to dissolve the House. Extraordinary activities then went on behind the scenes as each faction lobbied for support, and large sums of money changed hands. Before long a document was presented to the Governor which was signed by 65 Action Group regional MPs (a majority of the House), that asked for the dismissal of the Premier. The Governor acted on this document and dismissed Akintola as Premier. On 21 May he then swore in as Premier Alhaji Daudu Adegbenro who had been elected as leader of the Action Group parliamentary party in his place. On the same day Akintola filed a High Court action challenging the Governor's right to dismiss him without a no-confidence vote on the floor of the House. He also petitioned the British prime Minister and the Queen to dismiss the Governor. The Regional High Court quickly shifted the uncomfortable onus of the decision to the Federal Supreme Court. Meanwhile the civil service recognised Adegbenro as Premier. Akintola was physically locked out of the Premier's office. When he forced his way back into the office to assert his legitimacy, it was an action that altered nothing legally, but in the bizarre conditions of the time had a strangely telling psychological effect.

A meeting of the Regional House of Assembly was called for 25 May. The Action Group appeared to have a solid majority over the Akintola group, which could hope to muster only about ten or twelve members, and the NCNC which had 35 members in a house of 120. When the Assembly met in the morning, the sitting was disrupted by the MPs hostile to the Action Group. The police intervened by releasing tear gas and clearing the House. Earlier the Federal Prime Minister had instructed the Regional Police Commissioner to recognise neither Adegbenro nor Akintola as Premier. After the House had adjourned both factions contacted the Prime Minister. Awolowo (who had been in the Visitors' Gallery) and Adegbenro asked for police protection within the chamber. The Akintola group said that the House could not again be convoked without disorder. The Prime Minister said that he had no power to prevent the House from meeting. But if it met, he said, there would be 'no police protection within the chamber.' He went on: 'If . . . any party insists on being afforded police protection within the Chamber, the police may be so present, but the Federal Government will not accept any decision reached as a result of such proceedings in the Chamber. If in spite of all the efforts of the police, there should be an outbreak of violence or any disorder, the police have authority to clear the Chamber and lock it up.'[5]

Following this statement, Akintola's supporters had only to create further disturbance in the chamber to make the proceedings impossible. They proceeded to do just this in a meeting of the House convened two and a half hours after the first one. The police again cleared the chamber. The Prime Minister convoked the federal parliament in emergency session. In a one day sitting on 29 May a state of emergency was declared in the Western Region, and an Emergency Powers Act listed 13 regulations that enabled the federal government to appoint an Administrator for the region who had powers to set up a government, remove opposition, and outlaw criticism.

It was difficult to accept that a state of emergency existed in a real sense in the Western Region. The Prime Minister could easily have ordered the police to act on the instructions of the Speaker of the House, and remove those members who were creating a disturbance. The towns and the countryside were tranquil. It is true that there were two claimants for the post of premier, but there was a legal way to resolve that issue. It was difficult not to suspect collusion between the Prime Minister and the Western Region opposition in facilitating a disturbance in the House that would be used as a pretext to declare an emergency. The validity of the declaration of emergency was taken before the Federal Supreme Court. The relevant clause in the constitution (Section 65) read that a 'period of emergency' came into existence at any time when: '(b) there is in force a resolution passed by each House of Parliament declaring that a state of emergency exists . . .' The Supreme Court refused to consider whether a state of emergency existed. It simply noted that there existed a resolution of both Houses of Parliament on this point and refused to intervene. The effect of the emergency was to tip the scales of political power in the Western Region decisively against the Action Group.

The Prime Minister appointed as Administrator Dr Moses Majekodunmi, the Federal Minister of Health, who was a nominated coalition member of the Senate and a personal friend. Majekodunmi was an Egba Yoruba. The Administrator at once placed restriction orders on the leading Western politicians, including Awolowo and Akintola, banning some of them to remote areas. He enacted legislation that made political journalism well nigh impossible, and placed under restriction two leading Action Group journalists, Lateef Jakande and Bisi Onabanjo, for making what were reasonable and informed criticisms of his policies. He then continued his thrust against the majority faction of the Action Group by releasing its opponents within two months while keeping its leaders under detention. He kept Rotimi Williams, the constitutional lawyer who had retired from active politics but who had played a role in trying to reconcile the warring factions in the Action Group, under detention in spite of a High Court order to release him. Williams was released by the court, but immediately afterwards detained again on the Administrator's orders. Dr Majekodunmi, and the federal government which supported him, seemed oblivious of the harm that such obvious contempt for the legal processes would cause to government and administration. While the Administrator was letting the Action Group know that he could effectively disband its political organisation, government controlled news media and other sources were putting it about that Action Group leaders had only to show repentance for their erstwhile hostility to the federal government and give up campaigning outside the West and all would be forgiven them (many of them were in fact only too willing to adopt any attitudes that would see them reinstated in political power).

To restore government in the region which had been disrupted by the continuous politicking of the previous months the Administrator set up a cabinet of mostly non-political commissioners who then worked closely with their civil servants. He also included in his cabinet six Obas or paramount chiefs (five of whom had been ministers without portfolio in the Action Group government). These last appointments were made in an effort to conciliate the region's natural rulers and persuade them to throw their weight behind the new administration. Majekodunmi also tried to conciliate at another level by raising the price of cocoa by £5 a ton. This helped farmers who had been hit by the previous price fall. It also brought money to the middle level groups involved in the cocoa produce trade and related activities. But it strained the declining finances of the region and left the government that succeeded the Administrator with less room for financial manoeuvre.

In a move to discredit the Action Group in a sustained way the Administrator proceeded to set up a tribunal under Mr Justice Coker of the High Court to investigate the Western Region Marketing Board and nine other public bodies. Shrewdly Awolowo refused to assist with the work of the tribunal, affirming that no real justice could be done by what was not meant to be an impartial investigation. The Coker tribunal brought much large-scale financial corruption and administrative incompetence to light.[6] The Marketing Board had inherited almost £18m. from its federal predecessor when it was set up in 1959. By 1962 the net assets in its current account were down to £1.5m. The tribunal revealed that money had been recklessly invested in worthless ventures. Not a single one of the 16 industrial projects set up with Marketing Board funds was making a profit. Alfred Rewane, the political secretary of the Action Group, had run the Marketing Board as a one-man show. The centrepiece of the investigation into corruption turned out to be a property company, the Nigerian Investments and Property Company (NIPC), which was run by Action Group backers. One glaring NIPC deal concerned a piece of property that had originally changed hands for £11 000 but eventually realised £150 000. The tribunal reckoned that the Western Region had diverted £6.5m. of Marketing Board funds to the company, and that in all over £4m. had gone to the party. The NIPC had been founded to get round the banking ordinance of 1960 that made the banks much less safe for party funding. It had played the major role in financing the Action Group newspapers. There were many other deals too, including the placing of public money in privately owned banks without regard for the stated policy of government, proper financial administration, or proper standards of probity. It is fair to say that not all the Marketing Board funds spent had been misappropriated and that a considerable share had gone to finance development in the region. However, it must also be said that if the regional government's award of contracts and other activities had been investigated, there is little doubt that other malpractices would have been uncovered. One of the few bright spots in the tribunal's report mentioned 'some bold and courageous civil servants who stuck to their guns with remarkable fortitude in the face of circumstances of a most trying order.' But the majority of the civil servants had simply carried out the orders that their political masters had given them; and some had displayed little competence in the technical aspects of their work.

Another development took place while the regional government was suspended and the Coker tribunal was sitting. Awolowo and a number of political supporters and allies were charged with treasonable activities. He and others were convicted in the High Court. On appeal his conviction was upheld, but his sentence was reduced from 15 to ten years. There is much that is still unclear about the strength of the evidence brought against him. It seems enough to say here that opposition opinion – and much neutral opinion – considered that Awolowo did not receive a fair trial and that the federal government manipulated the judiciary and the legal system to eliminate opposition. The trial further eroded respect for the rule of law.

By mid-1963 a stability of sorts had been restored in the West. Akintola and other Action Group dissidents had formed the United Peoples Party (UPP). As a consequence of a Supreme Court decision (to which we shall come) he had been reinstated, and although there was an appeal to the Privy Council against this, he was now able to go ahead and form a coalition regional government with the NCNC. Those MPs who joined the new government coalition had, moreover, their salaries paid from the time of the suspension of the parliament, while the salaries of Action Group MPs who remained in opposition were withheld for that period. Akintola's return to power was clearly facilitated both by the fact that the Coker tribunal had exonerated him from complicity in the financial misdeeds that had taken place while he was previously Premier, and by his readiness to work closely with the federal government.

Akintola and his ministers knew, however, that for this and other reasons they were regarded with much hostility by the majority of the Yoruba population. But they did not have to face an election until 1965, and they reckoned that a repeat of the mixture of patronage and intimidation that had been part of the Action Group's own mobilisation of support could swing the region behind them by that time, particularly since the Action Group's organisation was in disarray and its leader in jail. There was however a hint of things to come when the Action Group mobilised Yoruba sentiment and won the Lagos Town Council elections in 1963 – a feat they had not been able to perform in 1959 when their organisation was at its peak and when they had been able to spend enormous sums of money to secure support. In many ways Akintola knew his people well, and was closer to them in outlook and feeling than Awolowo, but he held a low opinion of their political conviction and courage. He and his associates had now to reckon with the stubbornness of a people who felt their pride had been trampled on and whose hostility to a government they felt had been imposed upon them was sharpened by economic recession. They were to discover, moreover, that not every political activist could be bought or intimidated, and that in any case there were many activists ready to wager that the longer term political prospects were on the side of the Action Group.

LAW AND PRACTICE: JUDICIAL INTERPRETATION AND THE CONTEXT OF POWER

While the political *melée* continued in the Western Region, the constitutional issue involved in Akintola's dismissal as regional Premier had made its way quickly first through the Nigerian courts and then been appealed by Adegbenro to the Privy Council, which, under the 1960 independence constitution, was still the country's final court of appeal. In the Federal Supreme Court Chief Justice Ademola had argued that: 'Law and convention cannot be replaced by party political moves outside the House'.[7] In other words, the Governor of Western Nigeria could not dismiss his Premier on the ground that he no longer enjoyed the support of a majority of the legislature when no formal vote had been taken upon the matter. The crucial constitutional provision[8] ran:

> The Ministers of the Government of the Region shall hold office during the Governor's pleasure:
> Provided that – (a) the Governor shall not remove the Premier from office unless it appears to him that the Premier no longer commands the support of a majority of the members of the House of Assembly; and (b) the Governor shall not remove a Minister other than the Premier from office except in accordance with the advice of the Premier.

The formal respondent in this case was Akintola but the Attorney-General of the Federation became an intervener. The essence of their case was twofold. Mr Foster, QC, argued first, on their behalf, that if the Governor was allowed to base his judgment on information conveyed to him outside the House that would involve a line of demarcation which 'would be very difficult to draw and would be unsatisfactory, because even in the case of the letter signed by the 66 members it may well be that in a debate in the House certain factors that they did not know about would win them over. It might be that the letter was obtained by a mis-statement by the persons who obtained the signatures to it. In fact a substantial proportion of those who signed the letter afterwards voted in favour of the persons in whom they had said they had no confidence . . .'. Second, Foster argued: 'There is no instance of a Prime Minister in England being dismissed on the ground that he did not enjoy the support of the members of the House'.[9]

On appeal however, the Privy Council did not accept these arguments. Viscount Radcliffe, in delivering its judgment, dealt with the main points raised:

> What then, is the meaning of the words 'the Premier no longer commands the support of a majority of the members'? It has been said, and said truly that the phrase is derived from the constitutional understandings that support the unwritten, or rather partly unwritten, Constitution of the United Kingdom. It recognises the basic assumption of that Constitution, as it has been developed, that, so long as the elected House of Representatives is in being, a majority of its members who are prepared to act together with some cohesion is entitled to determine the effective leadership of the Government of the day. It recognises also one other principle that has come to be accepted in the United Kingdom: that, subject to question as to the right of dissolution and appeal to the electorate, a Prime Minister ought not to remain in office as such once it has been established that he has ceased to command the support of a majority of the House. But, when that is said, the practical application of these principles to a given situation, if it arose in the United Kingdom, would depend less upon any simple statement of principle than upon the actual facts of that situation and the good sense and political sensitivity of the main actors called upon to take part. . . .
>
> The difficulty of limiting the statutory power of the Governor in this way is that the limitation is not to be found in the words in which the makers of the Constitution have decided to record their descrip-

> tion of his powers. By the words they have employed in their formula, 'it appears to him,' the judgments as to the support enjoyed by a Premier is left to the Governor's own assessment and there is no limitation as to the material on which he is to base his judgment or the contacts to which he may resort for the purpose. There would have been difficulty at all in so limiting him if it had been intended to do so.[10]

This judgment raised three basic issues for the interpretation and practice of constitutional law in Nigeria. First, the judges agreed that the issue was justiciable – in spite of the bitter regional competition for power and the intervention of the federal government. Second, they rejected the British analogy. Viscount Radcliffe remarked: '. . . it is vain to look at British precedent for guidance. . . .'. No matter what the provenance of articles of the constitution they had to be interpreted in their own right and not in the light of British practice. Third, they gave their judgment on the basis of the written text of the constitution which did not require a formal vote in the legislature before a premier could be removed.

Three comments in respect of this judicial approach seem apposite. First, the British judges who must have had some idea of the Nigerian political situation did not appear sensitive to the consequences of giving a judgment that might prove ineffective. In this sense the Nigerian Supreme Court may have been closer to a judicial sense of constitutionalism when it nullified Akintola's removal. It is not possible to 'find a judicial remedy for every political mischief'.[11] Moreover, the ability of the federal government (which it quickly proceeded to exercise) to change the constitution called into doubt the wisdom of such intervention in this case. To say this is not to argue against judicial interpretation of constitutional law in circumstances such as those of Nigerian politics – in certain circumstances there may be no other legal or political device available to resolve a deadlock or to clear up a doubt – but a judicial role tends to take its strength from brokerage rather than king-making. Second, while it is historically interesting to look at various British-type constitutions imposed on or accepted by various colonies on independence in which British conventions were with increasing explicitness written into law, not least in blocking loopholes discovered in previous constitutions, it is clear that not only have constitutions to exist on their own once they have been promulgated – and in their own political context – but that law can never be framed to cater for every eventuality which may arise. Two politically sensitive lawyers have aptly written: 'It seems that the draftsmen of some of the Westminster model constitutions in various parts of the Commonwealth, being British or trained in the British system, fell too readily into an assumption that by encapsulating the legal position of the United Kingdom in the constitutions of newly independent Commonwealth countries they would reproduce the UK practice. This ignores the fact that the practice is as much a function of the political situation as of law.'[12] Third, the crucial factor in political practice is less the constitution than constitutionalism – a sense of just law and an acceptance of restraint in the use of power. Once politicians do not accept restraint on power – do not display a willingness to avoid driving opponents to the wall – there are no legal ways of resolving differences over power.[13] In that event one is sent back to the warning in Hobbes' famous pun: where there are no rules of the game, clubs become trumps.

POWER AND THE RULES OF THE GAME: THE EROSION OF CONSTITUTIONALISM

The split in the Action Group, the ensuing financial investigations, and the treason trials were a turning point in post-independence Nigerian politics. The break with constitutionality in the federal government's intervention in the West was clear to many at the time, and dismayed those who had hoped that the future lay in law and elections. The federal government's action suggested that its leaders had little respect for constitutional law and procedure, and that a combination of bitterness against the Action Group leaders and fear of oppositional politics overrode what respect they had. It seems possible to say now that the overthrow of the Western Region government by constitutional violence constituted the first major step on the road to the overthrow of the federal government itself by violence just four years later in 1966. It thus seems worthwhile to end by enumerating the implications of the Western crisis, anticipating somewhat in the process events which occurred later on. For the sake of clarity various factors are set out separately, but these, it should be emphasised, were linked and in various aspects reinforced one another.

1. As a consequence of the 1962 crisis the ablest Action Group leaders were removed from the play of politics. The federal government considered that it had made plain that it had the will and the means to put down those whom it considered to have broken the rules that it wanted to operate in Nigerian politics. It thus opened the way for a

regional government in the West which was willing to accept consensus politics. It was not, however, able to remove Awolowo from the actual play of politics; and in prison he remained a martyred symbol of Yoruba resistance. Nevertheless the federal government – and many observers – believed that opposition had been reduced to ineffectiveness. In taking the action it had it followed the letter of the constitution but little more. The dominant partner in the federal coalition, the NPC, was to pursue the same approach later in requiring the manifestly falsified 1963 census to be accepted. The ultimate logic of this approach came out in the 1965 Western Region elections when the government in power, sure of the federal government's support, used its control over the administration to declare itself re-elected in spite of the adverse vote of the electorate. A federal government which had declared an emergency where none existed, and which supported a regional government that did not have the consent of the people, was apparently insensitive to the dangers inherent in abandoning constitutionalism (that is, a just application of law and the acceptance of restraint in the use of power). Once opponents of the government were convinced that it was impossible to win by constitutional means, they were soon tempted to have recourse to non-constitutional means. The abandonment of constitutionalism was all the more serious in the case of a federal government whose dominant partner represented a section of the country that could claim to rule only by virtue of the constitutionality of its voting numbers and not by the spread of education, possession of places in the federal civil service and the officer corps of the army, or by its level of regional economic development.

2. Confidence in appeals to the courts was undermined, as judges were thought to act in a partisan or pusillanimous manner, or were seen to be by-passed by governmental action. In this respect the legal struggle over the premiership of the West reinforced the impression left by other constitutional cases and by the treason trials. When the Supreme Court's decision to reinstate Akintola as Premier was reversed by the Judicial Committee of the Privy Council, the regional government, by getting in one hour before the announcement of the Judicial Committee's decision, rushed a constitutional amendment through the House of Assembly that retroactively denied the Governor the power to remove the Premier without a vote on the floor of the House. Though the constitutionality of this legislation itself was doubtful, and though it was not clear that the regional parliament had passed the legislation by the majority required for a constitutional change, the federal parliament was convoked in emergency session the following week and ratified the change. It would

take very little more before the opposition would decide that the courts had nothing to offer them.

3. The attempt to discredit the Action Group through the Coker tribunal misfired. Not only did Action Group sympathisers believe that the investigation was partisan, but they were left unimpressed by the undeniable evidence of misappropriation of funds. Sophisticated supporters argued that money was needed to operate the party system, and that it was forthcoming only through contrived deals. Though politically-minded Westerners objected to money going into the pockets of private individuals, many of them also believed that less was lost in this way under Awolowo in the Western Region than in the other regions, particularly the Eastern. They believed, rightly as subsequent investigations were to prove, that if the other regions were investigated scandals similar to those unearthed by Coker in the West would come to light. If the Coker tribunal convinced educated Nigerians of anything, it was that all politicians were corrupt. The tribunal offered them concrete evidence for what they already believed. And that was one more factor in discrediting the political class.

4. The suspension of the Western government paved the way for slicing out a new mid-West Region (comprising Edo, Ibo and Ijaw areas) from the West. The NCNC gained control of the new region. But it did so just as a series of crises set the stage for a political confrontation between the North and the South. In the longer run, however, the creation of the new region had two fateful consequences. First, it set a precedent for establishing new states which in the period after 1966 and following the outbreak of Nigerian civil war became an issue of major importance and led to a profound modification of the federal shape of the state. Second, it brought official minority representation into the constitutional conference of September, 1966, where the Mid-West delegates provided a crucial resistance to confederal proposals put forward by the majority-led regions, and so impeded the dissolution of the federation. Their resistance gave enough time to Middle Belt Army elements to change their minds on confederation, and to pressure delegates to opt for a continuing federation.

5. Since Akintola's pro-NPC party – indeed a party entirely dependent on the NPC for survival – controlled the formal political and administrative structure of a Southern Region, those leaders who during the next two or three years wanted the South to move away from the North found themselves weakened, and were unable to secure the political agreement and co-ordinate the institutional measures that a dangerous secession manoeuvre required. By a strangely inverted trick

of fate unconstitutional action put in place an obstacle to the political dissolution of a country that was about to be sorely troubled by confrontation between North and South, on the census, on elections, and other issues too.

6. The most enduring consequence of the 1962 Western Region crisis was to bring together three factors that in their convergence eventually destroyed the stability of the first Nigerian Republic. These factors were: a lack of accepted rules in politicking between government and opposition; envenomed relations between major ethnic groups; and lack of confidence in the financial probity of political leaders. The court cases underlined the absence of 'rules of the game'. The belief came to be held among a great majority of the Yoruba that they were singled out for unfair treatment and oppression – and a similar belief generated a little later among other groups, not least the Ibo, set a bitter seal of distrust and dislike on inter-group relations. These were already bad, both because of the absence of a long history of co-operative co-existence, and the immediate history of competitive modernisation in the scramble for jobs and amenities that came from the control of the state apparatus as well as the exposure of corrupt and common practices among politicians through the Coker tribunal compounded the case by leaving the entire political class besmirched. No matter what directions politics might have taken in Nigeria immediately after independence, it is most likely that the legitimacy of new governments and the unbalanced shape of the federation (the Northern region being larger than all the other regions combined) would have been challenged and stability would at best have been fragile. Yet as history actually developed, there was a direct line from the Western Region crisis in 1962 to the fall of the federal government in 1966.

Notes

1. In describing relations between Awolowo and Akintola as well as between their respective factions I have drawn on interviews with politicians of all the main Nigerian parties as well as on interviews with federal and Western Region civil servants. Moreover, as the split about to be described developed, information on meetings and on negotiations and deals, accusations and counter-accusations and anecdotes poured on to the pages of the Lagos *Daily Express, Daily Times* and *West African Pilot*. I might add that I lived at Ibadan, the Western Region capital, during all this

period. The late John Mackintosh who draws on much the same sources as I do conveys vividly the flavour of the crisis and its aftermath in his *Nigerian Government and Politics* (London, 1966) pp. 427–60.

2. See *Daily Express* (Lagos), February 3–7, 1962.
3. *Constitution of the Action Group of Nigeria (as amended by the Congress of the Party held at Jos from February 2 to 7, 1962)*, Amalgamated Press, Lagos, 1962.
4. *Sunday Post* (Lagos), May 20, 1962.
5. *Daily Times* (Lagos), May 30, 1962.
6. *Report of the Coker Commission of Inquiry into the affairs of certain statutory Corporations in Western Nigeria* (4 vols)., Ibadan, 1962.
7. *Akintola vs. Governor of Western Nigeria and Adegbenro* (Federal Supreme Court 187/1962).
8. *Constitution of Western Nigeria*, 33 (8)
9. (1963) Appeal Cases at 623
10. (1963) Appeal Cases at 628–629
11. Justice Frankfurter cited in K. J. Keith, 'The Courts and the Conventions of the Constitution', *International and Comparative Law Quarterly*, 16, April 1967, p. 546.
12. Yash Ghai and Jill Cottrell, *The Head of State in Pacific Island States*, Warwick Law Working Papers, vol. 8, 1 (1986).
13. A case that bears considerable resemblance to the Nigerian case was one in which a Chief Minister of Sarawak, Ningkan, who was dismissed without a parliamentary vote filed an action in the Borneo High Court against the state Governor and a new Chief Minister. The defendants relied on the Privy Council decision in the *Adegbenro vs. Akintola* case which had accepted the right of the Governor to use discretion. The Borneo High Court ruled however that the cases were different and ruled that the dismissal was unlawful. In particular, Harley ACJ said that in Sarawak the Governor had to determine 'support' which was 'a term of art' implying a vote, moreover, in Nigeria – unlike Sarawak – the number of signatories constituted a clear majority. The defendants did not appeal the case and Ningkan was reinstated in office. The Malaysian government – like the Nigerian federal government – immediately acted politically. The government in order to oust the Chief Minister created conditions to justify a proclamation of emergency; and it then went on to change the constitution. See Yash Ghai, 'The Politics of the Constitution: Another Look at the Ningkan Litigation', *Singapore Law Review*, 7, 1968, pp. 147–173. Both cases are also carefully compared in Keith, *op.cit.*, pp. 542–549.

6 The Dismissal of a Prime Minister: Australia, 11 November 1975

D. A. Low

Soon after 1 pm on 11 November 1975 the Governor-General of Australia, Sir John Kerr, withdrew the commission of Gough Whitlam, the leader of the Australian Labor Party, as Prime Minister of Australia and shortly afterwards appointed in his place Malcolm Fraser, the leader of Australia's Liberal Party and hitherto Leader of the Opposition. Kerr gave as his principal reason that Whitlam 'could not obtain supply'. He now required of Fraser that he should 'guarantee supply', form no more than a caretaker government, and recommend an election. An hour or so later supply had in fact been secured, and on 13 December 1975 a general election was held that was handsomely won by the Liberal Country Parties' coalition under Fraser's leadership.

These events and the issues surrounding them have constituted the most contentious episode in Australian history. Their entrails have been picked over in a long continuing controversy which over a decade later has yet to be laid to rest. The present account seeks – perhaps in vain – to identify its barest bones.

For 23 years after 1949 a Liberal-Country Party coalition, for long under Robert Menzies Prime Ministership, ruled Australia. In 1972 their opponents, the Australian Labor Party, after two earlier near misses, finally won an election under Gough Whitlam's forceful leadership to the House of Representatives, but without winning control of the Senate for which there was no election in that year. The ALP had a long banked-up list of major reforms to carry through, and the floodgates were now opened. Conscription was ended. Draft dodgers from the Vietnam war were released. Communist China was recognised, and in the months that followed a whole raft of reforms was instituted in education, urban development, the arts, aboriginal rights, and much else besides. Australia's 'territory', Papua New Guinea, was advanced towards independence, and compulsory medical insurance was instituted for the first time.

Opposed to much of the new government's legislation, the Opposition used its majority in the Senate to prevent the enactment of several parts of it. With a view to circumventing this obstruction, Whitlam in April 1974 went to the length of offering the Irish Embassy to a former bitter opponent, Senator Vincent Gair, (who wanted it), in the expectation that through the labyrinths of the Senate's election procedures he would thereby critically increase his chances of procuring an additional Senate seat at the next election. But others could play the game too, and by the swift use of some further constitutional technicalities, the Queensland Premier, Bjelke-Petersen, baulked Whitlam's move, and amid the accompanying uproar the Liberal Country Parties, unable to shake off their presumption that they were the ordained parties of government, used their Senate majority to threaten to deny supply to the ALP government. The knives were now out, and in April 1974 Whitlam, within eighteen months of his 1972 victory, called a double dissolution to settle the issue so that not only the House of Representatives but – unusually – the whole Senate went to the polls.

At the general election in May 1974 Labor was returned with a reduced majority in the House, but with a better position in the Senate. This now divided 29–29. One independent rejoined the Liberals, which left Steele Hall of the breakaway Liberal Movement holding the balance. Whitlam in August 1974 then held the first joint sitting of the two Houses of Australian Parliament which with his House majority allowed his ALP government under a further provision of the Australian constitution to pass into law legislation the Senate had previously held up. Those measures were brought before the Australian High Court in 1975, but with one exception they were there declared to be constitutional. That was of major importance to Whitlam personally. Since the Court had struck down the Labor Party's Bank Nationalisation Act of 1947, he, a lawyer by profession, had been deeply committed to displaying to his own party that properly prepared social reforms need not again be frustrated by the Australian constitution.

Meanwhile, further new measures continued to tumble from the cabinet room; but ructions too, and following the first oil hike and a large internal wages rise the economic weather turned against Labor, and its government started to lose its bearings. Things were not helped by a rift with its senior Treasury and Bank officials who had mishandled a credit squeeze. There was a budget in the autumn of 1974 which did not enjoy Treasury approval, and soon Australia began to move into the highest unemployment for 40 years and the highest inflation for several decades. Already within two months of the 1974 election the polls had started to turn against Labor, and on the economic issue they persisted in doing so.

Over the following year a series of bizarre episodes followed. The most portentous and longest running of these was the so-called 'Loans Affair'. A sturdy, longstanding Labor stalwart, Rex Connor, who was Minister of Minerals and Energy, had become committed to developing Australia's major natural resources (for example in natural gas) not by turning to experienced international companies, nor by seeking capital in the world's established capital markets (which he despised), but by exploring novel capital sources of an unorthodox kind in the newly oil-rich countries in the Middle East. In December 1974 he secured formal authority from the Executive Council to raise no less than $4000 million in new capital loans through a Pakistani broker named Khemlani. These were deemed to be (very questionably) for 'temporary purposes' – so as to obviate the need to clear the matter with the long established Loans Council where sat a hostile phalanx of Liberal and Country Party state premiers. Connor's authority was soon rescinded, but then granted again at a reduced level, only to be finally rescinded in May 1975. Upon the first occasion that the Executive Council determined the issue it had met – as it was entitled to do – without the Governor-General, Sir John Kerr, in the chair and without his being told until afterwards. This episode was so handled, however, not least by Kerr himself, as to leave a sour taste both in Kerr's mouth and in that of the Opposition and its supporters. No $4000 million, nor the later figure of $2000, was forthcoming; but when the news of the government's actions became public, whilst the personal probity of the ministers was never in doubt, their financial and political judgement very extensively was.

The issue became compounded when it then emerged that Whitlam's deputy Prime Minister and second Treasurer, Cairns, who had succeeded the hapless Labor warrior Crean in that post in 1974, and had already become much embroiled in a very public affair with his media-chased assistant, Junie Morosi, had in March 1975 hurriedly signed an authorisation to an acquaintance to raise further loans of which he had next to no recollection. In July 1975 he was forced to resign for misleading the House of Representatives on this issue, and the Whitlam government reeled. Its nerves and its standing were then steadied by its third Treasurer, Hayden, who had been amongst the most successful of its ministers and had brought compulsory medical insurance into being. Amid the mounting economic crisis of 1975 Hayden in September managed to bring down a retrenchment budget which even received grudging approval in Opposition circles.

Meanwhile all had not been running smoothly on the Opposition side either. Snedden, the new leader of the Liberal Party after the Labor victory in 1972, had evidently mistimed the Opposition's threat to deny supply to Labor in April 1974 which had led Whitlam to call the 1974 election. Had he waited until the economic indicators and the polls had shortly afterwards turned against Labor, he might well have been Prime Minister before the end of the year. As it was, his much troubled followers, still greatly vexed at finding themselves excluded from government, and soon increasingly perturbed at Snedden's failure to withstand Whitlam's often biting rhetoric, began to move against him. Twice Malcolm Fraser was launched upon a leadership challenge. The second time around, in March 1975, this succeeded. Fraser's brief was thereafter plain: the Whitlam government had to go. But he was careful not to repeat Snedden's mistake by misjudging his throw, and at the outset openly declared that a government with a majority in the lower house was entitled to its three-year term unless something 'reprehensible' occurred.

In the six months that followed, four cumulative sequences brought Fraser to the brink. First there were the polls, where the Labor vote continued to slump. Their tale was confirmed by one dramatic by-election. On 2 June 1975 Whitlam appointed his Deputy Prime Minister, who wanted the job, to be Ambassador in Sweden. That left a by-election to be held, and on 28 June the Liberals won the ensuing Bass election with no less than a 17 per cent swing from Labor.

Behind this lay some deeply worrying economic indicators. Thanks in part to ministerial action and in part to pressure from the unions, wages had lately risen substantially, and despite Hayden's August budget Labor was soon in major trouble because of the very rapid inflation which seemed to characterise its economic management. By October 1975, as Melbourne's University Vice-Chancellor of the day was to put it, 'the land-owning, larger business and primary producers of Australia were feeling desperate and wondering whether they could stand the Government in Canberra one minute longer . . . Clear messages were reaching the politicians that if there was anything they could do . . . they should do it without delay'. Early in October a majority of the Liberal Party Federal Council made it plain at a meeting in Canberra that they expected Fraser to mount an assault forthwith.

They were supported in this by their Country Party allies who were now very fearful of the likely effects upon their position of the Labor government's new Electoral Bill by which the divergence allowed between different sizes of electorates especially in the countryside was to be reduced from 20 per cent to 10 per cent. The whole Opposition was much concerned too lest the Whitlam government's further Act to give for the first time two Senators to each of the Northern and Australian Capital Territories (which the High Court in October 1975 found to be constitutionally valid) might allow Labor to improve decisively its precarious position in the Senate. On both scores an ominous electoral clock was now beginning to tick.

Two sequential occurrences produced the vital lever. The first followed upon Whitlam's devious move in the Gair affair, and then upon his decision in February 1975 to appoint to a vacancy on the Australian High Court his Attorney-General, Senator Lionel Murphy. There was nothing unusual about such a clear political appointment, but personally Murphy was anathema to many of Australia's conservative lawyers. Much noise thereupon ensued, and amid the acompanying uproar Tom Lewis, the New South Wales Liberal Premier, decided to break the hitherto firmly established convention that 'casual vacancies' in the Senate would be filled by state legislatures at the instance of the Premier but always on the recommendation of the party to which the previous Senator had belonged, by appointing his own Independent nominee rather than Labor's chosen candidate. In the event the new Senator was careful not to upset the existing balance in the Senate. But a damaging precedent had been set – and later in the year it was eagerly capped by another Labor-hating state Premier, Bjelke-Petersen.

In June 1975 a Queensland Labor Senator, Milliner, died. In his place Petersen appointed an undistinguished trade union Labor Party member named Field, who announced outright that he would never support the Whitlam government in the Senate. Whilst Field soon found his appointment challenged so that temporarily he could not attend in the Senate, and whilst, to be sure, the Liberal's federal leadership was opposed to both these breaches of convention, their ability thereafter to destroy the Labor government rested critically upon the Field appointment. Steele Hall, the Liberal dissident, was soon denouncing them indeed for 'marching on the sleazy road to power over a dead man's corpse'. But even with his vote the Whitlam government was now in deep trouble. For in Milliner's absence the Opposition had a majority by which they could defer Bills in the Senate if they so wished.

Even so Fraser still hesitated. He wanted a clear-cut *casus belli*. Incredibly the day after the Liberal Party Federal Council in Canberra early in October pressed him to the attack, Labor gave him his opportunity upon a plate. An enterprising journalist had long been chasing Khemlani, Connor's Pakistani fund-raiser. Eventually he secured clear evidence that Connor had continued to use Khemlani to seek Arab money even when his authority had been finally revoked. There was nothing strictly unwarranted in such behaviour, but Connor had told the Prime Minister that he had not been doing this, and Whitlam had so assured the House of Representatives. Faced with damning evidence from Khemlani, Whitlam moved precipitously to stop the rot. Connor the old warrior was immediately replaced, but the damage was done. Fraser denounced the Labor government for 'reprehensible' behaviour, and the Opposition's Senators were instructed to refuse to consider Hayden's budget in the Senate. By using the Senate's power to reject or defer its passage, the Opposition sought to force Whitlam to the polls once again, this time in circumstances where he would almost certainly lose. From the outset there were several Liberal Senators who were ill at ease with this proceeding. One, Senator Bessell, publicly announced that he would never vote to reject supply, and for this and other reasons (and not least so as not to forego the possibility of finally securing supply for a new government) the Senate deferred its decisions on the Appropriation Bills rather than rejecting them outright. This prompted Whitlam to denounce it for failing in its constitutional duty to vote on the budget. But so far as his government was concerned it was now in an extremely dangerous political situation.

The battle was finally joined on 16 October 1975 when the Senate decided that because of 'the continuing incompetence, evasion, deceit and duplicity of the Prime Minister and his Ministers as exemplified in the overseas loan scandal; . . . the Prime Minister's failure to maintain proper control over the activities of his Ministers . . . and . . . the continuing mismanagement of the Australian economy . . . which have . . . created inflation and unemployment not experienced for 40 years' the Appropriation Bills should not be 'proceeded with until the Government agrees to submit itself to the judgment of the people'. On the same day the House of Representatives riposted: 'Considering that this House is the House . . . from which the Government of Australia is chosen' and that the Labor Party government had lately been 're-elected by the people of Australia to be the Government of Australia' it first declared its 'full confidence' in the Whitlam Government. It then affirmed 'that the Constitution and the conventions of the Constitution vest in this House the control of the supply of moneys to the elected Government and that the threatened action of the Senate constitutes a gross violation of the roles of the respective Houses of Parliament in relation to the appropriation of moneys'. It further asserted that 'the basic principle that a Government that continues to have a majority in the House of Representatives has a right to expect that it will be able to govern', and for good measure roundly condemned the Opposition's action 'as being reprehensible and as constituting a grave threat to the principles of responsible government and of Parliamentary democracy in Australia'. During the four weeks that followed, each House was to reiterate these statements upon a number of occasions, and the ensuing debate revolved around their contrasting propositions.

It was on the 16 October too that Ellicott, the recent non-political (for that is what he is in Australia) Solicitor-General, who not so long since had been officially working with Whitlam but was now one of Fraser's shadow ministers, issued a constitutional opinion on the crisis in the form of a press statement. This was to provide the rationale for the Opposition's case in the weeks that followed, and from the outset it served to bring the position of the Governor-General into play. For Ellicott stated as early as 16 October that immediately upon the blocking of supply, 'the Governor-General, in the performance of his role, would need to know immediately what steps the Government proposes to take to avert the problem of it being without supply in the near future'; and he went on to declare: 'He is not powerless'. In Ellicott's view if the Prime Minister did not forthwith advise a new election, 'it is then open to the Governor-General to dismiss his present Ministers and seek others who are prepared to give him the only proper advice open. This he should proceed to do'. It was a knuckle-dusting declaration, and whilst initially rejected by the Governor-General, it lay throughout on the tapis.

Back in September Whitlam had made his own position upon these issues clear in a speech in Goulburn. 'There is no obligation by law, by precedent or by convention', he declared, 'which sets out that a Prime Minister must go to the Governor-General and ask him to dissolve the House of Representatives if the Upper House refuses supply'; and as the crisis then erupted he was plainly deeply angered. For no previous Senate – on the 139 occasions since 1913, as he put it, when this would have been possible – had persisted to the end in denying supply to an incumbent government. Wherever parliaments on the Westminster model were to be found constitutional practice left both the making and the breaking of governments to the lower house alone. Once already he had gone to the polls in response to the Senate's intransigence. How often was this to be required of him? In any event after Field's appointment was the Senate not 'tainted'? Such fulminations were supercharged by a deeply laid personal point. For all his lately successful efforts to persuade his sceptical party that a reforming government need not be frustrated by the constitution, he now faced the prospect that this might have been in vain. He thus embarked upon a tearing assault upon his opponents in which all his portentous rhetorical skills were driven by a passionate belief in the correctness of his stance. As he propounded his case, so his party's spirits rose – and the polls too. For by this measure, upon the constitutional issue the great majority of Australians soon proclaimed that they opposed the Opposition's moves.

The Government's case was clearly supported, moreover, by Byers, Ellicott's successor in the official position of Solicitor-General. Byers made it plain that he was 'firmly of the opinion that Mr Ellicott's expressed views are wrong'. The Senate, he opined, 'has no express constitutional authority to impose' a condition before proceeding to exercise its legislative power; 'nor is there any implied authority'. 'There is no doubt', he went on, 'that the principles of responsible government permeate the Constitution'. 'It clearly cannot be said', he averred, 'that the Representatives in asserting the existence of the convention' – that the Senate should not frustrate supply – 'are acting unreasonably or without the most solid foundation'. The power had never once been used '– a fact suggesting the convention exists'. And on the central point that in the end was to dominate the case, Byers was especially emphatic. 'The mere threat of or indeed the actual rejection of supply', he declared, 'neither calls for the Ministry to resign nor compels the Crown's representative thereupon to intervene'.

As the public debate then mounted so Sir Robert Menzies, the great former Prime Minister, came out solidly for the Opposition's case. But there was much retort against it as well. Sir Norman Cowper, a leading Sydney lawyer, clove down the middle. Some of Whitlam's claims, he said, were 'manifestly untenable'; but nothing had occurred that justified the Opposition's action. Amidst all this contention the Law professors, Sawer, Howard and Stone publicly anticipated that the Governor-General would shortly begin to mediate.

The Governor-General, Sir John Kerr, came from a modest background. After a distinguished career as a right-wing Labor lawyer standing on the edge of politics, he had been appointed Chief Justice of New South Wales. He was then nominated by Whitlam in 1974 as Governor-General. From his boyhood he had known H. V. Evatt the High Court judge, who prior to becoming Labor's External Affairs Minister in the 1940s and President of the UN General Assembly in 1948, had published in 1936 an anxious study of *The King and His Dominion Governors*. With this Kerr had long been familiar, and it provided one of the few authorities to which he turned. As the crisis mounted not only did Kerr become increasingly troubled; he was clearly unsure as to how he should proceed. Throughout Whitlam was emphatic that 'the Governor-General must act on the advice of his Prime Minister'. Since Whitlam joked about 'who gets to the phone first, he to dismiss me or I to have him recalled', Kerr concluded that Whitlam was fully alert to the reserve powers of the Crown upon which Evatt had written, whereas to Whitlam this was part of the relieving banter of an ever heightening crisis.

The Governor-General was not, however, prepared to allow himself to be left out in the cold, and he secured Whitlam's agreement that on 21 October he should see Fraser, not to seek his advice, but to hear his views for himself. These were no less emphatic than Whitlam's. Resolutely Fraser affirmed that the Opposition stood solidly on course; and there was no discussion of any compromise. Over the following few days Fraser publicly announced more than once that if the Governor-General 'gives advice we would give the greatest possible weight to it'. Kerr, however, was clear in his own mind that 'there was no way in which, of my own initiative, I could assume such a role'. On 30 October he suggested to both sides that there should be a half-Senate election in the following May along with an undertaking that the Senate should not meet until 1 July 1976 so that no fortuitous advantage could be taken of the results in the new territorial seats. Neither party, however, at this stage displayed any interest in this idea. Over the first weekend of November the Opposition's federal and state leaders then gathered in Melbourne, and on 3 November Fraser told the Governor-General that they would now be ready to vote supply, and allow the Prime Minister to hold on till the following May, so long as there would then be a House election as well as one for half the Senate. Whitlam rejected these proposals out of hand. He had convinced himself that the opposition in the Senate would shortly break – there can be little doubt that several Liberal Senators were indeed very shaky – and he had no intention of embarking on a six-months'-long election campaign.

It was by now becoming clear that in a few weeks time the government's supply would begin to run out. Hayden, Whitlam's new Treasurer, thereupon worked out an elaborate scheme for the issuing of certificates of indebtedness to employees and suppliers who would then assign these to the banks and draw upon their credit. This, he allowed, would be undoubtedly 'messy', but the Law Officers had declared that it was legal. Following the troubles surrounding the Executive Council's decisions in the overseas loans affair, Kerr was understandably very apprehensive. He was increasingly troubled too by Whitlam's mounting affirmations that in no circumstances would he 'advise the Governor-General to dissolve both Houses at the behest of this tainted Senate'; and before very long Kerr came to the conclusion that Whitlam would not be persuaded to change his mind. On 6 November Kerr saw both Whitlam and Fraser and with both of them floated again the idea of a May Senate election. Fraser insisted that there must be a House election too, and declined to accept the two conditions which Whitlam said would require prior agreement, *viz.*, simultaneous Senate elections (so as to obviate the accompanying threat that hostile state premiers might advise their Governors not to issue election writs) and the new Senate preferential voting system. Fraser, moreover, now warned the Governor-General that if he now failed to act he would be endangering the reserve powers of the Crown for ever. Whatever his intentions Kerr in the course of these and other exchanges clearly left the impression on the one side that he would indeed shortly be ready to use the reserve powers of the Crown, and on the other that this was in no way his intention.

From the very outset he had felt that he might in the end feel bound to dismiss the Prime Minister, and after 6 November he decided to concentrate his mind upon the issue. The *denouement* he believed could not be long delayed. Some of the necessary supply granted by parliament would begin to run out by 30 November. Since the summer holidays begin in Australia around Christmas, the last day for an election would be 13 December. Because of the provisions of the electoral act, that implied that there should be a decision to hold one by 11 November.

Kerr now decided that if there was no break in the crisis he would dismiss Whitlam outright, instal Fraser in his place, dissolve Parliament forthwith, and call a general election. But he wanted to have just one reassurance. Early in the crisis he had asked Whitlam if he might consult Sir Garfield Barwick, the Chief Justice of Australia. But since Barwick was both a former Liberal minister and hostile to much of Labor's legislation, Whitlam vehemently opposed this. Kerr, however, now arranged to see Barwick on Monday 10 November to tell him what he intended to do and seek his opinion in writing. In the course of that day Barwick presented him with a letter (which would obviously be published) in which, after canvassing the issues as he saw them, Barwick proferred the opinion that if 'the present Government is unable to secure supply, the course on which Your Excellency has determined is consistent with your constitutional authority and duty'.

Thereupon 11 November 1975 became a dramatic day. At 9 am Whitlam and two of his colleagues saw Fraser, Fraser's deputy, and the Country Party leader, Anthony. Whitlam, who had been pondering this eventuality for some time now, told them that he had decided to recommend a half Senate election but if the Opposition agreed to pass the budget to defer it so as to ensure that the new Territorial Senators should not steal a march upon the others. The Opposition leaders made it plain that this was not enough. Whitlam then phoned Kerr to arrange a formal interview to advise him to grant a half Senate election forthwith; but since Kerr had to attend a ceremony at the National War Memorial, and Whitlam had to reply that morning to a no-confidence motion in the House, they arranged to meet at lunchtime. Since Whitlam was anxious to tell his party of his decision, he secured Kerr's agreement that he might do this before seeing him, and when he did so it was well received in his party room. The Opposition leadership, however, kept the news to itself lest, it seems, its ill-at-ease Senators seized the opportunity to break ranks. The House then debated the Opposition's no-confidence motion. Before Whitlam had finished his response, Fraser, having received a summons from Government House, very unusually left the chamber. There followed a sequence of sheer farce. Fraser's aides waited for Whitlam's car to leave for Government House first – but they did not check that Whitlam was in it. To their dismay it came back to pick him up. Fraser thus reached Government House first. Hurriedly his car was hidden around a corner, while he himself was ushered into a side room. When Whitlam arrived he was shown into the Governor-General's study. Before Whitlam could tender his advice, Kerr asked him to confirm that the 9 am meeting with the Opposition leaders had not brought any change in the situation. Whitlam readily concurred, whereupon Kerr told him in that case he had decided to dismiss him, and then handed him a letter, which he had already signed, which (as lawyers put it) 'determined' his commission as Prime Minister and that of his government with him. Whitlam had not entertained the slightest suspicion that this could really happen and he was very evidently taken totally by surprise. There is continuing dispute as to what reference he then made to 'the Palace', but he made no move to frustrate Kerr's decision, shook him wanly by the hand, and left. When he had gone Fraser was shown in, was asked to 'guarantee supply', form a caretaker government, and advise a dissolution, and upon agreeing to all three was forthwith sworn in as Prime Minister. Multiple copies of an already prepared statement by Kerr giving his reasons for his actions were then despatched to Parliament House for distribution to the press.

Meanwhile, Whitlam immediately returned to the Prime Minister's Lodge, ate a large steak, sent for his senior colleagues, and made arrangements for an immediate vote of no-confidence in Fraser. He failed to inform any of his Senate leaders of what had happened, and they only learnt of this when the Opposition unexpectedly agreed to pass the Hayden budget. This was done by 2.30 pm. Soon after 3 pm the House passed its no-confidence motion in Fraser. The Speaker was then instructed to take this personally to the Governor-General. By 3.15 the Appropriation Bills were received back from the Senate, and the House adjourned to await the Speaker's return from Government House. Had the Speaker withheld the Bills until he had seen the Governor-General and/or had referred them back to his own House – as would not indeed have been unprecedented – the day's outcome could have been disruptively different. But he signed them, and as soon as they got to Government House, Kerr did as well. Australia's government accordingly had supply. Thereafter Kerr refused to see the Speaker until 4.45. In the meanwhile he saw Fraser, who now asked for a double dissolution of all the Senate as well as the House, and by the time Kerr eventually saw the Speaker, Kerr's Official Secretary was already standing on the steps of Parliament House reading the dissolution proclamation. This ended 'God save the Queen'. From amid the attending crowd Whitlam exclaimed: 'but nothing can save the Governor-General'. He then proceeded to denounce Fraser as 'Kerr's cur' (Fraser had formally countersigned the Governor-General's proclamation), and called upon his audience to 'maintain your rage'.

In the aftermath there was an enormous and continuing furore. Australia's next Labor Prime Minister, Hawke, who at this time was President of the Australian Council of Trades Unions, had to use all his very considerable influence to keep the unions off the streets and prevent a protest strike. Even the respected Melbourne *Age* declared the next morning: 'Sir John was *wrong*'. And (as a personal recollection) there is not much doubt that the pro-Labor meeting in Canberra on the eve of the December poll constituted – such was the public excitement – much the largest gathering ever to have congregated in the grounds of Australia's Parliament. But whilst the polls had swung sharply in Whitlam's favour over the constitutional issues, they swung no less sharply back to Fraser, over inflation and related issues, once the general election had been announced; and on 13 December 1975 Labor found itself out of office through two more elections for the next seven years. Prior to the 1983 election, Labor were only indeed in office at the federal level for three of the previous 34 years. So one can understand not only why they felt quite so bitterly about 1975, but why the Liberal Country Parties saw themselves as the natural parties of government. As for Kerr, and Fraser, and their supporters, they earnestly believed that the 1975 election result had handsomely vindicted their stand, and it was never indeed to be challenged in the courts. By a constitutional amendment in 1977 the former convention about the filling of Senate vacancies was written into the constitution, and a seemingly unending sequence of constitutional discussions, some of them of a formal kind, was soon instituted. But when the new Labor government came back into office in 1983 it appeared concerned to distance itself from the Whitlam years, while both the Leader and the deputy Leader of the Liberal Party (who was shortly to supersede him) immediately commited themselves against repeating their predecessor's move in 1975.

That was not, however, the full measure of the outcome. 1975 not only broke entirely Whitlam's parliamentary and political career – he lingered on until after the 1977 election and then resigned his party's leadership – it gravely damaged both Kerr and the Governor-Generalship too. Wherever Kerr went thereafter, he seemed to be boycotted, pelted and hissed at, and even his supporters soon began to distance themselves from him. Under the strain he could become inebriated in public, and eventually resigned early, and took himself off to England. That left his successor, Sir Zelman Cowen, with the unenviable task of restoring the office's standing. It was now necessary, as Cowen put it, 'to bring a touch of healing' to the scene. November 1975 also gravely damaged those two redoubtable double cousins, Chief Justice Barwick, and the Liberal lawyer, Ellicott. Arguably the most distinguished advocate Australia has ever known, Barwick came to be mercilessly pilloried, while Ellicott failed in his great ambition to be his successor, since even his Liberal colleagues could not bring themselves to appoint to the Chief Justiceship of Australia the widely accepted intellectual architect of the 1975 *denouement*. In a way even the immediate victor Fraser seemed eventually to pay a price. For he seems to have so judged the mercilessness of Australian politics, to which he had been such a conspicuous contributor, that when he lost the election which he prematurely called in 1983, he not only lost his composure publicly, but took himself, at the prime age of 53, out of Australian politics altogether. Nemesis, it seems, was a harsh destroyer.

These were only the more salient of the personal consequences. In the meanwhile the decibels in the public debate continued to reach high. In 1978 Kerr published his apologia, *Matters for Judgment*; Whitlam riposted at the end of the year with *The Truth of the Matter*; Barwick followed five years later with *Sir John did his Duty*. Typically Whitlam was vigorously denounced in other quarters, for being 'implacable – indeed obsessive'; for his 'unpardonable lack of circumspection'; 'of turning the clock back and of forgetting the lessons of the last five hundred years', and a good deal else besides. From the other side, Kerr's former associate, Labor's Senator James McClelland, brutally denounced him for wanting 'a place in history and he certainly got one – just like Judas did'. Australia's prophet-historian, Manning Clark, asked, 'Are we a nation of bastards?'. And Australia's hitherto insubstantial republican movement clearly received a considerable boost.

In this toing and froing the attempt of Mr Justice Eggleston to argue that the *ipsissima verba* of the constitution did not give the Senate the right to deny supply made no headway, whilst the argument of the distinguished Professor Sawer that the Governor-General should not have consulted the Chief Justice fared ill against the precedents soon adduced. The assiduous Clerk to the Senate meanwhile rejoiced in having his view of the Senate's power vindicated. Many, like Melbourne's distinguished legal Vice-Chancellor, Sir David Derham, were strongly of the view that Kerr's actions had been thoroughly well warranted, as further afield were those as various as Britain's Lord Chancellor Hailsham, Canada's constitutionalist Senator Eugene Forsey, and the University of Oxford's Australian Professor D. P. O'Connell.

On the other side, most of the journalists' instant histories supported the Labor case. Australia's major literary figures ranging from the Nobel Laureate Patrick White, to the poet Judith Wright, the journalist Donald Horne and the author Geoffrey Dutton, were amongst the most notable of those in the community at large who were utterly affronted by the Governor-General's actions. Whilst there were many notable opinions expressed in support of Kerr's actions, all three of the most sustained legal commentaries on the affair, by Sawer, Cooray, and above all Winterton, came down against Kerr. Winterton roundly affirmed, for example, that 'there was, in fact, no Emergency in November 1975' that called for the Governor-General's intervention; that 'the point is that the framers' of the executive provisions of the constitution 'intended all the powers to be subject to the principles of responsible government, regardless of the formula used when vesting them in the Crown'; and that 'any attempt to ground an independent vice-regal discretion in the language of the Constitution is futile'. So the issues churned debate.

It is a rash exercise amid the forest of this still continuing controversy to attempt an objective commentary, yet something has to be attempted. The personalities of the principal actors were very pertinent to the case. Whitlam's stance and style allowed no room for questioning: 'crash through or crash' as he himself described it. Enmeshed in his own hubris, witty and biting in his arguments, roused to a peak of rhetoric by his impassioned belief in the rightness of his cause, he rode the crisis high. How were the mighty fallen! Meanwhile all the hardness to be found in Fraser was much at work too, in its dour and gnarled way. Affronted by the government's casuistry in the loans affair, and by all the ministerial flounderings, he shared the electorate's near panic at the worrying state of the nation's economy. At the same time he had, of course, his eyes focussed closely both on the enticing possibilities of office, and on the short shrift he could expect from his own side of politics were he to flinch at the climax. When that arrived Kerr was in no doubt, and had none later, that what he did was right. The legal issues were always to him quite clear, and have remained so ever since. Yet as the crisis overtook him he displayed none of the *savoir faire* which it called for. Elated by the trappings of office, he lacked the personal resource to face his Prime Minister, and the wise circumspection that the crisis demanded.

There were issues of politics, government, law and the constitution as well. The Senate, it seemed, did have power to deny supply, and the Prime Minister was clearly determined to break this decisively. The Governor-General did employ constitutional authority to dismiss the Prime Minister – and the furies loosed against him were grievious to behold. There was clearly much public dismay throughout the affair over several aspects of the government's doings, and it was proper to be worried at the implications of a government governing without the proper constitutional appropriation of supply. Kerr certainly did believe that he could not in the end proceed otherwise, and that it was democratically correct to leave the issue to the people.

Yet, following Bjelke-Petersen's appointment of Senator Field, the Senate was unarguably and critically 'tainted' (as the later Liberal minister Killen put it). By actually denying supply to a quite recently re-elected government the Senate clearly did break a long hallowed tradition of never actually doing so whatever the Opposition majority there might be. Dismissing a Prime Minister was, moreover, a peculiarly brutal way of settling the crisis – and the precedents were at best uncertain. The Governor-General gave no indication (as Sir Philip Game did to Premier Lang in New South Wales in 1932) that he was seriously contemplating using the reserve powers in the extreme form that he did (and the suggestion that he feared to do this lest he be dismissed from office not only traduces his procedural understanding, but his political judgement and sense of honour). For a government to be broken, moreover, by the combined actions of an upper house and the head of state when it still comfortably possessed a not long since renewed mandate in the politically predominant lower house jarred with all the fundamental instincts of democratic parliamentary government. Hayden's financial contingencies were no doubt messy, but (with the New South Wales Game-Lang affair evidently in mind) they were in no way brazenly illegal. As for the suggestion that the Liberal Senators were 'solid', that was simply wrong.

The fundamentals of the conflict lay, one perhaps can now see, in a peculiarly sharp confrontation in an unusually finely balanced parliamentary situation between, on the one side, an ebullient reforming party which had only lately emerged from over two decades of being confined to the Opposition benches – and which was now deeply imbued with a palpable sense of mission as well – that now saw itself being wantonly deprived of its hard-won right to a period in office by a totally unscrupulous Opposition, and so turned to fight it with every means at its disposal, and, on the other, a profoundly angry Opposition, still totally unreconciled to their unwonted relegation from office, that was soon increasingly perturbed at many of its opponents' measures (not to mention some of the antics of its ministers) who then became deeply concerned at the exceptional unemployment and inflation that seemed to be overtaking the country, and so likewise felt a sense of mission – to rid the country of what they saw as this now quite impossible government. In the encounter that ensued no holds were barred; while in the midst stood a man who if he read his law aright had considerable difficulty in allowing that there are other things to constitutions than lawyers' words can tell.

Notes

In a contribution of this length it is well-nigh impossible to give detailed references for each statement since a summary bibliography could now readily produce a hundred items, very many of which traverse much of the same ground. Among the more important books are: J. Kerr, *Matters for Judgment* (London 1978); G. Whitlam, *The Truth of the Matter* (Harmondsworth 1979); G. Whitlam, *The Whitlam Government 1972–1975* (Ringwood, Victoria 1985); G. Barwick, *Sir John did his Duty* (Wahroonga 1983); D. Marr, *Barwick* (Sydney 1980); A. Reid, *The Whitlam Venture* (Melbourne 1976); R. Hall & J. Iremonger, *The Makers and the Breakers* (Sydney 1976); C. Lloyd & A. Clark, *Kerr's King Hit!* (Melbourne 1976); L. Oakes, *Crash through or Crash* (Richmond 1976); D. Solomon, *Elect the Governor-General!* (Melbourne 1976); P. Kelly *The Dismissal*

(Sydney 1976); G. Evans, ed., *Labor and the Constitution 1972–1975* (Melbourne 1977); M. Sexton, *Illusions of Power* (Sydney 1979); G. Sawer, *Federation under Strain* (Melbourne 1977); L. J. M. Cooray, *Conventions, the Australian Constitution and the Future* (Sydney 1979); G. Winterton, *Parliament, the Executive and the Governor-General* (Melbourne 1983); H. V. Emy, *The Politics of Australian Democracy*; H. O. Browning, *1975 Crisis: an Historical View* (Sydney 1985). There have been innumerable journal articles. Since 1975 the quarterly *Quadrant* has been especially notable for carrying these. The weekly *The Bulletin* published several retrospective articles in September and October 1985. Among articles of note elsewhere, R. Cranston and B. J. Galligan, 'Comment', *Public Law* Autumn 1976, pp. 217–21, and D. Derham, 'The dismissal of the Prime Minister on 11 November 1975', *Law Institute Journal* 1985, pp. 1174–1186, should not be overlooked. The present author's earlier comments are in 'Wearing the Crown: New reflections on the Dismissal 1975', *Politics*, 19, May 1984. For a more substantial bibliography see Winterton op. cit.

7 The Governor-General's Part in a Constitutional Crisis: Fiji 1977

David J. Murray

In March 1977 a general election in Fiji produced an unexpected result. The opposition party emerged with half the seats and as the largest party. There followed a constitutional crisis which centred on the action of the Governor-General in appointing a Prime Minister and subsequently dissolving the Parliament. The episode was important for the development of Fiji's constitution and of the office of Governor-General. In addition, because the office of Governor-General is similarly constituted elsewhere, the episode in Fiji has a wider significance more possibly in the issues it raises than for the answers it offers.

Fiji had become independent in 1970 with a constitution that had been developed to take account of the racial composition of the population. According to the most recent census which had been taken prior to independence, that of 1966, indigenous Fijians constituted 42 per cent of the total population, Fijian citizens of Indian origin 51 per cent and others seven per cent. As a result the constitution contained five specific safeguards for the indigenous Fijians. In the upper house of the bicameral legislature Fijians were guaranteed a majority. Existing laws safeguarding the separate administration of Fijians, their control of land, the basis for leasing land to non-Fijians and the administration of Fijian development funds were entrenched in the constitution and could only be amended with the agreement of Fijians. The electoral system provided for a complex system of communal representation which ensured that Fijians would fill close to half the seats in the House of Representatives. Among fundamental rights individuals were protected against discrimination on the grounds of race but this did not apply to existing law (thus, for example, safeguarding Fijian interests including those in land). Finally recruitment to the public service was to ensure that each community received fair treatment in the number and distribution of appointments. There was no mention however of the composition of the army which was almost entirely Fijian. Fijian citizens of Indian origin accepted the provisions (and omissions) with expressed hesitation, but did so in the belief that the working of the constitution combined with their majority position in the population would enable them to gain greater influence and share in the exercise of power.

Beyond containing unusual provisions designed to safeguard Fijians, the constitution conformed to the Westminster export model, but as one of the later such constitutions it sought to avoid leaving uncertainties about the rules of the political game. Unlike the earlier constitutions, notably of Ceylon (now Sri Lanka) and Ghana, prescriptions were avoided which referred to convention and practice in Britain. Institutions, powers, procedures and operating arrangements are as specified in the constitutional instrument. The office of Governor-General, though carrying a title that is to be found in many states, has, therefore, the particular characteristics specified in the relevant constitution. It is limited, as the judgement in the case of Adegbenro *vs*. Akintola made clear by the wording of the constitution itself, 'and this wording can never be overridden by the extraneous principles of other constitutions'.[1]

In Fiji's constitution the Governor-General has three politically sensitive functions in the exercise of which he has a degree of discretion. These are appointing a Prime Minister, removing a Prime Minister and dissolving the Parliament. When taking these steps, the Governor-General's exercise of his discretion has sufficient political importance for constitutional provisions to have been included to clarify how the discretion is to be exercised.

The relevant sections of the constitution in Fiji – and the drafting of them – reflected experience gained elsewhere. Becoming independent in 1970, Fiji's constitution was prepared using the Mauritius constitution as the immediate model, but it was influenced also by the thinking developed in drafting other constitutions. Of particular relevance here is the assessment that there was advantage in being explicit in the provisions that treated political processes which were potentially tricky to handle. This thinking is reflected in de Smith's comment that 'There are very strong grounds for making a constitution speak as unequivocally as possible on those issues where it falls for the Governor-General to exercise important and potentially controversial personal discretion.[2]

The terms in which the Governor-General's exercise of his discretion in appointing the Prime Minister as set out has reflected the aim of specifying precisely the limits to this discretion. In Fiji this is expressed as:

> The Governor-General acting in his own deliberate judgement shall appoint as Prime Minister the member of the House of Representatives who appears to him best able to command the support of a majority of the members of that House.[3]

This particular formulation was the product of a refinement of wording which in Ceylon and Ghana, for instance, had been expressed by reference to the constitutional conventions applicable to the exercise of similar powers in Britain by Her Majesty.[4] Subsequently, and starting with the constitutions of Malaysia and Nigeria, the formula was that the appointee should be the person who appears likely to command the support of the majority of members of the lower house of the legislature. The wording used in Fiji was favoured as a more precise formulation.

Similarly in Fiji the Governor-General's discretion in removing a Prime Minister and dissolving Parliament is expressed in an explicit and circumscribed way:

> 1. If a resolution of no confidence in the Government is passed by the House of Representatives and the Prime Minister does not within three days resign from his office the Governor-General shall remove the Prime Minister from office unless, in pursuance of section 70(1) of the Constitution, Parliament has been or is to be dissolved in consequence of such resolution.
> 2. If at any time between the holding of a general election and the first sitting of the House of Representatives thereafter the Governor-General, acting in his own deliberate judgement, considers that, in consequence of changes in the membership of the House resulting from that general election, the Prime Minister will not be able to command the support of a majority of the members of the House, the Governor-General may remove the Prime Minister from office.[5]

As regards dissolution the constitution sets out the power of the Governor-General and the extent of discretion in the following terms:

> 1. The Governor-General, acting in accordance with the advice of the Prime Minister, may at any time prorogue or dissolve Parliament: Provided that –
>
> (a) if the House of Representatives passes a resolution that it has no confidence in the Government and the Prime Minister does not within three days either resign from his office or advise the Governor-General to dissolve Parliament within seven days or at such later time as the Governor-General, acting in his own deliberate judgement,

may consider reasonable, the Governor-General, acting in his own deliberate judgement, may dissolve Parliament;

(b) if the office of Prime Minister is vacant and the Governor-General considers that there is no prospect of his being able within a reasonable time to appoint to that office a person who can command the support of a majority of the members of the House of Representatives, the Governor-General, acting in his own deliberate judgement, may dissolve Parliament.[6]

The Governor-General's discretion is thus strictly limited and this contrasts with wider discretions which existed in earlier – and indeed in some later – Westminster model constitutions.

A final point of additional clarification is contained in an interpretative section. This is explicit that the Governor-General may act in his discretion only where it is expressly stated that he shall act in his deliberate judgement.[7] None of the powers and discretion which form a part of the royal prerogative in Britain are thus among the powers of the Governor-General as representative of the Queen as Queen of Fiji.

As one of the later constitutions to be drafted the Fiji constitution reflects a concern to be explicit about the Governor-General's functions, the extent of personal discretion and, in the selection of a Prime Minister, how this is to be exercised. The general election in March 1977 and its aftermath provided evidence on the practical operation of these constitutional provisions.

In Fiji's bicameral legislature, the Senate has 20 appointed members and the House of Representatives 52 members. In March 1977 an election was held to the House of Representatives. The Governor-General, Ratu Sir George Cakobau, was a former politican in the ruling Alliance Party and senior Fijian chief who had become the first Fijian Governor-General.

Before the election the position in the House of Representatives was that the Alliance Party had 32 seats and the National Federation Party 19. One member, elected as an Alliance Party member had, during the Parliament, left that party and formed the Fijian Nationalist Party. Prior to the election the Prime Minister was Ratu Sir Kamisese Mara, the leader of the Alliance Party, and S. M. Koya was the leader of the National Federation Party and Leader of the Opposition.

The Alliance Party drew its main support from Fijian voters, and particularly from the hierarchy of Fijian chiefs and those supporting an established order, from voters who were neither Fijian nor Indian, and from certain groups of Fijian Indians (notably part of the Muslim community). The Fijian Nationalist Party directed its efforts to attracting Fijian voters and particularly commoners. The National Federation Party was in origin a party supported by Fijian Indians and though the Party sought to widen its appeal its main support remained among Fijian Indian voters.

The general election results announced at the beginning of April showed that the National Federation Party had won 26 seats, the Alliance Party had 24, Fijian Nationalist Party one and there was one Independent. The loss of eight seats by the Alliance Party had not been anticipated. The result was due to a split in the Fijian vote between the Alliance Party and the Fijian Nationalist Party.

When the results were known on Monday 4 April, Mara made a broadcast anouncing that he was resigning.

> I will tomorrow morning tender my resignation and that of my government to His Excellency the Governor-General. I have accepted the verdict of the people of this country arrived at by democratic processes and I am proud to do so. Nothing else would accord with this political philosophy of ours in respect for Parliamentary institutions which my Party stands for. We have lost the general elections and the National Federation Party have won. It is not only their right, it is their duty to form a government. I thank all who have supported me throughout these ten exciting and rewarding years. I thank my colleagues and I thank the people of this country who gave us the opportunity of this role. Meanwhile, good luck to the new government as they take on the burdens of office. I hope they will find it tremendously satisfying, as we, ourselves, have found it in serving the people of Fiji in this high office. May God bless you all and our beloved country.[8]

Thereafter the sequence of events was as follows:

Monday, 4 April. Koya informally approached Mara proposing the formation of a coalition, if necessary as a caretaker government. In part this reflected unease about whether Fijians would accept a Fijian Indian dominated government.

Tuesday, 5 April. Mara submitted his resignation as Prime Minister and this was accepted. The National Federation Party decided, in a party meeting on a vote of 24-2, to seek a coalition with the Alliance Party under Mara as Prime Minister. A letter was signed by the president of the National Federation Party and addressed to Mara inviting the Alliance Party to join in a coalition, but not stating that the coalition would have Mara as Prime Minister. An immediate reply was requested but none was forthcoming and late in the evening it was agreed that the president of the party should contact Mara first thing the following morning.

Wednesday, 6 April. The president of the National Federation Party telephoned Mara but Mara declined to comment on the proposal for a coalition until after an Alliance Parliamentary Party meeting. After this meeting Mara, as the re-elected leader of the Alliance Party, informed the president of the National Federation Party that he would not talk about a caretaker or coalition government unless the Governor-General summoned a meeting.

Koya attended a meeting with the Governor-General who asked Koya if he would be able to form a government. Koya stated that the party would do so, but wished first to explore further the possibility of a coalition. At Koya's request the Governor-General summoned a joint meeting of a delegation of four from each party to discuss the question of a coalition government for the following day.

The National Federation Party chose four members, but Koya was not amongst them for the reason that the poor personal relations between Koya and Mara were seen as a possible impediment to fruitful discussions on a coalition. Various reports appeared, and attention was drawn to them by Mara in a broadcast, that the one Independent member was associating with the National Federation Party.

Thursday, 7 April. The National Federation Party delegation attended the joint meeting summoned by the Governor-General. The Alliance Party declined to do so. The Party was prepared to attend a meeting to discuss the formation of an Alliance government on a caretaker basis but not a coalition. At the meeting the Governor-General read a prepared statement covering four points. As reported by the president of the National Federation Party these were:

1. The Alliance was prepared to form a caretaker government which would not include any National Federation Party members in the Cabinet. It would run for three months, after which a fresh general election would be held.
2. The Alliance was not prepared to talk about coalition.
3. The Governor-General invited the National Federation Party to 'now form a government'.
4. If the National Federation Party did not form a government, he would ask the Alliance to do so.[9]

In the absence of Koya, the secretary and the president of the National Federation Party informed the Governor-General that the National Federation Party would form a government. As reported in a statement by the secretary, what the delegation informed the Governor-General was that the party would proceed without delay to:

a) form the next government of Fiji;

b) elect a leader under its prescribed procedure which provided that the elected Members of the House of Representatives of the National Federation Party should elect a Party Leader from within its ranks;

c) request his Excellency to appoint the Party Leader as the Prime Minister of Fiji;

d) ask his Excellency to swear in the Prime Minister and members of his Cabinet today.

The National Federation Party then proceeded to hold an election to the post of leader of the Parliamentary Party. Members were divided over whether a Fijian member, Captain Atunaisa Maitoga, should be elected to reassure Fijian opinion, or whether Koya should be re-elected. On the first ballot each candidate received the same number of votes. In a second election Koya was re-elected by 14 votes to 12 with Captain Maitoga as deputy.

At 3.15 pm Koya rang the Governor-General and made an appointment to attend at 4.30 pm to present his list of ministers and to be sworn in as Prime Minister.

Shortly after 3.45 pm, the Governor-General appointed Mara as Prime Minister.

At 4.30 pm Koya kept his appointment to be told that Mara had been appointed as Prime Minister. On asking why he had acted in this way Koya reported the Governor-General as saying that the appointment of Koya would create instability.[10] A special edition of the *Fiji Times* newspaper announced the appointment of Koya as Prime Minister, to be followed by a replacement issue reporting the reappointment of Mara.

Obviously the check on the Governor-General that is expected to operate in such a situation lies with the House of Representatives. Parliament met on 28 April. A Speaker in the House of Representatives was elected from the Alliance Party, thus leaving the effective numbers in the parties as Alliance Party 23, National Federation Party 26, Fijian Nationalist Party one, Independent one. The House of Representatives then went into a four-week recess.

Immediately before the House reconvened the 26 members of the National Federation Party signed a letter to the Governor-General. This stated:

> We, the undersigned members of the House of Representatives request you to invite the Leader of the majority party in the House of

> Representatives namely the Hon. Mr S. M. Koya to form the government of Fiji who in our considered view commands support of the majority of the members of the House of Representatives.
>
> We assure your Excellency that we stand as a united party and that each and every signatory to this letter will serve as a Minister under (the) Hon. S. M. Koya as such responsibility is allotted to him under the Constitution of Fiji.[11]

When the House reconvened on 28 May the Alliance Party introduced a motion of confidence in the government of the day. To this the National Federation Party moved an amendment in the following terms:

> This House expresses its considered view that the will of the people of Fiji as expressed through the secret ballot should be respected in order to maintain parliamentary system of the government in Fiji and therefore requests the Governor-General not to dissolve Parliament should an advice in that behalf be tendered but to invite the leader of the majority party in the House, namely, the Leader of the Opposition, to form the government.[12]

The amendment was carred by 26 votes to 23 with the one Independent member abstaining and the Fijian Nationalist Party member absent.

The following day, 29 May, Mara as Prime Minister advised the Governor-General to dissolve the House, which he did. The House was dissolved in the middle of a debate on a motion to lower the voting age from 21 to 18 years.

The sequel was that a further general election was held in September 1977. The Alliance Party had an apparently sweeping victory winning 36 seats, the National Federation Party won 15 and the one Independent retained his seat. The principal reasons for the election result were a split in the National Federation Party and a reuniting of the Fijian vote behind the Alliance Party. There was only a marginal change in the total number of votes cast in support of the Alliance and National Federation Parties as between the March and September elections. This change does appear to have contributed to the loss by the National Federation Party of two seats. Otherwise the split in the National Federation Party, with candidates of the two factions standing against each other, let in seven Alliance Party candidates on a minority vote. The National Federation Party lost two other seats which it had won in the March election on a minority vote due to support, in that election, for the Fijian Nationalist Party. The final seat, won by the Alliance Party, was at the expense of the Fijian Nationalist Party.

The Governor-General, in appointing Ratu Mara as leader of the minority party rather than Koya, had justified his action in an official statement which ran:

> In the recent elections the people of Fiji did not give a clear mandate to either of the major political parties. It therefore became the duty of the Governor-General under the Constitution to appoint as Prime Minister the member of the House of Representatives who appeared to him best able to command the support of the majority of the members of the House. The Governor-General has not been able to act sooner as it was not until this afternoon that he was informed who had been elected leader of the National Federation Party. The Governor-General, after taking all relevant circumstances into account, has come to the firm conclusion that the person best able to command the support of the majority of members is the leader of the Alliance Party, Ratu Sir Kamisese Mara. In compliance with the Constitution and acting in his own deliberate judgement, the Governor-General has accordingly appointed Ratu Sir Kamisese Mara as Prime Minister. The Prime Minister is now in the process of forming a government.[13]

It is worth pointing out that the Governor-General did not justify his action on the grounds of the balance of support in Parliament as a whole. Because of the composition of the Senate, there was – and would remain – a majority there opposed to the National Federation Party. The wording of the constitution makes it clear that it was support of a majority in the House of Representatives that was the intended criterion for deciding on who was to be appointed as Prime Minister, and the Governor-General did not refer to the situation in the Senate in his statement.

The Governor-General thus gave a broad interpretation to his powers in selecting a Prime Minister. He did not consider himself to be limited by the apparent facts about the strength of the two parties in the House of Representatives. The leader of the party with 24 seats could only appear better able to command the support of the majority of the members of the House of Representatives than the leader of the party with 26 seats if the Governor-General knew that there was some member or members of the majority party who would favour Mara and was willing to cross the floor. Subsequent disclosures indicate that this was not so. Whatever the justification for his action, the Governor-General placed on Section 73(2) an interpretation which in effect gave to him the power to appoint as Prime Minister whomever he regarded as appropriate.

Once the Prime Minister was appointed the episode showed the significance of the Governor-General's power and the limitations of various strategies for enforcing the principle, which supposedly underlay the constitution, that the Prime Minister and Cabinet owed their position to majority support in the elected House of Representatives rather than to the Governor-General. On the face of it there were two alternative routes open to the majority party. The first, political, route involved passing in the House a motion of no-confidence. The weakness here – as had applied incidentally in Ceylon (as it was then) in 1959 when the opponents of the Prime Minister faced a comparable position[14] – was that to remove the government in this way depended on the Governor-General not granting the Prime Minister a dissolution. So long as the Prime Minister acted in a way that was consistent with Section 74 (1) of the constitution in advising the Governor-General to dissolve the House, the Governor-General could be expected to act in accordance with that advice. In these circumstances the Prime Minister would remain in office pending the outcome of a fresh election. As with the Sri Lanka Freedom Party in Ceylon in 1959–60 the National Federation Party failed to prevent this happening. When dissolving the House the Governor-General justified his action with the following statement:

> The Constitution provides that the Governor-General may dissolve Parliament at any time, but in so doing, he shall act in accordance with the advice of the Prime Minister.
>
> Acting in accordance with the advice of the Prime Minister, and in compliance with the Constitution, the Governor-General by proclamation has now dissolved Parliament and has so advised the Speaker of the House of Representatives.[15]

The National Federation Party did consider alternative courses of action. Three of these involved action through Parliament. First, there was the possibility of preventing any Speaker from being elected, and thus making it impossible for the House to transact any business. This, it was recognised would precipitate a dissolution and would not therefore achieve what was sought.[16] Second, the possibility was raised of moving a motion of no-confidence, but this was rejected on the grounds that this also would result in an immediate dissolution. The third possibility of leaving an Alliance Party government but passing motions and Bills to give effect to National Federation Party policy (such as lowering the voting age to 18) was superseded by the Alliance Party motion of confidence in the government of the day.

What the circumstances of April and May 1977 showed was that the House of Representatives was powerless itself to reverse the action of the Governor-General and so secure a Prime Minister and Cabinet which owed its position to the support of a majority in the House rather than to the favour of the Governor-General. The episode revealed that the replacement of Mara as Prime Minister through political processes could only have been achieved as the result of a further general election.

As an alternative to political action in the House there was the possibility of seeking in the Supreme Court a ruling on the Governor-General's action in appointing Mara. The constitution gives to the Supreme Court of Fiji original jurisdiction in constitutional questions 'if any person alleges that any provision of this Constitution . . . has been contravened and that his interests are being, or are likely to be affected by such contravention, then, without prejudice to any other action with respect of the same matter which is lawfully available, that person may apply to the Supreme Court for a declaration and for relief under this section'.[17] In terms of this section Koya, and arguably others, was a person who could seek relief from the Supreme Court, and Koya was publicly urged to do so.

The difficulty with taking this option immediately following the appointment of Mara as Prime Minister lay in the likelihood of the Supreme Court adopting a subjective interpretation of the discretion conferred on the Governor-General and thus declining to investigate the Governor-General's exercise of judgement. The problem of challenging the way the Governor-General had acted was increased by the Governor-General's formal statements. Whether intentionally or not these statements were drafted in a way that meant there was nothing on the record which could serve as the basis for a case in the Court. For the Court to adopt a subjective interpretation was the more likely because, though not himself responsible to Parliament, the Governor-General's action was in theory reversible at the will of Parliament. This would have been so if the person appointed as Prime Minister did not gain the support of a majority in the House of Representatives, and additionally he chose to resign from office without recommending a dissolution. Alternatively the action of the Governor-General could be reversed through the political process by the electorate and a new House of Representatives.

There were, in addition, issues about what relief the Court could have provided. Had Koya sought relief immediately after Mara's appointment the Court could have declared improper the Governor-General's action in appointing Mara. Once events became enmeshed in the parliamentary political processes, removal of the Prime Minister would have presented significant practical difficulties (as the comparable cases in Malaysia and Western Nigeria had shown).[18]

Finally, there were certain difficulties of a different nature surrounding any action in the Courts. First, the Chief Justice was known to have played a part in the events leading up to the reappointment of Mara both in advising the Governor-General and in drafting the statements which the Governor-General issued. The Chief Justice had not, however, made public his own role or the nature of his advice – as had the Chief Justice in similar circumstances in Australia when Governor-General Kerr removed Whitlam as Prime Minister. An action in the Supreme Court would have placed the Chief Justice, therefore, in a difficult position. To disqualify himself would have made public his own role; not to have done so would have invited a challenge to his impartiality in hearing the case. Whichever happened the standing of the Courts would not have been enhanced. Koya, however, was himself a lawyer with an active practice. He had a personal interest in sustaining the Courts and the legal process and he also had a deep commitment to doing so. At a personal level, moreover, Koya had a friendly relationship with Clifford Grant, the Chief Justice. Additionally, Koya appeared to make the assessment that action through the Courts would not bring political rewards.

In retrospect the Governor-General was taken to have been proved right by events. The National Federation Party split into two factions with the leadership of S. M. Koya as a main issue in dispute between the factions, thus reinforcing doubts about Koya's suitability as Prime Minister. The subsequent success of the Alliance Party in the September elections deflected criticism from the Governor-General. His judgement in rejecting Koya was taken to have been endorsed by the electorate. Koya was presented in press comment as having mishandled the situation.

This conclusion carried with it the implication that the Governor-General had, properly, the degree of discretion in choosing a Prime Minister which he had exercised. Whatever the words of the Constitution stated about the Prime Minister being the person best able to command the support of the majority the Governor-General was accepted as having a wider discretion. As a *Fiji Times* editorial expressed it: 'There is no questioning the Governor-General's right to act. The powers are there in the Constitution.'[19]

Because no-one sought a declaration from the Supreme Court on the constitutionality of the Governor-General's interpretation of his powers in appointing Mara as Prime Minister (and subsequently in granting Mara a dissolution), some ambiguity must surround the provisions in the constitution which specify the Governor-General's powers. There are two aspects to this uncertainty. One question concerns the standing of the stipulation that the Governor-General shall appoint as Prime Minister the member of the House of Representatives who appears to him best able to command the support of a majority. If a declaration were sought and the Court did indeed decide that it was not for the Court to inquire into the Governor-General's assessment, this makes the constitutional provision not an enforceable rule but a guide to what is expected of the Governor-General and thus no more than an influence on what developed as practice. If, on the other hand, the Court were to investigate the exercise by the Governor-General of his discretion, it is not clear what interpretation the Court would put on the section, and whether, therefore, the Governor-General's interpretation would be adjudged consistent with the provision.

In the absence of an application to the Supreme Court, the presumption is that the Governor-General acted within his powers. There remains, however, uncertainty about who could be understood in Fiji to be rightly or appropriately appointed as Prime Minister. The Governor-General's choice could lie between members of the House of Representatives regarded as individuals or his selection might be between the leaders of organised political parties. Mara, in his resignation broadcast, and in a subsequent extended interview, assumed that the Governor-General's choice was between himself as leader of the Alliance Party and the leader of the National Federation Party. The Governor-General's statement after appointing Mara did not clarify the basis for his choice. The immediate reaction in Fiji was that the choice should be between parties. In consequence the assumption was made that at least one member of the National Federation Party had communicated to the Governor-General a clear commitment to support Mara and the Alliance Party. The Governor-General's choice was assumed to be based on the strength of the parties as known to him. Subsequent clarifications established that this was probably not the case.

An alternative basis for choice was the degree of support for an individual. On this interpretation the Governor-General made an assessment of the support for Mara as an individual. Once re-elected as leader of the Alliance Party the support of the Alliance members for him was reaffirmed. Mara was also the favoured choice of a 25-2 majority in the National Federation Party. However, this support was only on the condition that there was a coalition government.

The Governor-General's own statement hinted at a further possibility. By attributing the delay to the fact that he was awaiting the outcome of the National Federation Party's election to see who was to be that party's leader, the Governor-General was hinting at some other consideration. Earlier disputes in the National Federation Party had cast some continuing doubt on Koya's capacity to command the support of his own party. On the other hand, Koya himself linked the statement to the nature of the choice made by the National Federation Party. He, as a Fijian Indian, had defeated a Fijian. Thus he publicly interpreted the statement to mean that a Fijian Indian was ineligible for appointment as Prime Minister.

Mara stated that the Governor-General had given no explanation for reappointing him. He did, however, seek to legitimise his own action, and that of the Governor-General, by linking to the authority of the Governor-General the authority of Ratu George Cakobau as the Vunivalu of Bau and thus as one of the senior chiefs in Fijian society. He also presented his own action as being that of a subordinate chief with a duty of obedience: 'I obeyed the command of His Excellency the Governor-General, the highest authority in the land and my paramount chief. I obeyed him in the same manner that thousands of Fijians obeyed their chiefs . . .'[20]

There is a further dimension to the appointment by the Governor-General of a Prime Minister on which the episode casts some light. Beyond the question of who is to be appointed as Prime Minister, there is the issue of how the appointment is to be made. Fiji's constitution is silent on the process of appointment beyond the requirement that the person appointed should take a prescribed oath. In this, Fiji's constitution is the same as other Westminster export model constitutions – until the last of those drafted provided for the election of the Prime Minister by the House of Representatives.[21] This silence is despite the view then current among those devising and drafting such constitutions that it helps to be explicit.

In the absence of specific provisions on the procedure of appointing a prime minister, practice in Britain might serve as a point of reference. The authoritative statement on this procedure is that appearing in Anson 'a man becomes Prime Minister by kissing the King's hands and accepting the commission to form a Ministry'.[22] Yet earlier twentieth century practice in Britain did not accord with this statement. If the appointment of Lloyd George in 1916 and Ramsay Macdonald in 1924 are used as examples, there were four stages in the appointing process.[23] First, an individual was invited to form a ministry; second, the individual accepted the invitation; third, the individual submitted a ministry to the King; and, finally, when the King had decided that a ministry could be formed, the individual was appointed Prime Minister.

In April 1977 in Fiji there were no clear-cut steps in the procedure followed by the Governor-General. Having accepted Mara's resignation on Tuesday 5 April, there were two days of soundings. Koya then interpreted the Governor-General's statement, not addressed to him but to the delegation, followed by his own telephone call to the Governor-General, to be an invitation to form a ministry. He understood that he had accepted this invitation, and he went to see the Governor-General to submit his ministry and to be appointed as Prime Minister. The procedure he followed accorded more closely with the earlier twentieth century practice in Britain. The Governor-General did not comment on what he regarded as the appropriate procedure, nor how he interpreted what happened between himself and Koya. What was explicit by implication was that he did not reject Koya at the final step in an appointment process because of the ministry he proposed.

The process by which a Prime Minister came to be appointed in April 1977 and, more significantly perhaps the steps taken which did not culminate in Koya becoming Prime Minister, indicates a second dimension to the Governor-General's power. Even if there was assumed previously to be some regular steps in the appointing process what happened on this occasion showed that the Governor-General was able to follow procedures of his own choosing.

The events in April 1977 have a significance for Fiji's evolving constitution. The Governor-General had to exercise the discretionary powers conferred on him under the constitution to appoint the Prime Minister and grant a dissolution. The way he exercised those powers and the fact that his exercise was accepted as being legitimate means that the relevant constitutional provisions have to be understood in the light of the way they were exercised. The Governor-General's discretion in appointing a Prime Minister may be taken to be wider than the words of the constitution indicate and there would appear, similarly, to be discretion in the procedure to be followed by the Governor-General before making an appointment. On the other hand, the constitutional provisions relating to the Governor-General's discretion in granting or refusing a dissolution is as constrained as the words suggest. Questions about the limits to the Governor-General's discretion over appointing a Prime Minister were not resolved by events. It is not clear whether the

Governor-General's choice relates to individuals or parties, nor is it clear how support is to be measured. Nor is it established what the steps are that come between soundings by the Governor-General and the Prime Minister taking the oath of office. The events did not establish new boundaries but did introduce uncertainty and ambiguity. Because, furthermore, no declaration was sought from the Supreme Court on whether the relevant constitutional provisions were justiciable and if so whether the Governor-General's interpretation of his discretion was correct, there remains a further element of uncertainty.

In the context of a review of the office of Governor-General in Commonwealth countries, the developments in Fiji have, I suggest, three points of interest: the standing of the constitutional provisions relating to the Governor-General's discretionary authority; the developing characteristics of the Governor-General's office; and finally, the effect of the attempt to be explicit.

The Governor-General's discretion is expressed in the Fiji constitution in terms which are identical or very similar to those in the constitutions of other countries.[24] The wider interest in the events in Fiji is that the issue of the standing of the relevant sections in the constitution was identified and discussed but no ruling was sought or given in the Supreme Court. The occasion could have prompted a declaration which would have been of interest to those operating under the comparable provisions elsewhere, and indeed of direct relevance given the nature of the legal system in operation.

If the Supreme Court does not intervene in Fiji (or elsewhere), the events in 1977 indicate the way political circumstances can mould the office of Governor-General. Clearly, however, the office will not evolve everywhere in the same way. The specific exercise by the Governor-General of his powers and the reaction to what he did will not be replicated elsewhere. Each office of Governor-General, even where provided for by largely similar constitutional provisions, will develop differently. Nevertheless, where there are similar provisions governing the appointment of a Prime Minister and the dissolution of Parliament the episode in Fiji demonstrates the potential significance of the power vested in the Governor-General.

In Fiji, Sir George Cakobau succeeded in widening the discretion of his office and creating a degree of ambiguity about his powers and the process of exercising them. Those convinced of the benefits of being explicit might suggest that what occurred could create difficulties for Fiji's Governors-General and for the office. The disadvantages of uncertainty were, indeed, evident in Fiji in 1977. Not only did the three-day interregnum give rise to concern about what might happen but the events left a sense of outrage and bitterness in Fiji's politics and undermined the authority of the constitution. On the other hand the events might be interpreted as suggesting some advantages in leaving room for the Governor-General to manoeuvre. The constitution did not recognise the existence of parties but they existed in practice. The party rules requiring the leader to be chosen by the party after the general elections and the delay in holding such an election in the National Federation Party added to an already complex situation, as the Governor-General made clear in his formal statement.

Whether the Governor-General was decided in the action he took by security considerations has not been conclusively established. A newspaper leader referred to this possibility at the time and there are grounds for this conclusion. Immediately after the election there were incidents in which stones were thrown at vehicles particularly in rural Fijian areas and Butandroka, the leader of the Fijian Nationalist Party, was reported in the press as making threatening statements. The National Federation Party was apprehensive about the possibility of disorder particularly among the Fijian population and in the army and police and this was an important consideration in seeking a coalition. In the event, as Mara subsequently confirmed – accurately – there was no direct threat to the constitutional processes from the army (a force drawn from the Fijian population) or police (whose paramilitary Mobile Force similarly comprised Fijians but which was otherwise an integrated force). Whether the army and police would have been willing to act to restore order among the Fijian population in the event of disturbances was not put to the test. Acting alone the police would have been effective but could have become over-extended. Whether the army could have been relied on, drawn as it was from the rural Fijian population, if it were to be required to act to suppress disorder in those areas, was more problematic. The Governor-General had, therefore, understandable and valid grounds for worrying about a possible threat to public order. The problem facing him in appointing a Prime Minister was that the constitution rested on the premise that political power would be exercised through elections and through Parliament and that the use of 'disorder' as a political instrument could be controlled by the institutions of government. It was on this basis that the Governor-General was to make his choice of Prime Minister. In fact he was apprehensive about trouble, particularly among rural Fijians, and about the capacity to deal with it. Whether the Governor-General was decisively influenced in the way he interpreted his own discretion in order to cope with what he perceived as a wider security situation, he never confirmed publicly.

It is possible, therefore, that the Governor-General acted in a way that went beyond what the words of the constitution provided because of what he thought was necessary to safeguard effective government under the constitution. If so, and if the Governor-General was making a reasonable assessment of what might happen, the episode might be taken to justify a greater degree of residual discretion that the constitution conferred so that the Governor-General could play a part in handling certain sorts of political crises. The British Foreign and Commonwealth Office showed a concern in the preparation of independence constitutions to avoid creating an office which would become embroiled in political controversy for reasons which did not arise from the needs of the new state but were because of the Governor-General's role as representative of the Queen. However, if the office is to have a residual political function, the fact that the Governor-General introduced uncertainties and ambiguities through his handling of events in 1977 may possibly prove in Fiji to be a useful outcome. Nevertheless, even if the actions of the Governor-General have produced conventions about his power which could be justified in the particular context of Fiji, the way this was achieved did not enhance the credibility of the Fiji constitution.

POSTSCRIPT

In a general election ten years later in April 1987 a National Federation Party – Labour Party Coalition defeated the ruling Alliance Party winning 28 seats to 24. The Governor-General appointed the leader of the Coalition as Prime Minister avoiding the delays that had occurred ten years earlier. Five weeks later there was an army coup. Prior to the election the Army Command had formally briefed the government both on the extent of the problem of maintaining or restoring order in the face of widespread disturbances in the rural areas and on the severe limitations in the capacity of the army. By 1987 there had been a marked decline in the efficiency and morale of the police as a first line of defence against disorder. Nevertheless the Commander of the Army made explicit his commitment to maintaining order under the legitimate government. Following the general election there was extensive disorder and the prospect of further disturbances parallelling what had been threatened in 1977. The military leader of the coup, the third ranking officer in the army, represented the disorders as warranting military intervention. The Army Commander deposed by the coup leader, on the other hand, asserted in a newspaper interview (*Fiji Times*, 4 June 1987) that there had been collusion between the coup leader and those fomenting the disorder.

Notes

1. Adegbenro *vs.* Akintola (Western Nigeria 1963), AC614 at 632.
2. S. A. de Smith *The New Commonwealth and its Constitutions* (London: Stevens 1964), p. 93.
3. The Constitution of Fiji, S73(2).
4. The Constitutions of Ceylon and Ghana, Part II, S4(2).
5. The Constitution of Fiji, S74(1)(2).
6. *Ibid.*, S70(1).
7. *Ibid.*, S78(1).
8. Recording of statement by Mara, broadcast by *Fiji Broadcasting Corporation*, 4 April 1977.
9. *Fiji Times*, 23 May 1977.
10. Personal communication of S. M. Koya as reported by the President of the National Federation Party.
11. Letter subsequently published in *Fiji Times*, 22 September 1977.
12. *Fiji Times*, 1 June 1977.
13. *Ibid.*, 9 April 1977.
14. A. J. Wilson, 'The Governor-General and the two dissolutions of Parliament', *Ceylon Journal of Historical and Social Studies*, Vol. 3 No. 2 (1960) pp. 187–207.
15. *Fiji Times*, 2 June 1977.
16. This consequence is argued in E. A. Forsey, *The Royal Power of Dissolution of Parliament in the British Commonwealth* (Toronto: O.U.P. 1968), second edition, p. 261.
17. The Constitution of Fiji, S97
18. Issues surrounding the intervention of the Courts are discussed in K. J. Keith, 'The Courts and the Conventions of the Constitution', *International and Comparative Law Quarterly*, Vol. 16 (1967), p. 542.
19. *Fiji Times*, 9 April 1977, p. 6.
20. *Fiji Times*, 11 April 1977, p. 2.
21. The Constitutions of the Solomon Islands and Tuvalu.
22. W. R. Anson, *The Law and Custom of the Constitution* (Oxford: Clarendon, 1935), 4th edition, Vol. II, Part 1, p. 130. see also F. M. Powicke, and E. B. Fryde, *Handbook of British Chronology* (London: Royal Historical Society 1961).
23. H. Nicholson, *King George V; His Life and Reign* (London: Constable 1952), p. 292, 384–6.
24. This applies to the Constitutions of Barbados, Dominica, Grenada, Jamaica, Mauritius, Zimbabwe; with regard to the appointment of Prime Minister the formulation is similar also in the constitutions of Malta, St Lucia and St Vincent.

8 Seeking Greater Power and Constitutional Change: India's President and the Parliamentary Crisis of 1979

James Manor

It is highly unusual for a head of state in a Westminster system to seek to increase his own power and to generate substantial constitutional change amid a succession/dissolution crisis. The formal institutions of state and the party system are usually too stable, and even an ambitious head of state is usually hemmed in by rules and precedents which are too widely and well understood to permit any such thought. It appears, however, that in mid-1979 this is precisely what the President of India, N. Sanjiva Reddy, sought to do. To be more specific, he appears to have sought partly to achieve and partly to catalyse a major revision of the constitution which would have made the President the pre-eminent figure in the political system. He failed, but in a manner that leaves open the possibility of a revival of such attempts.

He was not thwarted by formal institutions. They were reasonably strong, but in the absence of detailed rules and precedents, they presented few impediments. He was thwarted when the Indian electorate gave a new ruling party a sizeable majority at the next general election in the first week of 1980. But that result masked a continuing disintegration of parties and the party system upon which the President had counted for an opportunity to assert himself, and which may one day present a head of state with such an option once again.

On 11 July 1979, it became known that defections from India's ruling Janata Party's parliamentary delegation had deprived Prime Minister Morarji Desai's government of a majority in the Lok Sabha (House of the People), the lower and dominant house of the Indian Parliament. The situation was unprecedented and speculation immediately arose about the options open to the President, whose position is roughly akin to that of a British monarch, although he is elected to a five-year term by Members of Parliament and state legislators who have always followed the wishes of the Prime Minister. What, for example, could he do if Desai asked for a dissolution of Parliament? As India's parties and newspapers – and, not least, the President himself – hastily consulted learned opinion, it quickly became apparent that the answers were not entirely clear. The predominant view, however, was that the President had very considerable latitude. It was widely held, for example, that he was not bound to accept the advice of a prime minister who had lost majority support.[1] The reasoning that lay behind this view ran as follows.

India's constitution sets down the rules for what is clearly a variant on the Westminster model, indeed it bears a close resemblance in many respects to the last constitution of British India, the Government of India Act of 1935. It is also true that India's Supreme Court has ruled that the positions of the Indian President and the British monarch are analogous. But because the constitution establishes India as a sovereign republic, it frees Indian officials of the necessity of following British or other Commonwealth precedents. They are free to do so if they so choose, and on occasions that has occurred, but they are not bound to do so. Nor does the constitution provide the President with detailed guidance on how to proceed if the ruling party in Parliament loses its majority and several leaders seek the opportunity to form a new government.[2] The constitution is quite long and detailed as such documents go, but on relations between the President and ministers, only three Articles are germane.

> 74. (1) There shall be a Council of Ministers with the Prime Minister at the head to aid and advise the President . . . who shall, in the exercise of his functions, act in accordance with such advice . . . provided that the President may require the Council of Ministers to reconsider such advice, either generally or otherwise, and the President shall act in accordance with the advice tendered after such reconsideration.
>
> 75. (1) The Prime Minister shall be appointed by the President and the other Ministers shall be appointed by the President on the advice of the Prime Minister.
> (2) The Ministers shall hold office during the pleasure of the President.
> (3) The Council of Ministers shall be collectively responsible to the House of the People.
>
> 85. (2) The President may from time to time –

(a) prorogue the Houses or either House;
(b) dissolve the House of the People.[3]

Most analysts concluded that if advice to the President to dissolve Parliament came from ministers possessing a majority in the Lok Sabha, then it would have to be followed, but if the ministers had lost their majority, it was not binding. This view was based partly upon precedents from the state level in India's federal system where Governors – the President's equivalents and representatives in the states – had refused advice for dissolutions from outgoing Chief Ministers who had lost majorities.[4] But it was also anchored in Article 75 (3), which indicates that the authority of the Council of Ministers rests upon majority support in the Lok Sabha.[5]

Despite broad consensus on this viewpoint, it came as a considerable relief to many that the problem of the President's response to advice from the Prime Minister did not arise during the first stage of this crisis. On 15 July, four days after losing his majority, Prime Minister Morarji Desai submitted his resignation to the President without offering any advice on subsequent actions. President Reddy asked him to remain in office until alternative arrangements could be made, and took soundings from the wide array of parties in India's fragmented Parliament, represented in a rough diagram in Figure 1. The President had told numerous callers that he was 'anxious that the country should not be exposed to the turmoil of a mid-term poll at present . . . that every effort must be made to avoid it' and 'that he would strain every nerve to help form an alternative Government'.[6]

His first step was motivated more by a sense of procedural necessity than an expectation that it would produce results. On 18 July, Reddy invited the official Leader of the Opposition, Y. B. Chavan of the (non-Indira) Congress Party, to try to form a government. No one expected Chavan to succeed.[7] His party of 77 members was no longer even the second-largest force in Parliament – which is why it had initally been designated the official Opposition – because Charan Singh's block of just under 100 Janata defectors, now called the 'Janata–S' ('S for Secular), had more adherents. But by inviting Chavan to try, the President bought time in which various realignments of forces might occur, and in which confusion in what remained of the old Janata Party – which with about 200 members was still the largest force in the Lok Sabha – might clear up.

The confusion existed because Morarji Desai was refusing to follow his resignation from the prime ministership with a resignation from the

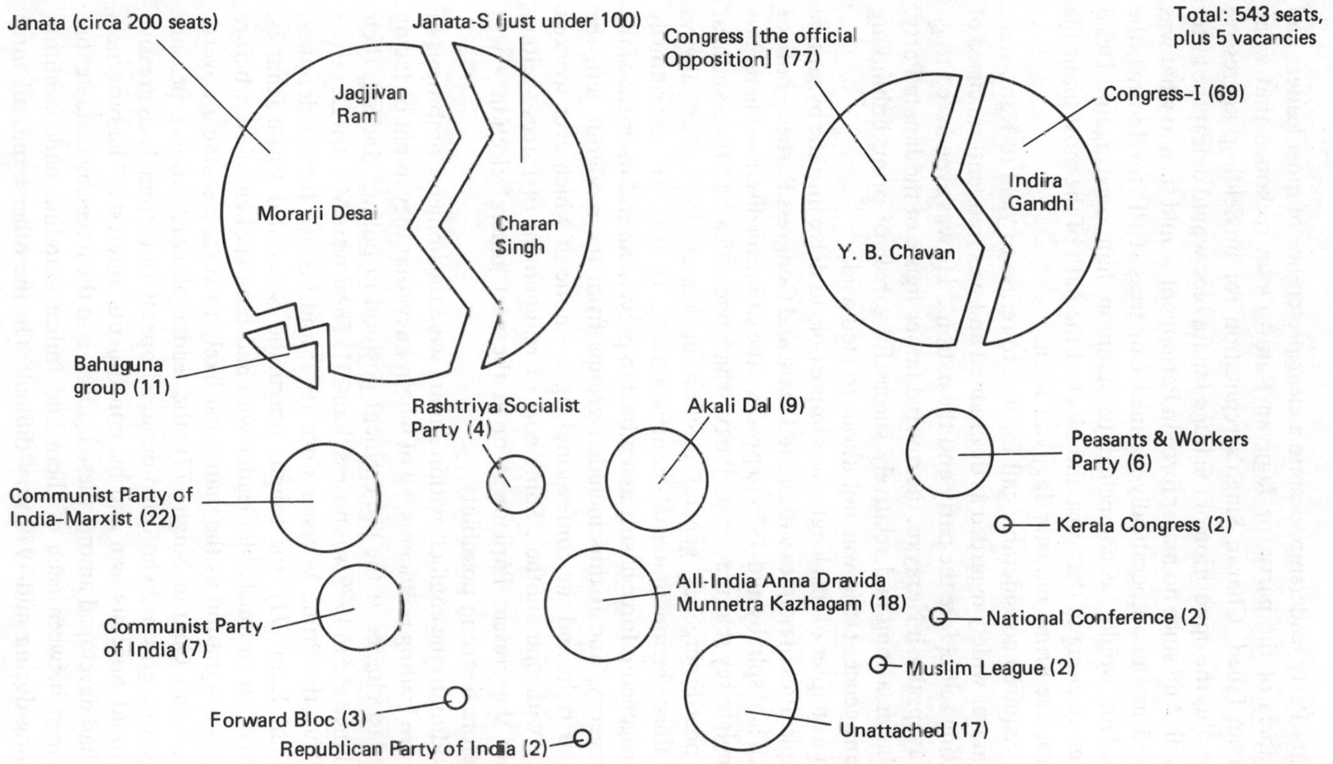

Figure 1 Position of the Parties in the Lok Sabha, July 1979

Janata Party leadership, despite a clear preference of most leaders and members of the party for Jagjivan Ram.[8] Desai reckoned that when Chavan failed, Charan Singh's reputation for unyielding, aggressive ways plus the opposition of the huge Janata bloc would defeat the latter as well. And since no major force in Parliament would turn to what was viewed as the autocratically-inclined Congress–I ('I' for Indira), the President would be compelled to summon him once again. Desai therefore clung to that post and blocked the path of the most plausible alternative prime minister Jagjivan Ram.

It required considerable gall for him to refuse to yield to Ram, since Desai was widely regarded as discredited and was frequently accused of 'putting self before the party and the nation'.[9] He was even asked to go by Jayaprakash Narayan, the revered father-figure of the Janata Party. But after a long and relatively successful career of prim, unblinking intransigence, Desai was not about to step aside.

In a chapter of this length, it is impossible to delve into the byzantine complexities of politics within the Janata and Congress Parties – both of which had split by mid-1979 to produce the situation discussed here. It is enough to say that the Janata Party, which had defeated Mrs Gandhi at the post-Emergency general election in March 1977, had always contained serious internal contradictions. It was an enormously heterogeneous force hastily assembled to prevent an endorsement of the Emergency, and it thus included groups from the moderate left, the secular right and the confessional right – none of which ever worked easily with one another. Some sort of realignment of forces – either within the present Parliament or at the next general election – was therefore a strong possibility.

Adding to the conflicts within Janata were the immense ambitions of its three leading politicians, all of whom knew that they might be facing their last chance at the pre-eminent position in politics. Indeed, their combined age in 1979 was no less than 231. These were Morarji Desai (83 in 1979), the Prime Minister since 1977; and his two former deputies, Jagjivan Ram (71), the tough, pragmatic Scheduled Caste (that is, 'Harijan' or untouchable) leader who had been spoken of even before Desai's resignation as the man most likely to sustain a stable government;[10] and Charan Singh (77), the leader of north Indian peasant cultivating groups, who often engaged openly in extremely aggressive acts to advance his own and his constituents' interests. The bitterness that had developed among these leaders, and the lingering distaste that remained between each of them and Indira Gandhi, made coalition building during mid-1979 very difficult. On the other hand, all three

Janata leaders were prepared (indeed they were compelled by circumstances) to include as a junior coalition partner the non-Indira Congress led by another pragmatist, Y. B. Chavan.

The canny Ram went quietly about his business, stressing his approval of the President's decision to invite the official Opposition leader to form a government and mustering pressure on Desai from within the Janata Party. The latter was a slow process. When a three-member committee of senior Janata leaders told Desai that he must step aside, he replied that 'they could do anything that they liked, but he was not going to resign', confident in the knowledge that the party remained sufficiently fractured that they could not muster the two-thirds vote needed to oust him.[11]

President Reddy meanwhile let it be known that whatever happened within the Janata Party, he was inclined to invite Charan Singh to make the next attempt at forming a government.

> The reasoning, based on Constitutional propriety, is that if the Lok Sabha had been in session [when Desai had resigned], Mr Charan Singh [whose defection caused the resignation] would have been designated Leader of the Opposition because of the higher strength of the breakaway Janata(S) group which he leads.[12]

This brought protests from no one. The President had thus far avoided controversy.

He had, however, begun to attract attention for what one editorial described as his 'extraordinarily active role',[13] consulting and reconsulting leaders and often members of every party and fragment in Parliament, large and small – all in the glare of intense media attention. Within a few days of Desai's resignation, this had convinced many MPs that President Reddy was seeking to establish in New Delhi the equivalent of 'President's Rule' – that is, a suspension of the legislature and direct rule through the bureaucracy – which had often been used when state governments became unable to govern. This was quite impossible, in both constitutional and practical terms, but the belief that it was occurring is indicative of how very assertive the President – who 'has indeed never concealed his own political ambitions' – had become. This prompted one analyst to appeal to him for statesmanlike restraint, lest institutions suffer damage.[14] As we shall see, however, Reddy remained highly energetic throughout this episode.

Once Y. B. Chavan had announced his inability to form a government, Ram ceased his attempts to force Desai to yield to him the leadership of the Janata Party. He did so for three reasons. First, he still had nothing like the two-thirds vote within Janata to oust Desai, second, he did not want to be seen to be adding further complications to an already baffling situation, and finally he ought to cultivate for himself the image of the accommodating statesman who lacked the unrestrained appetite for power which other leaders were exhibiting. This left two men seeking a summons from the President: Desai and Charan Singh, the leader of the Janata–S, the body of defectors that had deprived the old Janata of its majority. President Reddy asked each leader to prove his claim to majority support in the Lok Sabha by providing a list of backers. The lists that were submitted contained a large number of names in common, and after consulting MPs whose names appeared twice, the President determined that Charan Singh had broader support. Accordingly, on 26 July, Reddy invited him to form a government and directed him to seek a vote of confidence 'at the earliest possible opportunity, say, by the third week of August 1979'.[15]

Some people felt that a period of nearly four weeks would not bring results 'at the earliest possible opportunity', but this caused very little controversy amid the mounting distaste at the ceaseless expedient shifts of parties and factions behind this leader and that. As one editor put it, Charan Singh's putative government was 'born in sin out of crass opportunism'. He was referring not only to his role in undermining the old Janata government, but also to his reliance now for a parliamentary majority on the support of Indira Gandhi's Congress–I. No one had been more aggressive in seeking to bring Mrs Gandhi and her son to trial before special courts than Charan Singh, and no one had been more scathing about the record of her father, Jawaharlal Nehru. For them now to make common cause seemed 'a most shameful chapter in Indian political history . . . written by men and women solely guided by their greed for power'.[16]

The President's decision at last induced Desai to relinquish the Janata leadership and open the way for Ram who had a far better chance than both Desai and Charan Singh of reassembling a working majority. On 28 July, Charan Singh and a team of ministers were sworn into office, and on the same occasion, Ram was officially recognized as Leader of the Opposition. Ram took great pains to emphasise his certain faith that if the new Prime Minister failed to obtain a vote of confidence, the President would then summon him to seek the same.[17] There followed three weeks of hugely complex negotiations, rumours and jockeyings in which Charan Singh sought to find and solidify majority support. In the process, it became clear that several small groups in Parliament might back both Charan Singh and, if the need arose later, Ram. The most important of these, as we shall see later, was the regional party in the southern state of Tamil Nadu, the All-India Anna Dravida Munnetra Kazhagam (AIADMK) which had 18 MPs in the Lok Sabha.[18]

As he entered the third week of August, the week in which he had to face Parliament, Charan Singh encountered increasingly public signs that Mrs Gandhi's Congress–I might withdraw the support that it had promised him. The crucial issue here was whether he was willing to disband the special courts which were very near to convicting her son Sanjay on a number of criminal charges arising out of his normless behaviour during the Emergency, and which threatened eventually to find Mrs Gandhi guilty as well. Charan Singh had initially won Congress–I backing by implying a willingness to do so, but since being called to form a government, he had again become unco-operative. As a consequence, the Congress–I withdrew support on the morning of 20 August, the day on which the Lok Sabha had been summoned to meet, and Charan Singh immediately resigned, before the House could assemble.[19] Mythmakers who would like to depict Sanjay Gandhi as an ingenious tactician, which he assuredly was not, have argued that he cleverly arranged the withdrawal of Congress–I support in order to force a general election which, five months later, Mrs Gandhi won. But it was the special courts and not what was then a highly uncertain election that was the main concern of the Gandhis at that point. Indeed, they were prepared to back any prime minister who might subsequently be called, providing he was willing to dispense with the courts and drop charges.[20]

When he resigned as Prime Minister, Charan Singh sought to deny others the opportunity to assemble a majority by advising the President that the Lok Sabha be dissolved so that 'arrangements may be made for a fresh mandate being obtained from the people'.[21] With the situation delicately poised, the Janata Party, which now sought to gain Ram the chance to form a government, rushed a team of three prominent leaders to Madras to court the Chief Minister of Tamil Nadu, M. G. Ramachandran, leader of the AIADMK. He was thought to be hesitant, but he had earlier agreed to support both Y. B. Chavan and Charan Singh after a little zealous wooing. That is what he was given on 22 August by the high-powered Janata delegation, which was building upon a visit ten days earlier by Jagjivan Ram himself.[22] The 18 MPs of the AIADMK were enough to gave Ram a bare majority on paper. Once again, Ramachandran proved amenable and at midday a member of the Janata group used a telephone in the Chief Minister's office to inform the President of the agreement. The three jubilant Janata men then entered a car for the 40-minute drive to Madras airport to catch a flight back to Delhi. When they reached the airport, they were informed that All-India Radio had just broadcast the news that the President had dissolved Parliament and called for a general election.[23]

The decision astonished many people from a wide array of parties and angered those who had hoped to make common cause with Ram. A crowd of several dozen politicians, including Ram, attempted a protest march to the President's residence but were turned away by several hundred police who reminded them that they were now merely ex-MPs who had no special access to the head of state. The marchers offered rhythmic cries of 'Impeach him, impeach him' and – for a moment – 'Sanjiva Reddy Murdabad' ('Death to Sanjiva Reddy') until the leaders put a stop to this latter chant. They wanted to maintain a strict sense of decorum since they now wished to present themselves as patriots seeking to restore the dignity of the presidency by removing its current incumbent.

Ram, who had met the President on the morning of 22 August, appears to have been flabbergasted at the announcement of a dissolution shortly thereafter. He was particularly exercised about comments attributed to the President, to the effect that it was during their meeting that the latter had concluded that Ram could not form a stable government. Ram released a letter that he said was written to Reddy immediately after their meeting but before the dissolution decision, which indicated that the President had given no hint of the impending decision.

> You were good enough to say that while you would like to have the matter settled quickly, you were in no special hurry and would still take some time to consider the questions involved further. I took [it] that you would be prepared to wait for a further communication from me, giving details of my support.

He added in interviews that the President had said that Ram could submit a list of supporters in Parliament 'by this evening', a statement which Ram now regarded as 'double talk'.[24] For four days the President's office made no reply to or comment upon the letter, and then it issued a brief statement denying the accuracy of Ram's account, without elaboration.[25]

The only other point of substance to emerge from the President's side was a statement that Reddy had felt constitutionally bound by Charan Singh's advice to dissolve the Lok Sabha, because the latter was the outgoing Prime Minister.[26] This argument was scarcely credible. A small army of constitutional authorities had agreed only the previous month that the President was bound by no such obligations, and Reddy himself had reportedly told a group of MPs on the day of Charan Singh's resignation that his request for dissolution 'carries no weight'.[27] The widespread consensus in mid-July that the President need not accede to any advice from Desai seemed to apply with much greater force to Charan Singh. Desai at least had once enjoyed the confidence of a parliamentary majority, whereas Charan Singh had declined even to set foot on the floor of the Lok Sabha as Prime Minister. Reddy would have been better off remaining silent on this point. The lameness of his justification lent substance to suspicions that his decision in favour of dissolution was based on a desire to keep Jagjivan Ram from becoming Prime Minister. It must of course be stressed that the President did not violate the letter of the constitution by dissolving the Lok Sabha, but there are serious doubts about both the constitutional propriety and the justice of his decision. As two distinguished commentators – N. A. Palkhivala and Rajni Kothari – have separately argued, dissolution of a body that had completed only half of its term should have been an option of last resort, and Reddy's action was mainly objectionable because 'it did not allow the political process to find its own solution to the situation . . .'.[28] After emphasising his intention to 'strain every nerve' to avoid a mid-term election, he had denied the most plausible candidate for the prime ministership the opportunity to form a government.

Why might Reddy have wished to thwart Ram? There are three possible explanations which are not mutually exclusive. The one which has achieved broadest currency[29] is the least worthy: that the President was prejudiced against Ram because the latter was a Scheduled Caste (that is, a 'Harijan' or untouchable) leader. This is usually linked to the accusation that Reddy, who came from a cultivating caste that was dominant at the village level in much of his home state in south India, was favourably inclined to Charan Singh who was the leader of such a caste group in north-central India. In fairness, it should be said that the composition and logic of the regional caste systems in north and south differ markedly. But given Reddy's long-standing link to the dominant landed stratum, it is possible that he preferred to avoid being known as the head of state who put the first Scheduled Caste Prime Minister in office.

The second explanation, which emphasises Reddy's resentment against Ram's role in denying him the Indian presidency in 1969, has received less attention in the press but is taken seriously by many politicians.[30] It was in that year that Mrs Gandhi decided to use the choice of a new Indian President as a means of splitting the Congress Party, the first major step in her drive to political supremacy. Reddy, who originally believed that he had the nation's highest honour securely in hand, was grievously disappointed to find himself the candidate of the lesser, anti-Indira faction of the party. Mrs Gandhi's version of the Congress was referred to in radio reports, day in and day out for years, by the name of its official head as 'the Congress owing allegiance to Mr Jagjivan Ram'.

A third explanation emphasises Reddy's ambitions for greater influence in the political system rather than his resentments against Ram. If the President hoped for changes that would strengthen his position, and it appears that he did, then he had a strong interest in avoiding the emergence of a Prime Minister who could in time build a solid majority government. Instead, he wanted a Lok Sabha in which no party had an overall majority so that it became necessary to form coalition governments. In the making and the functioning of such governments, an activist President might informally acquire considerable influence, and such changes might eventually be formalised through constitutional changes.

President Reddy, who was both intelligent and experienced in party work, could see that all of the centrist parties (which is to say all of the parties which could play leading roles in coalition-building) had suffered serious internal fragmentation and decay,[31] and that the party system in general was undergoing disintegration. This led him and others to the very plausible presumption that future elections might well yield Lok Sabhas in which no party had a majority or anything else close to it.[32] In the midst of this crisis, he indicated in his Independence Day broadcast to the nation that this appeared to necessitate constitutional change – indeed, that theme formed the main headlines in several papers on the national holiday. The President also poured scorn on unsavoury 'power politics' and 'politicians' who had generated a 'spirit of confrontation' and a 'crisis of character'.[33] This led many to conclude that Reddy sought to portray himself as an altruistic figure above the unseemly political battle – which is the way Presidents tend to be perceived in any case – in order to lay the groundwork for first a *de facto* enhancement of his powers over a fragmented parliament, and then a *de jure* ratification of that change through a revision of the constitution.

Suspicions of Reddy's ambitions grew when, soon after the dissolution it was announced that he had invited Charan Singh and his ministers to remain in office as a caretaker government even though a delay of three or four months was expected before a general election could occur, owing to necessary revisions of voters' rolls and other procedural problems. It had been widely understood before the dissolution that a 'national government' composed of most or all major parties could not be formed because of bitter resentments between various parties and leaders, but *after* the dissolution, it seemed not only feasible but fair and important that such a broad-based caretaker regime be assembled. Many observers had wondered whether the President had initially given Charan Singh nearly a month to hammer together a parliamentary majority because he seemed likely to build an unstable coalition, over which the President would be able to assert himself. Now it was alleged that Reddy had 'deliberately elected to invite (as caretaker) . . . the most pliable head of government'. The President had sought out 'a weak Prime Minister the better to be able to control him. None filled the bill better than Charan Singh'. Reddy's aim was 'a wholly new relationship between the offices of the Prime Minister and the President . . . the strengthening of the office of the President, and making it more explicitly political, less ornamental'.

Since the election was expected to produce a hung parliament, 'the final politicisation and activisation of the office of the President can be taken up at the conclusion of the elections'.[34] We now know, of course, that the election in the first week of 1980 yielded up a new Prime Minister, Indira Gandhi, with an impressive majority – just the sort of thing to dash the dreams of an ambitious President. But in August of that year, no one expected that result.

On the other hand, President Reddy well understood that Jagjivan Ram had the kind of broad support, and the managerial and manipulative skills to have a good chance of entrenching himself in a reasonably strong position if he was allowed to form a government. Ram had, after all, been regarded as a strong candidate for the prime ministership, on both counts, even before Desai had lost his majority.[35] And given the appeal of an able Scheduled Caste leader to Members of Parliament from numerous disadvantaged and minority groups, he might even have managed to initiate a major realignment of poorer social groups behind him, as Rajni Kothari has suggested.[36] That would have pleased neither an ambitious President nor the conservative landed groups that had long provided Reddy with a political base. The threat from Ram seemed far more proximate and compelling in August of 1979 than the hypothetical prospect of an electoral landslide for Indira

Gandhi or anyone else. It is probable that some combination of these three explanations accounts for President Reddy's decision to dissolve the Lok Sabha.

After issuing his brief denial of the truth of Ram's version of their final meeting, President Reddy said very little about the dissolution in the hope that the episode would fade in importance, amid more urgent concerns during the election campaign. The Janata Party sought to keep the controversy alive, but they encountered problems on two fronts. First, the constitutional niceties involved could not be easily or compellingly explained to ordinary voters. It was indicative, for example, that Janata protesters shouting 'Impeach him' had to use the English word since there was no easy translation into Hindi or other indigenous languages. Their second problem was the reluctance of the Indian press to criticise the President severely – partly out of respect for his office and partly out of anxiety that the authority of the office might be damaged if Reddy's actions were too closely analysed.

The result was very gentle treatment of the President. For example, when Reddy visited the great Hindu temple at Tirupati in his home state of Andhra Pradesh in early September, the press dealt with it by noting his remarks that his recent decision had been dictated by his conscience and then by reporting straight that he had come to the shrine to seek 'guidance' from the god. The story then continued:

> Mr Reddy prayed for courage and strength to face the challenges ahead. Prostrating before the idol of Sri Venkateshwara, the President lost himself in deep meditation for a few minutes and prayed to the Lord to held [*sic*] him keep his mouth shut.[37]

By that time, only ten days after the dissolution, references to the controversy were fast disappearing from even the most lively newspapers[38] and within another ten days, the ever-pragmatic Ram was distancing himself from what was clearly an unpromising issue.[39] The President had been right to presume that the controversy would die amid the excitement of an election campaign in which other issues came to the fore.

Four months later, the 1980 general election – much delayed by painfully slow preparations – unexpectedly provided Indira Gandhi with a large parliamentary majority. This ended whatever hopes President Reddy harboured of asserting himself in a hung parliament. In some assessments, the result also 'saved the President from further embarrassment and the [dissolution] issue was consigned to history',[40] but this sigh of relief may have been premature.

It is quite possible that the issue will arise again under another head of state. The underlying conditions which appear to have tempted President Reddy to seek to enlarge his role still exist. All of the parties of the broad centre in India have continued to suffer decay and in several cases fragmentation since 1980. Rare attempts at rebuilding party organisations have met with failure, and the party system has thus grown less stable than it was.[41] The Congress–I majorities at the elections of 1980 and 1984 were achieved despite appalling organisational problems within the party. The 1980 victory was mainly the result of a negative vote from an electorate that was deeply exasperated with Janata's failures in power and its unseemly, often vicious internal feuding. In 1984, a party that was still more fragmented and criminalised, and which in ordinary circumstances could probably not have gained a majority, won thanks to a massive sympathy vote for the young Prime Minister, Rajiv Gandhi, amid an extraordinary national trauma and anxiety in the wake of his mother's murder.[42] In future elections the disarray within the major parties and the party system is likely to be reflected in the number of Lok Sabha seats won by various parties. There is thus a significant chance that hung parliaments will occur and perhaps even become the rule, which would revive not just the memory of President Reddy's attempt to enhance the powers of his office but possibly even the attempt itself under another head of state.[43]

Notes

1. See, for example, *Statesman* (Delhi) 12–15 and 19 July 1979.
2. Article 105 (3) states that the 'powers, privileges and immunities of each House of Parliament, and of the members and committees of each House, shall be such as may from time to time be defined by Parliament by law, and, until so defined, shall be those of the House of Commons of the Parliament of the United Kingdom, and of its members and committees at the commencement of this Constitution'. But none of that yields guidance for India's President in a case such as that examined here. *The Constitution of India (As modified up to 1st April 1958)*, (New Delhi, 1958) p. 44.
3. *Ibid.*, pp. 39 and 53, and the text of the 42nd and 45th Amendments given in *Statesman*, 26 August 1979.
4. *Statesman*, 21 August 1979.
5. The constitution does not provide for a limited period of direct rule over India's central government by the President that would be analogous to President's Rule in the states of the Indian federal system, which is discussed elsewhere in this volume by Douglas Verney (ch. 12).

6. *Statesman*, 15–16 July 1979.
7. *Ibid.*, 15–19 July 1979.
8. *Ibid.*, 15 July 1979.
9. See for example, S. Sahay in *Statesman*, 19 July 1979. See also, S. Nihal Singh, *Statesman*, 18 July 1979.
10. See for example, *Economic and Political Weekly* (Bombay), 7 July 1979, p. 1111, and 14 July 1979, p. 1143.
11. *Statesman*, 17–19 and especially 20 July 1979.
12. *Ibid.*, 20 July 1979.
13. *Economic and Political Weekly*, 18 August 1979, p. 1393.
14. The quotation is from *Economic and Political Weekly*, 25 August 1979, p. 1441. See also, 14 July 1979, p. 1178.
15. Lok Sabha Secretariat, *Journal of Parliamentary Information*, xxv, 4 (October–December, 1979) p. 537 and *Hindustan Times* (Delhi) 24–27 July 1979.
16. *Statesman*, 27 July 1979.
17. *Ibid.*, 29 and 30 July, and 1 and 7 August 1979.
18. *Ibid.*, 5 August 1979.
19. *Journal of Parliamentary Information* . . ., p. 538.
20. These comments are based on two dozen interviews with politicians, including numerous Congress–I leaders, New Delhi, December 1984.
21. *Journal of Parliamentary Information* . . ., p. 538.
22. *Statesman*, 7, 12, 14 and 18 August 1979.
23. Interviews with a member of the Janata delegation, 13 and 19 November 1985.
24. *Statesman*, 23 August 1979.
25. *Ibid.*, 26 August 1979.
26. *Ibid.*, 22–26 August 1979.
27. *Ibid.*, 22 August 1979.
28. *Ibid.*, 23 August 1979 and R. Kothari, 'Delivering the Goods', *Seminar*, (October, 1979) p. 13n.
29. See for example, numerous reports in *Times of India* (Bombay) and *Statesman*, 22 August 1979, and *Economic and Political Weekly*, 1 September 1979, p. 1485.
30. This is based on interviews with two dozen national-level politicians, New Delhi, December 1984.
31. See in this regard, J. Manor, 'Indira and After: The Decay of Party Organisation in India', *The Round Table* (October, 1978) pp. 315–24.
32. Jagjivan Ram himself felt it necessary to emphasise 'that he did not agree with those who said that the days of single-party Governments were over and that the coming years would be the days of coalition Governments'. *Statesman*, 24 August 1979. See also, the views of the editor and Romesh Thapar in *Economic and Political Weekly*, 25 August 1979, pp. 1442 and 1445.
33. See for example, *Statesman*, 15 August 1979, and *Economic and Political Weekly*, 18 August 1979, p. 1393 and 25 August 1979, p. 1445.
34. *Economic and Political Weekly*, 25 August 1979, pp. 1441–42.
35. See for example, *Economic and Political Weekly*, 7 July 1979, p. 1111, and 14 July 1979, p. 1178.

36. Kothari, 'Delivering the Goods', p. 13.
37. *Statesman*, 3 September 1979.
38. *Indian Express* and *Statesman*, 25 August to 3 September 1979.
39. *Statesman*, 15 September 1979.
40. See for example, V. B. Raju, 'Correctives Needed', *Seminar* (April, 1981) p. 19.
41. See in this vein, J. Manor, 'Party Decay and Political Crisis in India', *The Washington Quarterly* (summer, 1981) pp. 25–40, and 'Parties and the Party System' in A. Kohli (ed.) *India's Troubled Democracy* (Princeton, forthcoming).
42. See J. Manor, 'The Electoral Process amid Awakening and Decay: Reflections on the Indian General Election of 1980' in P. Lyon and J. Manor (eds.) *Transfer and Transformation: Political Institutions in the New Commonwealth* (Leicester and Salem, N.H., 1983) pp. 87–116; 'The Indian General Election of 1984', *Electoral Studies*, iv, 2 (1985) pp. 149–152; and 'Appearance and Reality in Indian Politics: The 1984 Election in the South' in P. R. Brass and F. Robinson (eds.) *The Indian National Congress: The First Hundred Years* (New Delhi, forthcoming).
43. Indeed at this writing, President Zail Singh has brought a bitter dispute with Prime Minister Rajiv Gandhi into the open, in an apparent attempt to mobilise dissenters within the ruling Congress–I Party behind his bid for re-election in mid-1987. This attempt indicates that we have not seen the last of ambitious Presidents. See *India Today*, 15 April 1988.

9 A Revolutionary Governor-General? The Grenada Crisis of 1983

Peter Fraser

On 19 October 1983, amidst an internecine party strife, the Prime Minister of Grenada was murdered. Six days later the island was invaded, largely by US troops. They soon arrested the Prime Minister's opponents, and the island was then without a government. Into this breach stepped the Governor-General, Sir Paul Scoon. Using the undoubted final reserve powers of his office he assumed full executive and legislative authority in the country. Thereafter, however, he had to find the best way of relinquishing this. In the end, in December 1984, after new elections, a new government was installed and the Governor-General reverted to his more ordinary role.

There had been a protracted run-up to these events. Grenadian political life from the early 1950s to the late 1970s was dominated by Eric Gairy. Starting as an opponent of vested interests, he rapidly became a vested interest in his own right. Suspended from office in 1962 by the British government, he survived to become Grenada's first Prime Minister and to win the first election after independence in 1976. Despite strong popular support, his government became known for mismanagement and encouraging violence against its political enemies. Gairy himself exhibited various symptoms of bizarre behaviour, the least serious and most endearing being his belief in unidentified flying objects. Demonstrations against him and the prospects of independence under his government in 1973 and 1974 ended in violence with the opposition cowed, having failed to change his policies or to delay independence. At the first post-independence elections in 1976 a united opposition challenged him strongly but lost, alleging that electoral irregularities had denied them victory. By early 1979 the Gairy years had left Grenada with a ruined economy, growing discontent and strong pressure for change. On 13 March 1979, while on a foreign visit, Gairy was overthrown by the New Jewel Movement, the most radical section of the opposition to him from 1973. Despite the fact that three of its leaders were Members of Parliament, the NJM decided that the electoral process would always be rigged against them by Gairy and feared that he intended to have them assassinated. As Marxist–Leninists they did not believe that even with fair elections the parliamentary system was appropriate for Grenada. Within weeks of the almost bloodless and immensely popular overthrow of Gairy, however, they invited non-NJM members into the newly proclaimed People's Revolutionary Government (PRG) and in the People's Laws they promulgated they re-enacted large sections of the independent constitution of 1973. They also retained both the position of Governor-General and the incumbent, Sir Paul Scoon. Even if the new government was revolutionary it did not completely repudiate features inherited from the Gairy era. One feature it did reject was any national election, at least until a completely new constitution could be drafted. Grenadian, Caribbean and US opponents of the People's Revolutionary Government would base much of their opposition to the NJM on this failure to hold elections. In retrospect a more pragmatic (or cynical) approach to elections would have been some help to the PRG, relieving some external pressure from the USA and increasing support from the Commonwealth Caribbean. It may also have defused internal opposition and allowed the PRG to operate in a less charged atmosphere.[1]

Of the three main tasks the NJM set itself when it came to office the first, though difficult, was achieved. In its four and a half years in office it undid much of Gairy's legacy of mismanagement. The economy was restored to a condition equal to that of its more fortunate neighbours, and the project for an international airport to expand the tourist industry was near completion in October 1983. The welfare of the Grenadian people improved, and many interesting innovations in education were made. Internationally, Grenada became known for its progressive policies, rather than the oddity in belief and behaviour of its previous leader. Its other two main tasks were of a different order of difficulty. Like many other governments it wanted to develop the national economy: in Grenada these plans were made even more difficult by its small size, limited resources, vulnerability, and the neglect of the Gairy years. It was a task that would take many more than four years to accomplish and would require much patience and endurance from the Grenadian people. In some ways it was made much harder by the easier successes of correcting Gairy's mismanagement: both the people and some PRG members and supporters believed the PRG capable of economic miracles. The final task was to build socialism in terrain unpromising even in the eyes of the NJM. It was the means chosen to fulfil this task that undid the PRG and the NJM, left its most popular figure dead, and its surviving Central Committee members under threat of hanging at the time of writing. Here an analysis is offered of the destruction of that project of building socialism and the following period when the almost forgotten Governor-General played the leading role in creating a Grenada without either Gairy or the NJM as the dominant force. At the time of writing the fate of that experiment, like the fate of the condemned NJM members, remains uncertain.

Exactly a month after the revolution in 1979, the first signs appeared of the PRG's later fatefully obsessive concern with protecting the new order. In a speech on 13 April its leader, Maurice Bishop, claimed to 'know that the dictator Gairy is organizing mercenaries . . . to restore him to his throne'. A month later he extended the list of dangers to the revolution by accusing its opponents of unwarranted propaganda and economic destabilisation.[2] A year later he stated that 'national security and defence' was the 'second pillar' of the revolution, and that the PRG had a duty to ensure 'our people understand . . . why it is that imperialism *must* attack us – why, it is, therefore that the assassinations, terror, destabilisation, mercenary invasion, *must* be part of the agenda'.[3] A number of incidents encouraged these fears. The worst was a bomb at a rally on 19 June 1980: apparently intended to kill the PRG leadership, it killed three young women, and injured more than 90 people.[4] Manoeuvres by US armed forces meanwhile generated fears of invasion.[5] Internal security thus became a major priority, and the armed forces came to be increased with the help of agreements with Cuba, the USSR and other allies.[6] These agreements would have led by 1985 to an army of four regular and 14 reserve battalions, with armoured cars, cannons, anti-tank guns and mortars, and a small coastguard force.[7] Plainly this increase was designed to be a deterrent to large invaders and to any mercenary ventures. It had two dangerous effects. First, it exaggerated the role of the military pillar of the revolution when its two other pillars (the organisation of the masses and the building of a sound national economy) were shaky: a small group of military officers proved to be the main source of opposition to Bishop. Second, it symbolised a growing reliance on military-style solutions to non-military problems: by 1983 the PRG was studying, and a commission had recommended establishing, a labour army and introducing national service, preferably on 13 March 1984, when celebrations for the fifth anniversary of the revolution, and the opening of the new airport, would mute protest.[8]

But by 1983 the PRG began to feel more embattled. It now felt itself increasingly threatened internally by loss of popular support and signs of public dissent. It had never taken kindly to expressions of dissent. The launching of a newspaper called *The Grenadian Voice* by 26 prominent citizens in 1981 had caused it to believe that the counter-revolution was imminent.[9] One proposed solution was the nationalisation of banks, merchant houses and large farms. The solution adopted, however, was to arrest some of the 26 and seize their businesses. At the same time it moved against another dissident group, the Rastafarians. By 1982, however, the main internal opponent of the PRG seemed to be, in its eyes, the churches. That year they requested a report upon them by the Cubans. In 1983 they followed this up with their own investigation.[10] This found that the Roman Catholic church was seeking to challenge government youth groups with its own youth groups, and was educating its priests 'through materials distorting the teachings of Marxism–Leninism and offering Christianity as the only way to solve societies problems'. Whilst less influential the Anglican church was thought to be 'still a major threat to the Revolution', the Seventh Day Adventists were 'hostile', the Methodists, though weak, would support opposition too, and of the minor churches the Jehovah's Witnesses, the Church of the Open Bible, and the Baptists were felt to be 'most reactionary'. A few months later a further report described the ecumenical opposition to the PRG as a 'very dangerous' development due to 'the large percentage of Grenadians who have very deep trust in the church and also taking into account the weakness in all our mass organisations'.[11] The chief counter to the churches had been the innovations and improvements in education, but these had been left in disarray by the Gairy government. By 1983 what had appeared to be the chief glory of the revolution, its education policies, was fading, and the government accordingly now took steps to impose on the system people who would be more amenable to its views. The ideological, as well as physical, security of the revolution appeared to be under threat.

To an obsessive concern with security, and intolerance of dissent, an elitist arrogance came to be added. Despite Bishop's claim that 'the greatest single achievement, the thing that we are happiest about, is the community mobilisation, community involvement, community participation', and that the first pillar of the revolution was 'to fully involve the masses in whatever we are trying to do, to keep them fully informed',[12] the NJM had never been very open about its real aims or structure. Hudson Austin, Bishop's successor, commented ruefully on 16 October 1983: 'We have tried to keep the problems away from the masses in order to maintain the unity of the party and the prestige of the Grenadian revolution.'[13] But the party's failure to consult and involve the people lay much deeper than that. In a collectively drafted speech delivered only to party members in September 1982, Bishop had outlined the relationship of the vanguard party to the masses:

> It is the party [this said] that has to be at the head of this process building the revolution, acting as representatives of the working people and in particular the working class. This is the only way it can be because the working class does not have the ideological development or experience to build socialism on its own. The Party has to be there to ensure that the necessary steps and measures are taken.[14]

Secrecy and lack of consultation were thus intrinsic to the party's procedures. These tendencies may have remained innocuous had not two major crises faced the PRG from late 1982. One was national; the other internal to the party.

At the outset the PRG had enjoyed a period of about three years after March 1979 when its main task had been to correct Gairy's mismanagement of the economy. Its apparent success in these years was seen as proof of the superiority of the PRG's economic policies to those of other Commonwealth Caribbean countries. The chief evidence for this was the reduction in unemployment from 50 per cent to 15 per cent.[15] This latter figure excluded, however, approximately four per cent of the working population belonging to the armed forces, a proportion much higher than that of the other islands.[16] If these were included the actual Grenadian unemployment figures fitted into the 15–20 per cent range common in the region. Nonetheless by late 1982 the PRG seemed to have confronted successfully the problems of mismanagement inherited from the Gairy years. But it still had to confront the problems posed by small size, limited resources, open economies and dependency. It is noteworthy that the policies to relieve these suggested by a Czech economist in 1982 did not differ greatly from those given to any other, non-revolutionary, government in the region.[17] Moreover by 1983 the PRG decided to switch its emphasis to the previously despised tourist sector, although by then it faced enormous problems. The proximate causes were the worsening balance of payments due to low export prices and increased imports (especially for the new airport), and the shortage of investment and liquidity (again due to the new airport's heavy demands). Some relief was obtained by an IMF agreement,[18] but the crisis remained severe enough to endanger the existence of a government facing an election, though by 1984, with the opening of the airport the more pressing problems of the balance of payments, investment and liquidity would have eased considerably. That was not to be, for in the meanwhile within the PRG a crisis had arisen within the party.

The internal crisis directly reflected the situation external to the party. The masses were proving to be no more tractable than the economy. They remained attached to their churches. They took for granted the welfare benefits the revolution had brought them (the disease of 'economism'). They had withdrawn their support from the women's, youth and the PRG's other mass organisations. Even more disturbingly the militia had almost disintegrated, and many soldiers were considering leaving the army, and the island itself, at the end of their five-year contracts.[19] This collapse of support had many causes: the heavy demands made on party members and supporters, the worsening economic situation, the PRG's talent for alienating people, the end of a period of great popularity similar to those immediately after independence elsewhere in the Caribbean. More profoundly it was related to the nature of the NJM itself.

This collapse of popular support lends credence to the claim by a hostile source that the original JEWEL (Joint Endeavour for Welfare Education and Liberation) had not been founded by any of the NJM leaders, but had been taken over by them to provide a mass base.[20] After the 1979 revolution one of its founders wrote of Bishop 'that his first *coup* was not the one that overthrew Gairy but the one that captured the strength of JEWEL for his revolution'.[21] The NJM certainly appeared to lack any talent for mass organisation. It considered the Grenadian people backward, and judged its own action in the mass protests of 1973 and 1974 'ultra-leftism in action'. Its 'major weakness . . .', so it said, 'was . . . the fact that a Leninist approach to party building and to strategy and tactics were not adopted'. From July 1977 onwards this 'weakness' would be corrected so well that by October 1983 the NJM had only 346 members: 72 full, 94 candidate, and 180 applicants. There were also 150 potential applicants.[22] The reasons for this had been spelt out by Bishop:

> There is no doubt that the Party can be built more rapidly on the basis of lower standards but this will mean that the tasks we have set ourselves, including our historical task of building socialism, would not be accomplished. As Lenin told us a long time ago 'better fewer but better'. Immortal words that we must never forget . . . it is real life and the demands of the struggle that make it necessary for us to have these difficult conditions and for us to ensure that comrades who are

> full members, and also candidate members are truly the finest representatives of the working class.

Indeed some members were now suggesting the additional grade of 'Prospective Potential Applicant'.[23] Inexperienced in building mass organisations but experienced in building a tight little party the NJM reacted to its loss of popularity in the only way it knew – by looking to improvements in the party organisation and by making its membership even more selective:

> We believe [it stated] it must become more and more difficult for comrades to become full members and candidate members and it must become more difficult for new comrades to remain as members and candidate members: and those who are unwilling to live up to the demands of this membership would have to be moved.[24]

Despite the statement by Bernard Coard, one of its major figures, that the annual meeting of all members was the supreme body of the party, the controlling body was in fact the Central Committee, the elite of the elite, only 15 members strong.[25] The disaster of October 1983 would result from the finally unendurable strains in this small body.

Strain, in the clinical sense, was present there too. From mid-1982 onwards several Central Committee members were ill for longish periods.[26] In the end, however, the crisis had more to do with the internal workings of a small body than health, or the economy, or ideology. From the time of Bernard Coard's resignation in October 1982 (kept secret even from close advisors) the Central Committee began to concentrate on matters of leadership, organisation and discipline. Coard had resigned, he stated, because his role as the most prominent critic of the party's failings which were endangering the revolution minimised the chances of a successful solution to these problems, since other members were becoming too reliant on him. The meeting that was called to discuss his resignation set the terms of debate. It abruptly switched from a discussion of his decision, and his failure to appear in person, to matters of party organisation.[27] The conclusion of this meeting (lasting 32 hours over four days) were that the crisis within the party was due to the 'backward and underdeveloped nature of our society and the consequent existence of a large petty bourgeois influence in our society' that was reflected in the work of the committee; a failure to study, leading to a failure to adopt a Marxist–Leninist line; and the poor functioning of many party organs because of their non-Leninist practices. The party, it believed, could either degenerate into a social–democratic party with the consequent degeneration of the revolution, or follow the 'communist road – the road of Leninist standards and functioning, the roads to democratic centralism, of selectivity, of criticism and self-criticism, and of collective leadership.'[28] In passing we can note that at this time collective, not joint, leadership was recommended, and that there was an extraordinary 'bookishness' to the committee. Time and time again in its minutes there are references to Lenin's works, quotations from Lenin, while works by Soviet authors, regarded as experts on party organisation and revolution, were made compulsory reading. This 'bookishness' was symptomatic of a more profound disease: the failure to seek advice from anyone outside a charmed circle of initiates. In September and October 1983 when the crisis became unmanageable they sought first the advice of a few Marxist–Leninists with no experience of government (Trevor Munroe from Jamaica, Michael Als from Trinidad, and Rupert Roopnarine from Guyana).[29] To begin with they kept their problems from the Cubans (and presumably the USSR), but then on 12 October Bishop, followed by the majority a little later, spoke to the Cuban ambassador.[30] The NJM had entered into many secret agreements with Cuba and the USSR. It took very seriously criticisms by Cuban and East European comrades. Both the USSR since Stalin and Cuba from 1959 had considerable experience in containing conflicts within the elite, and thus they turned to them for advice. In retrospect this late recourse to their allies is one of the most surprising features of the final crisis.

Following Coard's resignation in October 1982 there had been a long pause until July 1983, since the scheduled March meeting in 1983 had to be cancelled because of an invasion scare. The July meeting lasted 54 hours spread over six and a half days. The conclusions did little to advance the debate beyond the point that had been reached earlier. There was now great concern about

> the emergence of deep petty bourgeois manifestations and influences in the party . . . in March the Party so it was said came dangerously close to losing its links with the masses . . . the continued failure of the Party to transform itself ideologically and organisationally and to exercise firm leadership along a Leninist path in the face of the acute rises in the complexities and difficulties . . . economic, political, social, military and international[31]

facing the country, were now felt to be quite intractable.

The pattern of long, often acrimonious, such meetings of about a dozen people can have done little to help to solve its problems; they also meant that since the Central Committee and the PRG were almost the same, the work of a government in crisis was several times brought to a halt. At a further meeting in August, Bishop concluded the discussion by agreeing that the party was close to disintegration, that another meeting should be held and that to prepare themselves committee members should discuss problems with party members and discover the reasons for public disenchantment with the party by talking to the masses and to people in various positions of authority. They should also 'study the history of the CPSU' and 're-read *Standards of Party Life* by Pronin'.[32] This temporary deviation into considering the problems of the revolution as perceived outside the party seemed to disappear entirely at the next meeting in September. At this, and all subsequent ones, attention was focussed solely on internal party matters, until, too late, the NJM discovered that both the Grenadian people legitimately, and foreign powers less so, had an interest in internal party matters, and their effect on Grenada and the region.

At the four-day-long extraordinary meeting of the Central Committee which started on 14 September 1983 the proposal that there should be joint leadership of the NJM, because of the complementary qualities of Bishop and Coard, was accepted by a majority, and so was the return of Coard to the Committee.[33] At a full meeting of party members on 25 September Bishop and Coard agreed to accept joint leadership, Bishop expressing his desire to 'use the criticism positively and march along with the entire party to build a Marxist–Leninist party that can lead the people to socialism and communism'. Both he and Coard agreed it was an historic day.[34] Coard's claim that the General Meeting of party members was the supreme decision-making body appears, however, quite theoretical: at this meeting and the later one on 13 October the membership accepted the line of the majority Central Committee. But agreement was not to last. Immediately after the 25 September meeting Bishop left for a tour of Eastern Europe. Any doubts which he may still have had about joint leadership were then revitalised by George Louison and Unison Whiteman. The party indeed was now deeply riven between Bishop's supporters and Coard's. Both sides, moreover, began to imagine the worst of each other, and by the time of Bishop's return on 8 October, the Coard camp had gone into hiding fearing assassination.[35] In an atmosphere of 'great tension among party members and in particular CC members . . . creating severe mental and emotional stress'[36] they emerged, however, to form a majority, discipline Bishop, and confine him to his house. This was done at the General meeting on 13 October, described by Vince Noel as 'a horrendous display of militarism, hatred and emotional vilification'.[37] Yet from testimony by George

Louison and Bernard Coard we know that meetings between the majority and Bishop continued until 18 October.[38] Indeed a meeting was scheduled for the 19 October. Clearly the most vocal critics of Bishop (Layne, James and Cornwall) were still being restrained by others on the Central Committee, and some sort of compromise seemed to be close. But on the morning of 19 October the much revered if backward masses intervened. Freeing Bishop, the crowd took over the military headquarters at Fort Rupert.

Ewart Layne described the reaction of the Central Committee members to this intervention:

> The situation with the Central Committee members was one of total paralysis, I could see that Comrades felt the situation was totally out of hand. While there we received a message that weapons were being distributed at Fort Rupert and that orders were issued by Maurice and Vince Noel to eliminate the whole Central Committee in particular myself, General Austin and Comrade Coard . . . I called General Austin outside and put it to him that the only way to save the revolution and the party was to move to recapture Fort Rupert and for the military to take control for a short period.[39]

In court Layne later repeated that he had given orders to re-take the fort, but denied ordering the killing of Bishop and the others with him.[40] Other members of the Central Committee deny that there was any meeting of the committee on that day. Austin claims to have only been there briefly, and Coard states that he and his wife were preparing to leave the country.[41] It appears that the attempt to recapture the fort was a military decision, taken by army officers who, from their later statements in court, believed themselves to be the real vanguard of the revolution. At the fort itself shots were fired, perhaps first by members of the crowd. Less than 15 minutes later Bishop and the others were dead. The nearest we can get to the truth of what happened is the statement by Callistus Bernard (Imam Abdullah), the officer of the detachment sent to recapture the fort. In court he denied giving orders to kill Bishop and the others, and explained the events which occurred in this way:

> There was confusion, chaos . . . Soldiers had been stripped and all kinds of things happened. It was in this atmosphere, in this context; it was in this way that a number of soldiers who went there to restore order, including myself, held a number of people prisoners; and it was in this atmosphere – in a situation of anger and rage –, in this situation of chaos and confusion, that a number of people died at Fort Rupert. It was in this tragic situation of rage, confusion, problems.[42]

Whoever gave the orders, the army thereupon took control, and the short-lived Revolutionary Military Council was then quickly formed.

The events of 19 October 1983 nevertheless remain a mystery. The trial of most of the surviving Central Committee members and some soldiers failed to provide much evidence of high quality. Conducted in a strange fashion, of dubious constitutionality, and with procedures of its own invention,[43] the trial at best threw some light on the events leading up to 18 October. All the confessions of the major defendants were repudiated; only one, Ewart Layne's, is in his own handwriting, and in this case Layne repeated in his statement to the court that he was responsible for sending troops to the fort. The statements to the court, some of the evidence given to it, and the documents released by the US government nevertheless allow some tentative conclusions.

These fall into four main categories:[44] matters are explained as the result of either an ideological conflict between Coard and Bishop, or a successful US conspiracy, or the Leninist structure of the party, or overwork, disintegration and confusion. A possible fifth explanation, the settling of old scores, seems to have no basis in reality whatsoever. Taking the major ones we can dismiss the first fairly easily. There is no evidence that there was any ideological disagreement between Bishop and Coard. All the evidence of party meetings suggests that the major issue was one of party organisation, and that the crucial differences arose over the question of joint leadership after the meeting of 25 September. One version of this theory emphasises Coard's desire to become leader, but again all the evidence points to Coard's appreciation of Bishop's special role in the revolution and his desire to maintain that role. The second explanation is the obverse of the first. The long history of US 'dirty tricks' in Latin America, the Caribbean and elsewhere lend this some plausibility. It is a version of events that the major defendants put forward in their defence, but there is no convincing evidence of direct US involvement: major defendants either named ex-comrades as likely CIA agents, spoke circumstantially, or referred to US hostility to the PRG; one of them, Bernard, in contradiction to this line, came close to stating bluntly that Bishop was killed by PRG soldiers in anger. The most that can be said for this explanation is that the USA did help to create the conditions for 19 October by its threatening military and naval manoeuvers, and may even have been in touch with anti-revolutionaries in the crowd at the fort beforehand. Combinations of the other two have much more plausibility. Thorndike in his most useful book on the affair points to the extreme difficulty of transplanting Leninist ideas to the environment of Grenada and 'the explosive mix of revolution and militarism' created thereby.[45] The Leninism the PRG espoused stressed the backwardness of Grenada and the necessity for a vanguard elite; popular involvement was always subordinate to the plans of that elite. By 1983 the PRG was much more isolated from the people even than it supposed, and seemed quite unable to re-establish its popularity. In this it was no different to many an elected government after four and a half years in office. What made the critical difference was the failure to concentrate on events external to the party, and adherence to an ideology which sought the opinion of the people only when they were ready to agree with the party. The exhaustion of over four dispiriting years in office had taken its toll on a tiny band of ideologues. This line of explanation was pursued by many of the major defendants in their statements to the court: clearly they had an interest in pursuing this, but the minutes of the Central Committee and other bodies reveal the numbers who were ill and absent, and the overwrought atmosphere amongst those who remained. The additional features which best explain the events of 1983, and in particular those of 19 October, are the militaristic tendencies which began to appear in the PRG's dwindling armed forces (a number of the army officers seemed to confuse military and revolutionary *esprit de corps*), and the astonishing immaturity of political judgement displayed by this same group of military men. Unlike Coard they had little appreciation of the special status and contributions of Bishop. All this rather than specific orders probably influenced junior officers in their actions. But the triumph of the military was brief.[46] On 25 October Grenada was invaded, proving the wisdom of Vince Noel's words: 'our Revolution is not irreversible'. The neighbouring Commonwealth states had been deeply concerned at the murder of Bishop and what appeared to be the slide into Leninist-inspired anarchy. They appealed for assistance to the USA. The US government, now finding its ideological opposition bolstered by this appeal, and by public concern about the safety of the US students at the medical school in Grenada, decided to send in its forces to overrun the island.

It was only after the invasion that the Governor-General became highly visible. This was not altogether unprecedented in Grenada. Since 1967 when the country had became an Associated State, Governors and Governors-General had not had easy lives. The first Governor, Mr Ian Turbott, had been asked to resign after differences with Gairy. He had been replaced by Dame Hilda Bynoe, apparently chosen by Gairy so that Grenada would be the first Commonwealth country with a female Governor. When strong opposition to Gairy surfaced in late 1973 and early 1974, Dame Hilda was attacked by demonstrators and promised to resign if people so wished. Gairy took this as an affront, deciding that only he could determine when she should leave. He thereupon requested her dismissal. Before this could be acted upon, she had left the island. Her replacement, Sir Leo DeGale, became Governor-General soon after independence in February 1974, but by October 1978 he too left hurriedly to join his family abroad.[47] Gairy then arranged for the appointment of his former Cabinet Secretary, Sir Paul Scoon, as Governor-General. The position had, by then, acquired little prestige and respect, least of all from the Prime Minister.

Described as 'urbane, dignified but rather indecisive',[48] Scoon was chosen by Gairy to be a more compliant person than his predecessors. Nothing of note seems to have occured in the brief remaining period of Gairy's government to the new Governor-General. When Gairy was overthrown, Scoon, like a majority of Grenadians, probably felt relieved. Of Gairy Sir Fred Phillips writes: 'The author, who during the mid-1950s had the painful experience of working in Grenada as the administrative head of ministry for which Gairy was the responsible Minister, is fully able to appreciate the trying circumstances in which these three unfortunate Heads of State must undoubtedly have had to discharge the functions of their office.'[49] Scoon is unlikely to have been so relieved that he 'pledged firm loyalty to the People's Revolutionary Government' as two authors state.[50] But the PRG did have something to gain from the relationship, and apparently felt that his retention conferred some measure of constitutional legitimacy upon them. On 25 March 1979 People's Law Number 3 at all events stated:

> The Head of State shall remain Her Majesty the Queen and her representative in this country shall continue to be the Governor-General who shall perform such functions as the People's Revolutionary Government may from time to time advise.[51]

Since the PRG had suspended the previous constitution (though it re-enacted large sections of it), and assumed both executive and legislative powers, the Governor-General became a mere figurehead. But all the evidence points to a fairly relaxed relationship between Scoon and the PRG. One legal advisor to the government between 1979 and 1983 remembers only three instances of disagreement: Scoon once questioned the order of precedence of the Prime Minister and the Governor-General; once he wanted a more expensive tea set for more dignified entertaining; and once he had difficulty over his request for a senior civil servant to decipher a cable about the engagement or marriage of the Prince of Wales.[52] The PRG's last Attorney-General, Richard Hart, confirmed that there was a formally correct, minimally troubled, relationship between Scoon and the PRG.[53]

The three references to him in the PRG documents confirm these views, and add some supporting evidence about PRG concerns in 1983. The first was in the Political Bureau minutes of 5 January 1983. This read: '*Venezuela House*: House near Personnel Security Unit reportedly bought by the Venezuela Embassy, sold by Paul Scoon. Cde. Bishop to speak to the latter, expressing Government's intention to buy said building.'[54] The concern here with security and the fear of foreign involvement are clear; the decision taken supports the view that the relationship was at this stage fairly harmonious. The second reference reveals a less harmonious side. At another meeting of the Political Bureau on 20 April 1983 the Minister of Education, Jacqueline Creft, submitted a letter. The notes, with their customary disregard for punctuation and grammar, record:

> The letter reflected a number of areas: not notifying the appropriate bodies before doing such; and a number of statements made in different activities at which the Minister of Education was present. Some of the points highlighted by the Political Bureau are as follows: He cannot contradict the Government's line; That there is a church input. Whenever he is visiting school the Ministry of Education should be contacted before entering the schools. Periodic sessions should be held with him so that he would be in line.[55]

By this time the PRG was feeling that even the education system had run into trouble and was likely to be used by counter-revolutionaries. The Governor-General could not be allowed to step out of line on this or other matters. His attachment to Christianity in particular was disturbing to people who were now increasingly afraid of church influence (at the October 1982 meeting a committee member was ousted for deviating 'into mysticism'). The final reference shows that even *in extremis* the soldiers who took charge after Bishop's murder had not forgotten Scoon. What appears to be a handwritten record of the last Central committee meeting on 24 October contains only one item (emphasis in original): '*Bogo to brief G.G. tomorrow*'.[56] What Major Leon Cornwall of the Revolutionary Military Council had been delegated to tell the Governor-General is not known; it may have been the plans to invite civilians into the government. The next day, however, Grenada was invaded, and the Governor-General came under the protection of the invaders on the 26 October, to discover that after his years of bit parts he was now the leading actor.

The Governor-General, it has been alleged, had requested the Organisation of Eastern Caribbean States to intervene. Described as 'the sole remaining source of Governmental legitimacy'[57] by a US official, Scoon had a few days after the invasion signed a letter appealing for intervention since 'there is a vacuum of authority in Grenada following the killing of the Prime Minister and the subsequent serious violations of human rights and bloodshed'.[58] Since no one takes this letter very seriously – it was signed after not before the invasion – more interesting is the statement that Scoon 'had used a confidential channel to transmit an appeal to the OECS and other regional states to restore order on the island.'[59] On this the British House of Commons' Foreign Affairs Committee later commented: 'Both the timing and the nature of this request, which is said by the United States Government to have been a critical factor in providing a legal justification for their decision to act, remain shrouded in some mystery, and it is evidently the intention of the parties involved that the mystery should not be dispelled.'[60] They concluded that Scoon probably knew of the likelihood of intervention some days before it occurred. On 24 October Scoon did talk with Brigadier Lewis, the commander of the military forces in Barbados, and did apparently ask for help, but does not seem to have sought a foreign invasion.[61] The late Prime Minister of Barbados, Tom Adams, revealed that the confidential channel Scoon employed was 'a friendly government, albeit non-participating',[62] but this has not been named. Had the confidential channel been a Grenadian citizen that would have been quite intelligible: but this has not been claimed. The most likely interpretation is that the confidential channel, like the letter, were fabrications. Had the Governor-General been found on 25 October rather than a day later, the letter would have been produced on the day of the invasion, complete with Scoon's signature. Resistance to the invasion was, however, much stiffer than expected, delaying production of the letter, and allowing doubts about its authenticity and that of any other request to surface. But in any case legal experts have questioned whether the Governor-General's request, even if authentic, could have served as the legal basis for the invasion.[63] That seems to have been principally based on *force majeure*.

In its aftermath Scoon's problems soon mounted. By December 1983 the Governor-General felt confident enough in an address to the nation to denounce the PRG and 'the actions of those who would prefer to see an alien culture imposed upon us – a culture supported by the gun and reinforced by an ideology which is hostile to our cherished Christian values and our democratic way of life'.[64] But if these values and way of life were to be restored what were the options available to him in late October? The most authoritative examination of the constitutional position has identified three. First, the Governor-General could have recalled the Parliament and Prime Minister deposed by the 1979 *coup*. Second, after a short interval he could have summoned a constituent assembly, since the 1974 constitution had manifest defects which allowed the conditions leading to the 1979 *coup* to develop. Third, he could have done more or less what he did do.[65] The advice given to the Governor-General on these matters will probably remain a mystery for some time. He now refuses to comment on the PRG years or subsequent events.[66] In place of detailed information an analysis of these choices suggests why he acted as he did.

The recall of the 1976 Parliament was never a genuine option. Phillips, the West Indies' foremost constitutional commentator, refers to the difficulty of recalling a parliament whose members had gone their separate ways.[67] In that Parliament, Gairy had had nine seats and the opposition six. Of the six opposition members two (Bishop and Whiteman) were dead and another (Coard) in detention; had they been alive and not in detention they would probably have forfeited their seats by their actions on 13 March 1979. These difficulties, however, were minor compared to the greater political problem of recalling Gairy, who was insisting that he was the legitimate Prime Minister. Though electoral support for him had remained at substantial levels, his years in power had not left Grenadians with pleasant memories. His recall would have been unpopular with many, especially those with influence, and it would have created grave difficulties both with the USA and the Commonwealth Caribbean. The USA had often been accused in the early years of the PRG of wanting to support an invasion by Gairy; had he now been asked to resume office, the justifications for the invasion – the PRG's violations of human rights, and the dangers of bloodshed – would have sounded very hollow. It was not an option that Scoon himself would have welcomed: the PRG might have treated him with public respect and private hilarity, but an older and resentful Gairy would have been uncommonly difficult to handle. The first of the three options was never a serious one.

Phillips preferred the second: a brief period of interim government during which a constituent assembly could have met to draft an improved constitution. But it is not obvious that the 1973 constitution was so defective that it needed to be replaced. It was basically the same as those of other Commonwealth Caribbean islands, and in these the same problems had not arisen. The Gairy regime was unique in the Eastern Caribbean. The basic problem in calling an early constituent assembly was the same as that which led to the delay in elections. No one could be sure about the support for the NJM or Gairy's party. If any sort of early election took place, what guarantee would there be that the NJM or Gairy supporters (both opponents of the 1973 constitution) would not dominate the assembly? If the Governor-General decided to avoid that problem by choosing its members, his actions would have been open to the same objections made against his actual conduct. There existed no parliament to choose the members; once elected or chosen the assembly could not be arbitrarily dissolved; so that the best choice was to avoid summoning an assembly. There was no universal feeling that such an assembly was wanted, and unpredictable in composition, it might have plunged Grenada back into a period of conflict. This was the last thing that most Grenadians wanted or deserved.

The Governor-General and his advisors decided instead that the best solution would be to have an advisory council which would run the country with him until elections could be held. It did not start without problems. The first person to be asked to serve as chairman refused on the grounds of ill-health; the second took some time to arrive in the island, and all its members did not manage to meet until December. Whatever its constitutional basis, it was at least preferable to the barely disguised rule by the US armed forces. Within a few days of its first meeting the Governor-General's legal advisor and Attorney-General, Tony Rushford, had resigned, complaining 'I have never known a situation where a Governor-General appoints himself saviour of his people, calls in foreign armies and then does very little to bring about the restoration of constitutional civil government . . .'.[68] While not entirely factually correct (Scoon had neither appointed himself nor called in foreign armies) many agreed with Rushford. This type of criticism failed to appreciate the difficulty that was facing the Governor-General. The advisory council managed to hold the line until the anti-Gairy and anti-NJM coalition was formed. This fought and won the December 1984 elections, but has subsequently shown by its internal disagreements and conflicts just how difficult it was to form in the first place. Initially the Governor-General and the council had had an equally difficult task: dealing with the US forces and diplomats who indubitably did regard themselves as saviours and were reluctant to return to more mundane activities.[69] It would have been difficult in the circumstances to do much better than Scoon did; easy to do much worse.

The most substantial criticisms of the Governor-General's actions have been those of Phillips. He examined the rather dubious constitutional basis for Scoon's assumption of both executive and legislative power, the curious retention of some of the People's Laws (themselves preserving parts of the 1973 constitution), and the granting to members of the advisory council of the immunities of an elected government. He concluded:

> Any pretence of constitutional succession exhibited by the interim regime must only be a fig leaf attempting to conceal the nakedness of the situation . . . the Governor-General, in taking the powers he did, was operating in the guise of a revolutionary . . .[70]

From the last judgement one feels compelled to dissent. In acting as he did the Governor-General was doing what was traditional, not what was revolutionary, in Grenada. Gairy had shown very little respect for the separation of executive and legislative powers; the NJM when it came to power followed in Gairy's footsteps (though it was starting discussions for a new constitution before it fell). At least the Governor-General moved Grenada away from these ways and allowed Grenadians to enjoy whatever benefits they could from a system of government that respects such separations. In his time as Governor-General Sir Paul Scoon must have had time to appreciate the profundity of the old Chinese curse, 'May you live in interesting times'.

Notes

1. Kai P. Schoenhals and Richard A. Melanson *Revolution and Intervention in Grenada: The New Jewel Movement, the United States, and the Caribbean* (Boulder: Westview Press 1985), W. Richard Jacobs and Ian Jacobs *Grenada: The Route to Revolution* (Havana: Casa de las Americas 1980), and Tony Thorndike *Grenada: Politics, Economics and Society* (London: Frances Pinter 1985) deal with the Gairy period.
2. Maurice Bishop *Selected Speeches 1979–1981* ed. Didacus Jules and Don Rojas (Havana: Casa de las Americas (1982) pp. 12 & 15 *et seq.*
3. Interview of 15 July 1980, reprinted in Steve Clark *Grenada: A Workers' and Farmers' Government with a Revolutionary Proletarian Leadership* (New York: Pathfinder Press 1980) p. 29.

4. Chris Searle *Grenada: The Struggle against Destabilization* (London: Writers and Readers 1983) pp. 40–41.
5. Schoenhals pp. 130–136 for US actions; Searle pp. 107–114 for Grenadian responses.
6. *Documents Pertaining to Relations Between Grenada, the USSR and Cuba* (n.p.: USIA n.d.) series 3 no. 102604 & series 4 no. H for internal security; series 1 no. 000191 for a typical military agreement. These are the documents of the PRG seized by the USA. (Cited as doc. series . . . no. . . .).
7. Doc. series 4 no. 103892 with hand-written notes (also appears, without notes, as series 2 no. 100355).
8. Doc. series 4 no. 102602.
9. Schoenhals p. 42; for a characteristically naive acceptance of the PRG version see Searle pp. 48–50.
10. Doc. series 4 no. II & JJ.
11. Doc. series 4 no. KK.
12. Clark pp. 27, 29.
13. Cathy Sunshine & Philip Wheaton *Death of a Revolution: An Analysis of the Grenadian Tragedy and the US Invasion* (Washington, D.C.: Epica 1984) p. 9.
14. *The Grenada Papers* ed. Paul Seabury & Walter McDougall (San Francisco: Institute for Contemporary Studies 1984) p. 73.
15. Trevor Munroe *Grenada Revolution, Counter Revolution* (Kingston: Vanguard 1983) p. 115 stresses this achievement.
16. Thorndike p. xix.
17. Doc. series 4 no. U.
18. Schoenhals pp. 47, 62; Thorndike pp. 126–127.
19. Doc. series 2 no. 100319.
20. Gregory Sanford & Richard Vigilante *Grenada: The Untold Story* (Lanham: Madison Books 1984) pp. 31–33.
21. Sanford p. 33.
22. *Grenada Papers* pp. 80–81; Thorndike p. xix for membership figures.
23. *Grenada Papers* pp. 83, 85.
24. *Grenada Papers* p. 86.
25. Bernard Coard 'Statement to the Court' p. 70.
26. Coard pp. 60–61.
27. Thorndike pp. 75–76 for Coard's resignation; Sanford pp. 148–152 contains the longest account of the subsequent meeting based on Bishop's notes.
28. Doc. series 4 no. 0.
29. Munroe pp. 100–101; Anthony Payne, Paul Sutton and Tony Thorndike, *Grenada Revolution and Invasion* (London: Crom Helm 1984) pp. 132–133.
30. *Grenada: The World Against the Crime* (Havana: Editorial de Ciencias Sociales 1983) pp. 9–10.
31. Doc. series 2 no. 100243.
32. Doc. series 2 no. 100319.
33. Doc. series 1 no. 000123.

34. 'Extraordinary General Meeting of full members of the NJM, *Caribbean Review* 12(4) 1983, p. 58.
35. Schoenhals p. 72.
36. Doc. series 3 no. 100270, letter to Bishop from Nazim Burke.
37. *Grenada Papers* p. 338, letter from Vince Noel.
38. 'Interviewing George Louison' *Caribbean Review* 12(4) pp. 17–18 and Coard p. 82.
39. Ewart Layne's 'Confession'.
40. Ewart Layne 'Statement to the Court' pp. 9–11.
41. Hudson Austin quoted in *The Grenada Newsletter* 14(13) 9 August 1986 p. 5; Coard p. 84.
42. Callistus Bernard 'Statement to the Court' pp. 22–23; also Thorndike pp. 159–163, Sanford p. 163 *et seq.* and Schoenhals pp. 75–77 for attempts to reconstruct events.
43. For details Tony Gifford *The Grenada Murder Trial No Case for Hanging An Analysis* (London: Committee for Human Rights in Grenada 1987) and Ian Ramsay 'Some Aspects of the Constitutional Problems of the Grenada 18 Trial' (typescript).
44. Sanford & Seabury adopt the first; most of the defendants the second (Schoenhals inclines towards this line); Hugh O'Shaughnessy *Grenada: Revolution, Invasion and Aftermath* (London: Sphere 1984) chooses the third; the defendants and Schoenhals stress the fourth. Thorndike and Schoenhals provide the most nuanced explanations.
45. Thorndike p. 178.
46. Thorndike pp. 163–170 for an account of the Revolutionary Military Council.
47. Sir Fred Phillips *West Indian Constitutions: Post-Independence Reforms* (New York: Oceana 1985) pp. 310–311.
48. Payne p. 179.
49. Phillips p. 311.
50. Jacobs p. 126; Schoenhals p. 35 repeats this unlikely statement.
51. Phillips p. 312.
52. Personal communication.
53. Conversation with Richard Hart.
54. Doc. series 2 no. 100276.
55. Doc. series 2 no. 100285.
56. Doc. series 3 no. unnumbered.
57. O'Shaughnessy Appendix 2 Kenneth Dam's speech, p. 246.
58. William C. Gilmore *The Grenada Intervention Analysis and Documentation* (London: Mansell 1984) p. 95.
59. O'Shaughnessy p. 246.
60. *Second Report of the Foreign Affairs Committee Session 1983–84 Grenada (15th March 1984)* no. 226, pxvi.
61. Fitzroy Ambursley & Keith Dunkerley *Grenada: Whose Freedom?* (London: Latin American Bureau 1984) pp. 87–88.
62. Gilmore p. 105.
63. Gilmore and Phillips agree on this.
64. 'Address to Nation 8th December 1983' (typescript) p. 1

65. Phillips pp. 20–52.
66. This was the response to my request.
67. Phillips p. 51.
68. Payne pp. 190–191.
69. Payne p. 189.
70. Phillips p. 51.

10 The Conventions of Ministerial Resignations: The Queensland Coalition Crisis of 1983

D. J. Markwell

Australian politics, both state and federal, have been characterised by long periods in office of one government. Queensland is no exception. There have been only two changes in the political colour of its government in over half a century – in 1957, when the long-serving Labor Government split and fell, to be replaced by a coalition of the Country (later National) and Liberal parties; and in 1983, when that 26-year-old coalition split and was replaced by a National Party government which, two elections on, is still in office.

This Chapter will set out the constitutional and political background to the 1983 crisis, describe its key events, outline certain conventions on ministerial resignations and consider the advice of the Premier to the Governor not to accept the resignations of the Liberal ministers, and the responses of the Governor and of the Liberal ministers to this.

CONSTITUTIONAL AND POLITICAL BACKGROUND

Queensland inherited from Britain the institutions of the Crown and of responsible government. The Queen is Queen of Queensland, as well as of Australia. She is represented in Brisbane by the state Governor, who (prior to the Australia Act of 1986) was appointed, and could only be dismissed, by the Queen on the advice of the British government. Normally, of course, this advice was really that of the Queensland Premier. However, in 1976, the British government declined to advise the Queen to re-appoint Sir Colin Hannah because in 1975 he had made partisan public remarks. Instead, the late Sir James Ramsay was appointed to be the new state Governor and he was in office during the 1983 crisis.

The Queensland constitution (as amended in 1977) provides (Section 14(2)):

> Officers liable to retire from office on political grounds [ie. Ministers] shall hold office at the pleasure of the Governor who in the exercise of his power to appoint and dismiss such officers, . . . shall not be subject to direction from any person whatsoever nor be limited as to his sources of advice.

Queensland is the only Australian state with a unicameral parliament. At the beginning of August 1983, its composition was: National Party, 36 seats; Liberal Party, 20; Australian Labor Party, 25; Independent, one. Although the Liberal Party is the largest non-Labor party in all other states, the National Party has always won more seats than it in the Queensland Parliament (though not always more votes). The coalition between the two parties was formalised in a written 'coalition agreement' authorised by the organisational wings of both parties and re-negotiated (sometimes with great acrimony) after each election. In 1980, it was agreed that there would be 11 National Party ministers and seven Liberals. The agreement also provided (as it had since 1957) that the leader of the National Party would be Premier, and the leader of the Liberal Party would be deputy Premier and Treasurer. Since 1968, the Premier had been Mr (now Sir) Joh Bjelke–Petersen.

At various times during its long history, but increasingly from the mid-1970's on, the coalition was severely strained over matters of policy and style of government. Many Liberals joined other political commentators in decrying alleged departures from the principles of the Westminster system. Both coalition parties wished to increase their relative strengths, and both became increasingly discontented with the constraints of coalition.

THE COALITION CRISIS[1]

The years of coalition in-fighting, during which the Liberals were widely perceived to be weak, erupted like Vesuvius in early August 1983. On 4 August, a Liberal minister, Mr Terry White, voted for a motion, moved by a Liberal back-bencher and supported by the Opposition, for Parliament to debate the establishment of a Public Accounts Committee; the motion was opposed by all other ministers who voted (one Liberal, Mr W. D. Hewitt, absented himself). Mr White rejected a call for his resignation from the Liberal leader and deputy Premier, Dr (now

Sir) Llewellyn Edwards; the state Governor subsequently dismissed Mr White on the Premier's advice. It was argued that Mr White had breached 'Cabinet solidarity', and counter-argued that a Public Accounts Committee was an 'open question' on which ministers were free to vote as they chose.

The political effect of Mr White's action was immediate and explosive. An apparent groundswell of public support, combined with the existing unhappiness of most Liberals with Dr Edwards, led the Parliamentary Liberal Party to dump him and elect Mr White as Liberal leader in his place (Tuesday, 9 August). However, the Premier, Mr Bjelke-Petersen, had warned that only Dr Edwards was acceptable to the National Party as leader of the Liberals, and that Mr White would not be accepted back into the cabinet. After Mr White's election, Mr Bjelke-Petersen continued to refuse to accept him back in the cabinet. The Liberals argued that this breached the coalition agreement provision that 'the leader of the Liberal Party shall be deputy Premier and Treasurer'. On Friday 12 August, the National Party organisation, backing the Premier, responded that Mr White had breached the coalition agreement by breaking cabinet solidarity, and that 'his party, by electing him as leader, adopted the breach of the agreement'. The Liberal Party responded with a press release headed 'Ultimatum', which gave the National Party 48 hours to change its mind. When the National Party did not respond, the Liberal Party state executive declared that the National Party's refusal to accept the Liberal leader had ended the coalition, and requested the Liberal ministers to resign their portfolios.

Early the next day, Monday 15 August, six of the seven Liberal ministers met with the Premier, and, according to Miller and Koch, 'he extracted from them a display of reluctance in tendering their resignations, an action, they told him, that was being taken only because their party wanted them to'.[2] The Premier later said that he told them of the advice he proposed to give the Governor, and that their facial expressions conveyed their assent. In the early afternoon, the ministers' resignation letters were collected by messengers and taken by the Premier to the Governor. However, the Premier advised that the Governor reject the resignations. It seems clear that the Premier spent an hour with the Governor (3.30–4.30 pm), and that the Governor's hand-delivered reply was in the Premier's hands an hour after the end of his interview with the Governor (5.30 pm). The Governor told the Premier that he had decided to accept his advice; the Premier announced this at a late afternoon press conference.

It is not known exactly what advice the Premier gave the Governor,

nor the exact terms of the Governor's reply. Nor is it known what informal advice, if any, the Governor sought from other sources. A request to the Premier in 1984 for access to the correspondence was declined because, it was claimed, 'the restriction of 30 years on general access to public records applies in this instance'.[3]

In the absence of those documents, and of any records there may be of the Governor's discussion with the Premier, we are left to rely on journalistic accounts. Miller and Koch say that the Premier 'recommended that the resignations not be accepted' because the ministers were reluctant to resign, they had done no wrong, and 'that if the Liberals were allowed to continue on in cabinet, Queenslanders could be assured of continuing stable coalition administration'.[4] An opinion prepared by the Solicitor-General at the request of the Attorney-General (a Liberal minister) on the day after the resignations were rejected contained this passage:

> As I understand the position, His Excellency has indicated that he is concerned that there be a stable Government until a general election can be held at the earliest convenient time. His Excellency has, I believe, stated that the interest of the State would be served better if Liberal Ministers continued in Office until a new government is formed following the general election.

The rejection of the ministers' resignations created even more political turmoil. The ministers, other than Mr Hewitt, were clearly very reluctant to resubmit their resignations, as urged by their Party organisation, parliamentary leader and back-bench colleagues. One minister would not comment to journalists, 'saying he could not make any statement on the ground that it would be insulting to the Governor'.[5] But 'the line [some] ministers took was that their resignations had been refused by the 'Queen's representative' and they therefore had "formal obligations as ministers of the Crown"' which precluded their resigning again;[6] the Solicitor-General's opinion took this line, though opinions obtained by Mr White from two Queen's Counsel (both later judges) argued that there was no reason at all for the ministers not to resubmit their resignations. After two days of very public bickering within the Liberal Party, the Liberal ministers resubmitted their resignations. (Five did so together on the Wednesday night, 17 August; another did so the next day, and the last on his return from a ministerial visit to Japan, commenced the day of his earlier [rejected] resignation.) Presumably because his political points – that it was the Liberals who were leaving the coalition, and that they were bitterly divided amongst themselves – had been made, the Premier this time advised the Governor to accept the resignations, which he did. National Party ministers were appointed to replace the Liberals, giving the state a National Party minority government pending the elections. It was announced some days later that the election would be on 22 October, two months away. Parliament, adjourned the day Mr White was elected Liberal leader, did not sit again between the ministerial resignations and the election.

We do not know the details of the discussions between the Governor and the Premier concerning the resubmitted resignations. However, Mr Bjelke-Petersen was quoted as saying that 'the Governor had not specified how long the minority Government could rule because supply was available into the immediate future'.[7] The Leader of the Opposition urged the Liberal Members of the Legislative Assembly (MLAs) to make a joint approach with Labor to the Governor for the recall of Parliament; Mr White rejected this, calling instead for an immediate election.

In the event, the election results were: National Party, 41 seats; Liberal Party, eight; Australian Labor Party, 32; Independent, one. However, two days after the election, two of the Liberals, both former ministers, resigned from the Liberal Party and joined the National Party. They returned to the cabinet, and gave the National Party a parliamentary majority in its own right. Mr White resigned as leader of the Liberal Party and was replaced by Sir William Knox.

SOME CONVENTIONS ON MINISTERIAL RESIGNATIONS

There is little dispute that, after the coalition split, it was proper for the Governor to allow Mr Bjelke-Petersen to remain as Premier, at the head of a minority government, pending elections. Constitutionally, the most controversial aspect of this crisis was the Premier's advice to the Governor to reject the Liberal ministers' resignations. This can best be understood in the light of the following conventions, which are evident in the past practice of ministerial resignations in Britain, Australia, Canada and comparable countries, and are reflected (though rarely made explicit) in writings on the Westminster system.

1. Formally, ministers are appointed by the Crown. The exact nature of this varies, of course, but in Queensland ministers are appointed by the Governor both as members of the Executive Council and as ministers. They hold office at the pleasure of the Crown, and so remain

in office (legally bound to fulfil their ministerial responsibilities) until the 'pleasure of the Governor' is that they should no longer hold office. That is, a resignation is not effective until it is accepted by the Governor. This is the formal, legal situation.[8] However, as in so many other contexts, the legal powers are, and should be, exercised in accordance with the conventions that have emerged from past practice. The following principles summarise some of these conventions.

2. Just as ministers are chosen by the Premier, so they resign by offering their resignation to the Premier;[9] this may be couched in terms of *offering* to resign or as actually doing so. This is reflected in all the cases listed under point 3. This principle was very clearly demonstrated in Canada in 1896 when seven members of Sir Mackenzie Bowell's cabinet tried to resign direct to the Governor-General, who replied that he could only receive such resignations through the Prime Minister.[10]

3. The Premier will either accept the resignation immediately (usually with a modicum of regret) or delay accepting it, perhaps while trying to persuade the minister not to go, or, as an element of that persuasion, telling the minister that the resignation is not accepted and that he should remain. British instances[11] of such delay before acceptance of a resignation include – Lord Randolph Churchill's resignation, 1886; Joseph Chamberlain, 1903; and Augustine Birrell, 1916. Instances of attempts at dissuasion, successful or not, include – the Duke of Devonshire, 1903 (temporarily successful); Beauchamp and Simon (successful), Burns and Morley (unsuccessful), 1914; Lloyd George, 1913, November 1915, April 1916 (all successful); Arthur Henderson, January and August 1916 (successful); Sir Oswald Mosley, 1930 (unsuccessful); Snowden, Samuel and other Free Traders, January 1932 (successful), and September 1932 (unsuccessful); two junior ministers (Mr Dick Nugent and Lord Carrington) over the Crichel Down affair, 1954 (successful); Lord Carrington (unsuccessful), (Sir) John Nott (successful), 1982; and Leon Brittan, 1986 (unsuccessful). In 1946, Sir Ben Smith delayed his resignation for almost two months 'in deference to the Prime Minister's wishes'.[12] It has been widely suggested that Attlee should have rejected Dalton's resignation in 1947. It seems that several of George Brown's resignations in the 1960s were ignored by Harold Wilson, at least one was withdrawn after talks, and the last was (unexpectedly) accepted.

In Canada in 1942, Mackenzie King sought to dissuade Ralston from resigning, and Ralston did not press his resignation. However, when King wished to expedite Ralston's departure from the government in 1944, he seems to have regarded Ralston's 1942 letter of resignation as not having been withdrawn and so open to acceptance by the Prime Minister at any time. King also believed that he had a right 'not [to] accept some of the resignations of Ministers' (at least for a time).[13]

In 1902, the Premier of Victoria, Peacock, refused to accept the resignations of several of his ministers. In the same year but at the federal level, Alfred Deakin withdrew his resignation after concessions and a personal plea from Barton. When in 1903, C. C. Kingston wrote to Barton to resign, Barton asked him to reconsider; when Kingston insisted on resigning, Barton said 'I must reluctantly consent to your action'.[14] When the cabinet (to whom Prime Minister Harold Holt had referred it) decided in 1967 that Peter Howson's resignation should be rejected, it was universally accepted that (in Sir Paul Hasluck's words) it was the Prime Minister 'in whose hands these matters finally lie'.[15] In October 1970, when he learnt that his then wife had appeared in an advertisement for Sheridan-brand sheets, Andrew Peacock offered his resignation to the Prime Minister, Mr (now Sir John) Gorton. Russell Schneider records:[16]

> Gorton, a knockabout chap at the best of times, laughed at the situation and when Peacock pressed the resignation called him a 'bloody fool'. But that night Peacock, enraged over the affair, humiliated and determined to quit the ministry, drafted his resignation and went back to his hotel for a near sleepless night. At 10 am the next day, 21 October, Peacock handed a brief letter of resignation to Gorton and remained in his office discussing the situation for almost an hour. Gorton, amused and bemused, steadfastly refused to accept. Finally, after thrice offering to leave the ministry, Peacock agreed to withdraw his resignation.

4. The decision as to how to react to a minister's resignation is a *political* decision; for the composition of the government is a political matter for decision by the Premier. He might *consult* cabinet colleagues, and perhaps the Crown, but the decision as to how to react is his. The Crown has, in this as in all other matters, the rights Bagehot made famous – to be consulted, to encourage and to warn. The Crown and the Premier might well discuss, at the initiative of either, the composition of the government and whether it would be desirable to discourage the resignation of a minister. It would not be improper for the Crown to discuss with a minister his intentions, and perhaps to discourage him from resigning. (When Malcolm Fraser resigned from the Australian cabinet in 1971, he spent an hour with the Governor-General, Sir Paul Hasluck, on the day of his resignation; it was reported that on the

following day both the Prime Minister and deputy Prime Minister tried unsuccessfully to have him withdraw his resignation.)[17] Discussions with the Crown affect neither the minister's right to proceed with and even insist on his resignation, nor the fact that it is for the Premier to decide whether or not to accept the resignation. The wishes of the Crown are not binding in character, and there is no disrespect to the Crown in a minister proceeding with a resignation the Crown has discouraged: for example, Lloyd George still intended to resign from Asquith's cabinet in April 1916 despite the efforts of Lord Stamfordham, the King's Private Secretary, to persuade him to stay (he remained in the cabinet only after concessions were made).[18]

5. It is taken for granted in all discussions of ministerial responsibility and related matters that ministers have a *right* to resign; no one imagines that Members of Parliament can be required – conscripted – to be ministers against their will. Prime Ministers may seek to dissuade them from going, and as part of that might initially refuse to accept their resignations, but if the minister insists on resigning, Prime Ministers accept that. This is evident in some of the exchanges referred to in this chapter. Sir George Grey in 1866,[19] Joseph Chamberlain in 1903,[20] Lloyd George in 1915[21] and, it seems, many other ministers have believed that they were entitled to *insist* on resigning. Lord Derby wrote to Lloyd George in 1918:[22]

> A man in office is not only entitled, but it is his duty, to resign if he thinks that the Government to which he belongs is doing something which he disapproves and which in his opinion is detrimental to the best interests of the Nation.

Lord Salisbury put the convention of collective responsibility thus:[23]

> For all that passes in Cabinet each member of it *who does not resign* is absolutely and irretrievably responsible, and has no right afterwards to say that he agreed in one case to a compromise, while in another he was persuaded by his colleagues.

Without a *right* to resign, this convention is unworkable. Dr Eugene Forsey, the great Canadian constitutionalist, has written that in the Canadian crisis of 1944, Mackenzie King propounded the 'highly original' theory that 'no Minister is entitled to resign from the Cabinet "in circumstances where as a consequence of [his] action the whole structure is almost certain to collapse," unless he is prepared to accept the premiership himself.' Dr Forsey continued:[24]

> Colonel Ralston's comment was: 'That is the strangest doctrine I have ever heard enunciated in this house. If I were not respectful of the Prime Minister, I would call it just plain nonsense.' Nonsense it is. Did anyone ever hear of this theory when Stanley and Buccleuch resigned in 1846, or Russell in 1855, or Cranborne in 1867, or Chamberlain and Trevelyan in March 1886, or Churchill in December, 1886, or Chamberlain, Ritchie, Hamilton, and Devonshire in 1903, or Mr Bevan a few months ago [1951]? If any British Prime Minister had talked in this vein, people would have thought he had taken leave of his senses.

Windeyer J in *Marks v. The Commonwealth*[25] concluded from his analysis of offices held 'at the pleasure of the Crown' that 'although at common law the resignation of an office was only complete in law when it was by acceptance assented to, yet in practice acceptance of a surrender or resignation in whatever form it was made was a formality that was sometimes deferred but not refused'. As Windeyer also said, the 'principle . . . that a man must remain at his post until relieved . . . is not incompatible with a right to be relieved'.[26]

6. If the Prime Minister wishes not to accept a resignation, he does not place the minister's resignation before the Crown; that is, he gives the Crown no advice at all, because it is not for the Crown, but for the Prime Minister, to decide whether or not to accept a resignation.

7. These conventions apply as fully in the case of ministers resigning on the withdrawal of their party from a coalition government as on any other occasion. (Instances will be mentioned later.)

8. The conventions are, of course, somewhat different when it is the Prime Minister himself resigning. Whereas the resignations of other ministers are resignations of individuals from the Prime Minister's government, the resignation of the Prime Minister is the resignation of the entire government. Where other ministers tender their resignations to the Prime Minister, the Prime Minister submits his resignation to the Crown. Like the Prime Minister with individual ministers, the Crown might well ask the Prime Minister to delay his resignation or even not to resign at all (but either stay in office or advise dissolution of the House, depending on the circumstances). If the Prime Minister insists on resigning, the Crown accepts this. There is no suggestion that insisting on such a resignation, contrary to the wishes of the monarch or her representative, is disrespectful to the Crown. For instance – in 1855, Lord Aberdeen's Government withdrew its resignation at Queen

Victoria's request; in 1866, Lord Russell's government left office despite the Queen's wish that they stay; in 1905, Balfour resigned against the King's wish; in 1908, Campbell-Bannerman (on his deathbed) resigned earlier than the King wished; after the December 1923 election, Baldwin complied with the King's request that he not resign immediately but face the new Parliament (Vernon Bogdanor has rightly deprecated the suggestion that the King might have *rejected* such a resignation);[27] in August 1931, the King three times dissuaded Ramsay MacDonald from resigning, though, as Kenneth Rose writes, 'had MacDonald persisted in his wish to resign, the King could not have prevented him'.[28]

MR BJELKE-PETERSEN'S ADVICE

In the light of these conventions, there are four key points to make about the advice of the Premier of Queensland to the State Governor in 1983: first, that it was clearly contrary to the established conventions, and (as best I can establish) without precedent; second, that it was unnecessary, as the Premier could himself have refused to accept the Liberal ministers' resignations (though not, I suggest, if they had insisted on them); third, that the Premier's advice was improper, in that it needlessly but deliberately brought the Crown into a political dispute; fourth, that there was no compelling reason for the resignations to be rejected or for the Premier to give such advice.

1. Past practice and lack of precedents. The conventions outlined above are so well established that action contrary to them at, say, Westminster or Canberra is unthinkable. By these conventions, the Premier had two options when the Liberal ministers submitted their resignations – either to accept them and transmit them to the Governor, or to decline to accept them and seek to dissuade the ministers from insisting on them.

I have not been able to find any instance in which a Premier or Prime Minister advised a monarch or his or her representative to reject the resignation of a minister or ministers. Rather, as already mentioned, Premiers and Prime Ministers have themselves declined to accept resignations; whenever they have transmitted resignations to the Crown, they have done so for the acceptance of the resignation. Mr Bjelke-Petersen himself was conscious of the lack of precedents for his action. He told journalists, 'this has never happened before in our State, but there it is'.[29]

2. Lack of necessity for such advice. It follows from the conventions

above that the Premier could himself have rejected the resignations. If he believed that stability of government demanded that the ministers stay pending elections, he should simply have told them that he was not prepared to accept their resignations and pressed them not to insist on them. There was no need to involve the Governor. The Premier's rejection of the resignations would have the same effect – preventing their becoming operative and so keeping the ministers in cabinet – as if the Governor himself rejected them. (Of course, had the ministers insisted on their resignations being accepted, the Premier should have accepted them.)

3. Embroiling the Governor. By advising the Governor to reject the resignations, the Premier embroiled the Governor in a political dispute. There are at least three elements to this. First, the Premier's advice confronted the Governor with the difficult decision of how to react, and whatever he did was liable to produce critical comment and bitter feelings in one quarter or another. His decision to accept the Premier's advice certainly did produce such comment.[30]

Second, the appearance was given that the Governor had a personal discretion on whether or not to accept the resignations. The Premier's advice was presented as a 'recommendation'[31] which the Governor was at liberty to reject; hence what he did was presented as *his* decision, the decision of the Crown. But there is, of course, a fundamental convention that the Crown appoints and dismisses ministers on the advice, and only on the advice, of the Premier. 'The Governor's decision' was made on the Premier's advice, and could not properly have been made except on the Premier's advice; moreover, it would have been unconstitutional for the Governor to act against the Premier's advice and accept the resignations. Under the principles of responsible government, it was for the Premier and his ministers, if they intended to remain in the government, to take responsibility for the Governor's acceptance of the Premier's advice, not to cast the onus onto him. Yet the Premier's involvement of the Governor left the Governor, rather than the Premier or the resigning ministers, being presented and seen as making the decision that the ministers must stay – a decision about the internal composition of the government, which was a political matter for the Premier himself to settle.

Third, if the Governor accepted the Premier's advice (as the Premier clearly intended he should), it was likely that he would be widely seen to have been used by the Premier for a partisan political end (*viz.*, the creation of further strife within the Liberal Party).

It is surely axiomatic that, in a constitutional monarchy, politicians –

especially ministers – should act to minimise the danger of the Queen or her representative being forced into political controversy; they must be, in Asquith's words, 'fully alive to the importance of keeping the name of the king out of the sphere of party or electoral controversy'.[32] As Bagehot put it, 'we must not bring the Queen into the combat of politics, or she will cease to be reverenced by all combatants; she will become one combatant among many'.[33]

4. No good reason for this advice. The reasons given by the Premier for the rejection of the resignations do not warrant such rejection, and most certainly do not warrant any breach of constitutional convention and embroiling of the Crown in politics to bring it about. (This is a criticism of the Premier's arguments, not of the Governor's decision, for it was not for the Crown to weigh up whether or not the reasons for rejecting the resignations were compelling; this was a matter for the Premier.)

First, the Premier's claim that the Liberal ministers were reluctant to resign is irrelevant: ministers are usually reluctant to resign, but, for one reason or another, feel compelled to do so. There have previously been cases when, on the break-up of a coalition, ministers from one party reluctantly resigned because of their party's attitude; the suggestion that the resignations should have been rejected seems not to have arisen. For example, Lord Templewood (Sir Samuel Hoare) recorded of the resignation in 1932 of Lord Lothian, who was his Under-Secretary at the India Office in MacDonald's National Government:[34]

> It was indeed a heavy blow to me when he resigned his office at the time that Samuel and the Liberal Ministers left the MacDonald Government over Imperial Preference. Lothian himself was so entirely enthralled by his Indian work that he was most reluctant to resign. Indeed, he told me, when the first rumours of a final rupture were becoming prevalent, that whatever his colleagues decided, he intended to remain in office. It was only after several days of reflection that loyalty to his Party forced him to give up a post that he not only greatly enjoyed, but filled with rare distinction.

Here, if anywhere, was a case for rejecting a resignation, but there was – as best I can ascertain – no thought of it.

In 1983, Mr Bjelke-Petersen could at most say that six of the seven Liberal ministers were reluctant to resign. Mr Hewitt had not been invited to the meeting at which the Premier apparently extracted that expression from his six Liberal colleagues. Yet Mr Bjelke-Petersen gave his advice on behalf of all the ministers. If the ministers' reluctance to resign was the reason for the rejection of their resignations, Mr Hewitt's should have been accepted.

The second ground apparently advanced to justify rejection of the resignations was that the ministers had 'committed no breach'.[35] But, as David Butler has pointed out, 'the vast bulk of ministerial resignations in Britain and Australia have been concerned with disagreements over policy', and have involved no 'malfeasance, actual or alleged'.[36] Indeed, ministers sometimes resign without giving reasons for their resignation. Resignations have been accepted in the past on the break-up of a coalition: for example, in the 1932 case already mentioned; when 'at the end of the First World War . . . the Labour Party instructed its members to withdraw from the Coalition Government' in Britain;[37] when the Country Party under Earle Page refused to serve under Menzies in Canberra in 1939; when the Victorian coalition broke on the withdrawal of Country Party ministers in 1935; and so on.

The third and main argument for rejecting the resignations was that this was desirable for stable government. The circumstances in Queensland in 1983 did not involve that element of grave international crisis or war that would make stability and continuity of government *especially* important, and 'stability' (to the extent that it is not just a political slogan) is not easy to define. Moreover, it was obvious (and, perhaps, the intention of the Premier) that the rejection of the resignations would cause yet more political turmoil and would *not* be conducive to 'stable coalition government'. It was inevitable that, with the resignations rejected, there would be great pressure from the Liberal Party organisation and back-benches for resubmission of those resignations, and a sense of turmoil and uncertainty in the community. The inevitable happened: and within two days, five of the Liberal ministers were resigning again because they found themselves 'under intolerable pressure to such an extent that I will be unable to fulfil the high duties that are cast upon me as a Minister of the Crown'.[38]

Nor was there ever any reason to think that, between the coalition split and elections, a minority National Party government would be any less 'stable' than a coalition government repeatedly racked by disagreements. It is clear that, in fact, the Premier was keen to see a National Party-only government. Miller and Koch record:[39]

> On 10 August, [five days before his advice to the Governor] Bjelke-Petersen announced plans to promote seven National Party backbenchers to cabinet, take the Treasury himself, and barnstorm the state in

> a bid to decimate the Liberals. In one of the more memorable quotes of the whole affair, he said: 'This is a tremendous opportunity to capitalise on circumstances I have never had in my political lifetime.'

This is not consistent with the view that 'continuing stable coalition administration' was important enough to justify rejecting the ministers' resignations.

THE GOVERNOR'S REACTION

Notwithstanding that the Premier's advice was improper, did the Governor have any alternative to accepting it? As already suggested, it would have been wrong for the Governor to have accepted the resignations of the ministers against the Premier's advice. But it is also important to remember the rights of the Crown 'to be consulted, . . . to encourage, . . . to warn'.[40]

It was clearly open to the Governor to exercise these rights on this occasion. Indeed, it follows from the analysis given here that the Governor's reaction to the Premier's advice should have been to remind him that the composition of the government was a political matter over which the Premier had effective control, that if he wished to reject the resignations he could do so himself without involving the Governor, and that the Governor was not to be involved in this way. This could have been done politely but firmly. It would not have required rejecting the Premier's advice, but would have meant expressing strong reluctance to accept advice that should not have been given. The Governor might also have reminded the Premier that if ministers insist on resigning, they must be permitted to do so. Furthermore, the Governor should have said to the Premier that the attempted departure of the Liberal ministers raised the question of whether or not his government commanded the confidence of the Legislative Assembly, and that this should either be put to the test in Parliament or elections held as soon as possible. The Governor might, if he wished, have told the Premier that on such a matter he, the Governor, was perfectly at liberty to consult anyone he wished, and that he was going to consult, say, the Chief Justice of Queensland; he might also have consulted the ministers whose resignations were in the balance. (The Governor's right to consult in this way, though always beyond doubt, is guaranteed by Section 14(2) of the State Constitution.)

We do not know how Sir James Ramsay's approach to the Premier varied from this. In particular, we do not know if, and in what ways, he questioned or resisted the Premier's advice, nor in what ways the Premier pressed it upon him, nor what (if any) conditions the Governor placed on rejection (and the subsequent acceptance) of the resignations. In the absence of such information, we are left to wonder whether the Governor was, perhaps, too ready to make a political decision or whether he thought he had no alternative but to act without delay on the Premier's advice. We are also left to wonder whether the Governor's response to the Premier within an hour of their interview gave the Governor himself, or anyone whom he consulted, adequate time in which to think through the matter. (We do not know whether the Governor was aware of the Premier's intended advice before their interview on the afternoon of 15 August, nor whether the Governor did consult the Chief Justice or anyone else.)

There seem to me to be no grounds for criticising the Governor's decision to allow Mr Bjelke-Petersen to remain in office with a minority government, pending elections: the incumbent Premier led the largest party in the House, stood a very good chance of being able to sustain his new government on the floor of the House, and elections were due within a few months in any case.

However, it is at least strongly arguable that the Governor should have insisted that either the Premier face Parliament soon, or that elections be held expeditiously. The two-month delay between the formation of the minority government and the holding of the elections was twice as long as the time normally needed to arrange elections. It left Queensland politics for some weeks in a state of suspended animation, under a government that had never faced the Parliament. The 65 days between the acceptance of the ministers' resignations and the elections compares with 32 days between the dismissal of the Whitlam government and the 1975 Australian elections, and 36 days between the defeat of the Callaghan government in the House of Commons and the 1979 British elections.

THE REACTION OF THE LIBERAL MINISTERS

Whether the Liberal ministers resubmitted their resignations, as many urged, was a matter for them to decide. It is possible that the six who were reluctant to do so were genuinely unwilling out of deference to the Crown, but their actions are open to criticism on these grounds:

1. That if the Premier's statement that he forewarned them of his plan

and that they assented is accurate, they were party to the Premier's improper embroiling of the Governor in the dispute.
2. That their argument that they could not resubmit their resignations because of 'the Governor's decision' was both wrong in principle and improperly placed reliance on the Crown for political purposes.

As already mentioned, the Attorney-General (a Liberal minister, Mr Sam Doumany, who was strongly insisting that the ministers should not resubmit their resignations) had the Solicitor-General prepare an opinion on the matter. The opinion was released to the media.[41] The kindest thing that can be said for it is (as one Queen's Counsel, later a judge, put it) that 'it was clearly written for its audience'. The Solicitor-General: (1) asserted that Mr White had breached cabinet solidarity and should have resigned, a claim that was, at best, irrelevant to the issue at hand; (2) repeatedly referred to the rejection of the resignations as 'His Excellency's decision', without any reference whatever to this being on the advice of the Premier, thus clearly seeking to imply that it was the Governor's own judgment that rejection of the resignations was desirable (e.g. the opinion declared that 'Stable Government is and should be the aim of all civic minded persons and His Excellency has clearly illustrated his concern in this regard'); (3) argued that 'it would seem to me to smack of irresponsibility if Ministers flew in the face of the specific indication which His Excellency had given in the interests of stable government pending an early election' by resubmitting their resignations; (4) left open the extraordinary possibility that people urging the ministers to resign again might be in breach of a provision of the State Criminal Code designed to prevent deliberate interference with 'the free exercise' of their duties by the Governor and ministers.

It is clear beyond doubt that until their resignations are accepted, ministers are legally bound to fulfil their duties as ministers.[42] However, as suggested above, ministers are free to resign at any time and to insist upon their resignation being accepted; rejection of a resignation does not preclude the resubmission of it, and, especially as the rejection was on the advice of the Premier, resubmission could not be taken as in any way disrespectful to the Crown.

As the acceptance and rejection of resignations is properly a matter for the Premier and not the Governor, the Liberal ministers should, if they wished their resignations to be accepted, have pressed the Premier to accept them. This is, of course, what did happen. Had the Premier rejected the resignations or repeated his advice that the Governor reject them, it would have been proper for the ministers to inform the

Governor directly that they wished to be relieved of their offices. The Governor should not have accepted those resignations without advice from the Premier to do so; but he might then have referred the matter back to the Premier with a clear intimation that he believed the resignations should be accepted. Given the importance of keeping the Crown out of politics, it would have been best for ministers insisting on their resignations not to have recourse to the Governor except as the last resort. In the event, this was not necessary.

CONCLUSION

Consideration of the 1983 crisis in Queensland is clearly hampered by the fact that the correspondence between the Governor and the Premier has not been made public. The practice at the federal level in Australia is that correspondence between the Governor-General and the Prime Minister over requests for dissolutions of both Houses of Parliament and such matters are published, usually immediately or not long afterwards. There is no suggestion that a '30 year rule' applies; and any such rule in Queensland could be overcome if the Premier and Governor agreed to publication of the correspondence. It is unclear what public interest, if any, is served by not releasing the 1983 correspondence. On the contrary; the study of the precedents in which our constitutional conventions are reflected and developed depends on the availability of such documents.

Even without them, however, it is possible to reach certain clear conclusions – that the advice given by the Premier to reject the ministers' resignations was improper; that the Governor should have told the Premier that this was so and that it was for the Premier himself to resolve the matter; that the Liberal ministers were wrong to claim that 'the Governor's decision' precluded their resubmitting their resignations; but that, when their resignations were accepted, it was right that the Premier remained in office at the head of a minority government pending elections. Had greater regard been paid to the conventions of the Constitution, this outcome could have been reached without embroiling the Crown in such political controversy.

Notes

1. An account of the crisis can be found in Ian Miller & Tony Koch, *Joh's K. O.* (Brisbane: Boolarong, 1983).
2. *Ibid.*, p. 33. See also, e.g., *The Courier-Mail*, Brisbane, 16 August 1983.
3. Letter from Co-ordinator-General to the author, 9 March 1984.
4. Miller & Koch, *op. cit.*, p. 35.
5. *Australian Financial Review*, 16 August 1983.
6. *The Australian*, 17 August 1983.
7. *Ibid.*, 19 August 1983.
8. See, e.g., Sir Ivor Jennings, *Cabinet Government* (Cambridge University Press, 3rd ed., 1969) pp. 83, 88, 207; *Halsbury's Laws of England* (London: Butterworths, 4th ed., 1974) vol. 8, pp. 599–600; *Marks* v. *The Commonwealth* (1964) C.L.R. 549.
9. A. Berriedale Keith, *The British Cabinet System* (London: Stevens, 1952) p. 83.
10. J. R. Mallory, *The Structure of Canadian Government* (Toronto: Macmillan, 1971), p. 80; see also p. 85.
11. The reader can readily check these cases by referring to the biographies or autobiographies of the ministers and Prime Ministers involved, diaries (e.g. Lord Riddell, Richard Crossman), histories, and Hansards and newspapers of the time. See also: R. K. Alderman & J. A. Cross, *The Tactics of Resignation* (1967); S. E. Finer, 'The Individual Responsibility of Ministers', *Public Administration*, 34 (1956); P. J. Madgwick, 'Resignations', *Parliamentary Affairs* 20 (1966–67); D. J. Markwell, 'The Politics of Ministerial Resignations', in Patrick Weller & Dean Jaensch, *Responsible Government in Australia* (Melbourne: Drummond, 1980).
12. Finer, *op. cit.*, p. 392.
13. J. L. Granatstein, *Canada's War: The Politics of Mackenzie King's Government, 1939–1945* (Toronto: OUP, 1975), pp. 236–241, 353–6.
14. *Commonwealth Parliamentary Debates* (Australia), 24 July 1903, pp. 2590–1.
15. *Ibid.*, 8 November 1967 p. 2839.
16. Russell Schneider, *The Colt from Kooyong* (Sydney: Angus & Robertson, 1981) pp. 48–9.
17. *Sydney Morning Herald*, 9 & 10 March 1971.
18. See, esp., *Lord Riddell's War Diary 1914–1918* (London: Ivor Nicholson & Watson, 1933) p. 174–5.
19. *Letters of Queen Victoria 1837–1861* vol. 3 (London: John Murray, 1907) pp. 94–5.
20. Julian Amery, *The Life of Joseph Chamberlain* vol. 5 (London: Macmillan, 1969) p. 403.
21. *Lord Riddell's War Diary*, *op. cit.*, p. 136.
22. Quoted from Lord Beaverbrook, *Men and Power 1917–1918* (London: Collins, 1956) p. 374.
23. Quoted from Madgwick, *op. cit.*, pp. 59–60; emphasis added.
24. Eugene Forsey, *Freedom and Order* (Toronto: The Carleton Library, 1974) p. 90.

25. *Supra*, at p. 590.
26. At p. 579.
27. Vernon Bogdanor, *Multi-party politics and the Constitution* (Cambridge: Cambridge University Press, 1983) p. 97.
28. Kenneth Rose, *King George V* (London: Weidenfeld & Nicolson, 1983) p. 378.
29. *The Australian*, 16 August 1983.
30. See, e.g., Miller & Koch, *op. cit.*, p. 37.
31. *Ibid.*, p. 43.
32. Quoted from George Burton Adams, *Constitutional History of England* (London: Jonathan Cape, 1948) p. 484.
33. Walter Bagehot, *The English Constitution* (London: Collins, 1963) p. 100.
34. Viscount Templewood, *Nine Troubled Years* (London: Collins, 1954) pp. 70–1.
35. Millcr & Koch, *op. cit.*, p. 35.
36. David Butler, *The Canberra Model* (London: Macmillan, 1974) p. 67.
37. Alderman & Cross, *op. cit.*, p. 38.
38. Miller & Koch, *op. cit.*, p. 43.
39. *Ibid.*, p. 26.
40. Bagehot, *op. cit.*, p. 111.
41. *Courier Mail*, 17 August 1983, p. 1. Thc opinion was dated 16 August 1983.
42. See footnote 8.

11 Princes and Politicians: The Constitutional Crisis in Malaysia, 1983–4

A. J. Stockwell

In late July 1983 the government of Datuk Seri Mahathir Mohamad tabled in the Malaysian parliament a bill to amend the constitution. Among its 22 provisions were three curtailing the authority of the King (Yang di-Pertuan Agung) and Their Highnesses the State Rulers. The Barisan National (National Front), a coalition dominated by the United Malays National Organisation (UMNO), had no difficulty securing the necessary two-thirds majority. Although the public were not made aware of the issue at the time, it became a *cause célèbre* because the Yang di-Pertuan Agung, backed by the rulers, withheld his assent.

THE YANG DI-PERTUAN AGUNG[1]

Malaysia's Head of State is the Yang di-Pertuan Agung, a constitutional monarch who is elected every five years by and from the hereditary rulers of nine Malay States meeting in conference. Malaysia is unique in its elected monarchy. The office of Agung was created by the Reid Commission in 1956–7 but is to be explained by reference to the longer history of Anglo–Malay relations.

Britain acquired power in the Malay states from 1874 through agreements with their rulers. Although the British came to assume *de facto* control in the states, they accepted the sovereign status of the sultans since it legitimised British 'protection' and fortified the British position behind the throne. Later, however, 'Malay sovereignty' obstructed schemes for administrative rationalisation and constitutional change. When in 1945 Sir Harold MacMichael concluded fresh treaties conferring upon King George VI 'full power and jurisdiction' in a Malayan Union, Malays, believing that 'the removal of their ceremonial rajas would bring an era of utter confusion'[2] campaigned against the change. In 1948, after lengthy negotiations with political and royal representatives, the British reaffirmed their recognition of the rulers' 'prerogatives, power and jurisdiction' within a new constitution, the Federation of Malaya. Significantly, the instrument by which power was transferred to independent Malaya in August 1957 was an agreement signed by the High Commissioner 'on behalf of Her Majesty on the one part' and Their Highnesses the Rulers 'of the other part'.[3] The rehabilitation of the traditional Anglo-Malay alliance yoked Malay support to counter-insurgency during the Emergency but also hampered the construction of a multi-racial nation. As the British prepared to decolonise they wrestled with the conflicting tasks of preserving Malay special rights and safeguarding the interests of all who regarded Malaya as home.

Federal citizenship was introduced in 1948 but it did not embrace all residents nor was it synonymous with 'Malayan' nationality. Malays resisted the non-Malay claim to *jus soli* and insisted that nationality involved allegiance to state rulers. In 1956 the Reid Commission of Commonwealth jurists was deputed to draft the constitution for independent Malaya in such a way that a strong central government, Malay rights and equality before the law would all be guaranteed.[4] As an aid, the constitution-mongers conjured up the Yang di-Pertuan Besar (later renamed the Yang di-Pertuan Agung) who, as head of state, would be a 'symbol of the unity of the country' and as a traditional Malay ruler would also embody the rights of the *bumiputras* (princes of the soil). At the time the constitution was agreed, the Malayan Chinese Association (which with the Malayan Indian Congress partnered the dominant UMNO in the Alliance government) was persuaded to accept the special provisions for Malays in the belief that they would wither away before long. This has not been the case; on the contrary, Malay privileges have acquired an aura of sanctity and amendments to the constitution in the two decades after 1957 added to the Agung's functions in the spheres of Islam and Malay rights.

The Agung is bound by his oath of office to perform 'duties in the administration of Malaysia in accordance with its laws and constitution' and to act upon the advice of the federal cabinet, though he may not be removed except by a resolution of a majority of the hereditary rulers meeting in conference. The constitution endowed the Agung with a number of discretionary functions: one of these was the appointment of the Prime Minister; another provided for the withholding of consent to a request for parliamentary dissolution; a third related to the convention of the 'Conference of Rulers'; a fourth concerned certain public service appointments; and a fifth granted the Agung discretion to declare a state of emergency. In addition, his assent was required before any bill that had passed through both Houses of the federal parliament could become law. Although constitutional authorities have debated the extent of these discretionary powers, 20 years after independence F. A. Trinidade remained confident in 'the enduring quality of the institution' of Agung and stated that he had encountered 'hardly any criticism' of it.[5] Indeed, the right of the Agung, for example, to veto federal legislation was not put to the test until the Constitutional (Amendment) Bill of 1983.

The clauses of the 1983 measure which directly impinged upon the Agung and state rulers were as follows:[6]

(1) Clause 12: legislation in future would become law automatically within 15 days irrespective of whether it had the assent of the Yang di-Pertuan Agung;
(2) Clause 20: power to declare an emergency would be transferred from the Agung to the Prime Minister who might act without reference to cabinet, parliament or the Courts;
(3) Clause 21: States would be bound to bring their separate constitutions into line with federal changes thus making 'deemed-assent' (as per (1) above) the law for all state legislation and effectively removing the royal veto.

Mahathir stated that the Bill was a codification of existing practice but the fact that it shattered the habitually calm surface of Malaysian politics suggests that there was more to it than a desire to tie up loose ends.

Before we move to the politics of the Amendment Bill, the procedure regulating the Agung's election requires clarification. It should be noted that the Governors of Malacca, Penang, Sabah, and Sarawak, being non-hereditary members of the Conference of Rulers, play no part in this election. An important feature of it is the election list. For the first election in 1957 the list comprised states of all nine hereditary rulers in the order in which Their Highnesses then recognised precedence amongst themselves. In effect this meant that the order was based on the dates of accession to their several state thrones. For subsequent elections the list was altered according to the following rubric: states whose rulers had already served as Agung were omitted while states where there had been a change of ruler were transferred to the end. In 1983 the Sultan of Pahang entered his final year as Agung and only two rulers remained from the original list, Perak and Johor. Previously the Sultans of these states had declined nomination but in 1983 Idris of Perak and Mahmood Iskandar of Johor appeared eager to assume office and promulgate their strong opinions on monarchy. The personalities of princes were, indeed, a pungent ingredient of the 1983–4 crisis.

PRINCES AND POLITICS

Since the late 1970s there had been a series of disputes between state rulers and their Chief Ministers (Mentri Besar) which brought government into disrepute and increasingly irritated the UMNO high command. One notorious case was the running conflict between the Sultans and Chief Ministers of Perak. Similar tension occurred in Pahang after its Sultan was elected Agung in 1980; his son, automatically deputising as state ruler, quarrelled violently with the Mentri Besar and refused to sign money bills. The Mentri was forced to resign despite the fact that he had been nominated by the Pahang division of UMNO and enjoyed the confidence of the state legislature.[7] The Pahang problem was festering when, in 1981, conflict surfaced in Johor. Like the Hanoverians, fathers and sons in the Johor royal family have rarely seen eye to eye. One of Sultan Abu Bakar's aims in drawing up the state constitution in 1895 had been to curb his heir, Ibrahim, who himself during a long reign (1895–1959) went out of his way to humiliate his sons, Ismail and Abu Bakar. Sultan Ismail (reigned 1959–81) in turn disinherited his eldest son, Tunku Mahmood Iskandar, in 1961. Twenty years later as he lay dying, the 85-year-old ruler reinstated Tunku Mahmood Iskandar as the Tunku Mahkota or Crown Prince. Within two weeks Mahmood Iskandar had ascended the Johor throne to the dismay of his younger brother (who had fully expected to succeed Ismail) and of the Mentri Besar who had been kept in the dark about these changes. Relations between the new Sultan and the Chief Minister deteriorated with the result that the former actually moved into the latter's office in September 1981. Subsequently the Sultan withdrew and allowed his Chief Minister to resume the management of state administration.

These instances of obstructionism won the rulers little credit. Writing his regular column in *The Star*, an English-language tabloid published in Penang, former Prime Minister Tunku Abdul Rahman gave a warning:[8]

> The situation in Johore and Pahang is beginning to look serious, and I should hate to see it get worse because it could lead to a severance of the good relations between the Rulers and the people. This may result in an amendment to the Constitution which can affect the position of

the Rulers, *vis-à-vis* constitutional monarchy. What the Prime Minister does with one he can also do with the other.

In June 1983 a dispute over the dates of Ramadan, the fasting month, once again called into question the extent of royal prerogative. The government planned to fix dates for the Federation as a whole. However, the rulers are the religious leaders in their respective states and the Sultans of Perak and Johor were angered by this example of central interference.[9] Mahmood Iskandar had already stressed his independent religious function in 1981 when, three days after coming to the throne, he had preached a sermon at the Sultan Abu Bakar Mosque (Johor Bahru) and, in the presence of the then Prime Minister (Hussein Onn) had 'cited the case of Abu Bakar Al-Sidiq, who had told Muslims when he was appointed the first Caliph after the death of Prophet Muhammad to give him their undivided loyalty if his leadership was not found wanting'.[10] That said, His Highness's private life left much to be desired; he had, for example, been found guilty of culpable homicide in 1977 only to be rescued by his father's royal pardon.

Such royal wilfulness in the sphere of religion provoked much anxiety within the Malay community. A wide range of opinion, including Tunku Abdul Rahman, ABIM (Malaysian Islamic Youth Movement) and various branches of both UMNO and its rival PAS (Parti Islam), called for constitutional changes to prevent Islam becoming a tool in the rulers' hands and thereby causing divisions between Malays. It is improbable, considering the time needed for parliamentary drafting, that the dispute over Ramadan was the immediate cause of the Constitutional (Amendment) Bill which was introduced into Parliament a month later. It was, nonetheless, symptomatic of the growing unease felt by Malay politicians about the intractability of certain princes. While the Sultan of Pahang had been an exemplary Agung, the rulers of Perak and Johor were strong-willed, jealous of their prerogatives and likely to embarrass the federal government in the event of either of them being elected Agung in 1984.

Mahathir was the first Prime Minister not to have come from the Malay aristocracy nor to have personal links with a royal family. A vehement critic of Prime Minister Tunku Abdul Rahman at the time of the 1969 communal riots, he was banished to the political wilderness. Later reinstated, he brought a new vigour to government when he succeeded Hussein Onn as Prime Minister and UMNO leader in 1981. It is tempting to interpret the Constitutional (Amendment) Bill as part of the radical strategy he espoused that required civil servants to clock on and 'buy British last', as the blow of the meritocrat and democrat against feudalism and the divine right of kings. Yet the picture of rakyat (people) pitted against rajas is misleading. Given the communalism of Malaysian politics, Mahathir fully recognised the uses of consensus and conservatism for sustaining Malay solidarity and dominance. Let him speak for himself:[11]

> The Malay is courteous and self-effacing. His world is full of nobility and he is never far from his rajas and chiefs. He gives way and shows them deference. It is good manners to do so. It is not degrading. . . .
>
> Formality and ritual rate very high in the Malay concept of values. What is formal is proper. To depart from formality is considered unbecoming, rude and deserving of misfortune or punishment by God and man. . . .
>
> In itself the feudalist inclination of the Malays is not damaging. It makes for an orderly law-abiding society . . . People who accept that a society must have people of varying degrees of authority and rights easily make a stable society and nation. A revolution in such a society is unusual unless led from above. A feudal society is therefore not necessarily a dormant or retrogressive society. It can be a dynamic society if there is dynamism at the top. But when the top fails, or is preoccupied with its own well-being the masses become devoid of incentive for progress.

Mahathir was by no means innovative in stressing the importance of responsible leadership since the quest for the just king (*raja adil*) lies as firmly in Malay traditions as in western political philosophy. He was certainly committed to the consolidation of prime ministerial power and the reduction of royal caprice but, for all the populist rhetoric trumpeted during the later stages of the constitutional crisis, Mahathir did not introduce the Bill in a spirit of egalitarianism or with a view to seeking confrontation with the princes. Anticipating difficulties that might arise if the next Agung (say Perak or Johor) proved uncooperative, yet aware of the importance of precedent and agreed practice in the conduct of Malay affairs, Mahathir hoped to amend the constitution with the minimum of publicity and disturbance. He was punctilious in consulting the Agung and may yet have retained his support for the measure had not its 'flow-on' effects struck at the interests of all the rulers and provoked royalist resistance on a wide front.

THE CRISIS[12]

The constitutional crisis passed through two phases before a compromise was agreed in mid-December and implemented early the following year. The first stage lasted from late July to mid-October when cloak and dagger were joined by publicity and demonstrations in a two-month spate of popular politics.

The Bill passed both Houses with ease and without press comment; the Barisan's huge parliamentary majority and control of the media ensured silent acquiescence. In October news began to leak out. On 3 October Datuk Senu Abdul Rahman, a respected UMNO politician and former Minister of Information, addressed an open letter to the Prime Minister in which he questioned the legality of the Bill. Although the authorities successfully muzzled reports of Senu's press conference, his letter was not kept under wraps for long. Ten days later (12–13 October) the rulers held their 128th Conference in Kota Kinabalu, the state capital of Sabah. At the time it was not clear whether the conference reached any decision on the constitutional issue and the absence of the Agung, who had suffered a heart attack in late September, suggested irresolution. However, when Parliament reconvened on 17 October, the Speaker departed from the practice of announcing the Bills which had received the Royal Assent during the recess. It was now clear that the Agung, supported by the state rulers, had withheld his approval from the Constitutional (Amendment) Bill.

Although the prime target of the Bill was the Agung's prerogative, it was the 'flow-on' change to the 8th Schedule bringing state constitutions into line with reforms at the centre which hit all rulers in their heartlands. Their case was that the Bill contravened Article 38(4) of the constitution which stipulated that:[13]

> No law directly affecting the privileges, position, honours or dignities of the Rulers shall be passed without the consent of the Conference of Rulers.

Whatever Mahathir may have told the Agung before the Bill came to Parliament, the rulers as a body had not been consulted in advance. The Attorney-General (Tan Sri Talib Othman) countered with the argument that since the Bill 'pertained to the function and power of the Rulers' and did 'not affect the special rights of the Rulers' it 'therefore fell outside Art. 38(4)'.[14] This did not convince the rulers. Their resistance stiffened, their alliance was cemented in adversity and, while it had hitherto not been their style to court popularity, their predicament won Malay and some non-Malay sympathisers. For example, Lim Kit Siang of the opposition Democratic Action Party, who had been a stern critic of Malay feudalism in the past, now espoused the rulers' cause with relish. He had spoken against the Bill in Parliament; the amendment transferring from Agung to Prime Minister the power to declare an emergency would, he affirmed, further reduce civil liberty in the land.[15]

This was, however, essentially an intra-Malay crisis throughout which it was UMNO, rather than the Barisan as a whole, that devised government strategy. The Prime Minister was taken aback by the rulers' stubbornness and perturbed by the cracks now appearing in UMNO unity. Not surprisingly, ambitious politicians seized the opportunity to square up to each other. Anwar Ibrahim, a rising star who led the UMNO Youth movement and was Minister of Culture, Youth and Sport, urged the Prime Minister to press ahead with the reforms, regardless of the rulers, and gazette the Bill immediately, thereby giving it the force of law. Other key UMNO figures, like Datuk Harun Idris of Selangor, and Tunku Razaleigh of Kelantan, took the rulers' part. Razaleigh, who was a member of the Kelantan royal family and Finance Minister, also had his sights on the deputy presidency of UMNO. Outside UMNO's supreme council many Malays were unnerved by the prospect of confrontation with the Sultans, for whom they bore an instinctive allegiance. Adversarial politics were alien to them; consensus and conciliation were the hallmarks of their guided democracy. Party faithful, who remembered the deal worked out between rulers and politicians in 1956–7, feared that hotheads were bent on driving a coach-and-four through an arrangement which for a generation had secured the paramountcy of Malay conservatism. Former Prime Minister Tunku Abdul Rahman, the venerable *Bapa Merdeka*, who had earlier condemned the petulant autocracy of some sultans, now urged the government 'to postpone the operation of this amendment Bill until every step has been taken to remove its ambiguity',[16] and suggested the appointment of a royal commission to review the working of the constitution. UMNO's problems with the rulers, some feared, might be seized by religious fundamentalists of the Parti Islam (PAS) to embarrass UMNO in the competition for Malay votes or, worse still, open the door to militancy of Iranian dimensions.

Once it had reached the public domain, the King's matter entered a new phase – a phase of manipulated popular politics. The press was 'turned on', and mass rallies were stage-managed by a government anxious to win the people's acquiescence but not their participation in the way the country was ruled.[17] On 4 November, 1500 youth leaders pledged support for the reforms; it was the first open demonstration on an issue which hitherto had not existed officially. The rulers then countered in public and mustered support in their states: Perlis made their position clear at a tea party attended by hundreds of his subjects; Perak addressed 650 eminent persons at a dinner in the Station Hotel, Kuala Lumpur. While Their Highnesses lacked press publicity, they gained valuable television coverage as they assembled in conference at Shah Alam (Selangor) on 20 November. A film showing thousands of loyal Malays seeing the Kelantan ruler off at Kota Bahru airport, at a gathering doubtless organised by Tunku Razaleigh's aides, was broadcast, as were pictures of the grand arrival of the Sultans of Perak and Johor symbolically attired, the one in combat dress and the other in military uniform. Naturally playing on the primordial loyalties of their Malay subjects, skilfully presenting a reasonable argument, and deftly maintaining a united front, the nine hereditary rulers put on an impressive display at Shah Alam on 20 November. UMNO delegates, who humbly presented Their Highnesses with a compromise proposal, returned with their tails between their legs.

Mahathir was in a quandary. He had gone too far in winning support for the reforms from party, cabinet and Parliament to backtrack at this stage without undermining the legislative authority of Parliament and damaging his political reputation. Yet he could not afford a prolonged *impasse*. Not only were the rulers threatening to hold up money bills but also the quarrel was delaying other important amendments to the constitution, notably the provisions affecting the constituency boundaries. If these were to be redrawn in time for the next federal elections, as the government wished, it was necessary to proceed with the package of reforms without more ado. Furthermore, the Kuala Lumpur stockmarket was reacting unfavourably to the stalemate, which, if allowed to continue, might prise open federal and communal fissures. Mathathir had to act and take risks. As he prepared his counter-offensive all leave for police riot squads was cancelled.

On 26 November Mahathir addressed a rally at Alor Star, the capital of his own state of Kedah. Here, and again at Bagan Datoh in Perak a few days later, he declared he would not quit since he had been elected by the people and was answerable to them alone. It was an odd message, because the media had not so much as hinted that the Prime Minister's future was in question. There followed other demonstrations throughout the peninsula culminating at Batu Pahat on 8 December. These were big occasions which UMNO was experienced in organising. Even so, the press exaggerated attendance figures and the set-pieces largely failed to spark spontaneous expressions of UMNO solidarity at branch level. As pressure was brought to bear upon them, so Their Highnesses accepted that they could not indefinitely block legislation which the Prime Minister was determined to get through, if need be by gazetting the Bill. Mahathir, for his part, wanted to avoid humiliating the rulers, and thus incurring the wrath of his own community. Both sides worked towards a compromise.

THE OUTCOME

On 15 December the Timbalan Agung (the ruler of Negri Sembilan) who had been deputising for the King during his illness, agreed to sign the Bill on condition that the government incorporated certain revisions at a special session of parliament in the new year. The three significant alterations to the original Constitutional (Amendment) Bill were as follows.

1. Although the Agung would lose his power of veto, he would in effect gain the power to delay legislation for a total of 60 days provided he gave reasons for his action. If he had objections to a Bill, he could make them known to parliament within 30 days of receiving any measure that had passed through both Houses, but, if on reconsideration Parliament abided by its original proposals, he would be obliged to give his assent after the lapse of a further 30 days.
2. The power to declare a state of emergency would remain with the King who would be obliged to act on the advice of his Cabinet.
3. The provision (Clause 21 amending the 8th Schedule of the constitution), which would have made royal assent superfluous in the matter of state legislation, was withdrawn, although the Prime Minister was given an oral undertaking that the rulers would not withhold their assent unreasonably.

Who had won? In the eyes of some who watched the events of the next three years (1984–6), Mahathir's maladroit handling of the rulers combined with other developments – such as financial scandals, the difficulties of the MCA (one of UMNO's partners in the coalition), political crisis in Sabah, and the resignation of Musa Hitam, Mahathir's deputy in government and party – served to reveal the limitations of prime ministerial power. In the constitutional crisis of 1983–4 his 'policy of thorough' appeared to founder on the bedrock of Malay conservatism.[18] After all, the fundamental ambiguity of a sovereign constitution that can be altered by a sovereign parliament was no nearer resolution.

Moreover, if the crisis had helped clarify the relationship between King and Parliament, it had done so, in the opinion of some, to the definite advantage of the former. According to this interpretation of events, the compromise amounted to a derogation of parliamentary control, since the Agung, who had never attempted to withhold assent from federal bills until the 1983 crisis, had gained unprecedented power to interfere with legislation and delay its passage up to 60 days. Instead of clipping the rulers' wings the government had conceded a good deal of room for royal manoeuvres. Their Highnesses, whose relations with each other had been rarely cordial, and with their subjects scarcely political, had in public mounted a united front and forced the government onto the defensive.

Mahathir's worst fears were, it seemed, realised when Sultan Mahmood Iskandar of Johor was elected Agung in February 1984.[19] The favourite candidate, Idris of Perak, died suddenly at the end of January and, although for a time it looked as though his successor in Perak, the eminent jurist Raja Azlan,[20] might be elected the eighth Agung, the Conference of Rulers followed the election list and voted in the Sultan of Johor. Sultan Mahmood Iskandar had the reputation of a reprobate, which the government had exploited at the height of the constitutional crisis, but which it now took pains to rehabilitate in the interests of national prestige. The deputy Prime Minister, Datuk Musa Hitam, himself ate humble pie when on 30 June in the National Mosque he publicly retracted disparaging remarks he had previously made about Mahmood Iskandar. At the swearing-in ceremony on 29 April the new Agung astutely committed himself to the good causes of defending religious equality, fostering consultation between politicians and civil servants, improving the lot of the *orang asli* (non-Malay aborigines), and abstaining from interference in parliamentary legislation. He gained further credit by ostentatiously donating his Agung's salary (though he retained his state salary) to scholarships open to Malaysians of any race. In November 1984 he intervened in a statesmanlike manner to cancel a planned television debate between UMNO and PAS representatives on the grounds that it threatened to divide the Muslim community.

On the other hand, it can be argued that the terms of the compromise were to Mahathir's advantage. The revised legislation did not depart from the original version in fundamentals: it elucidated the Agung's functions and established the principle that parliamentary legislation proceeds to the statute book at both federal and state levels. Politically, indeed, Mahathir more than survived, and went on to hammer home his advantage both within government and UMNO. By the middle of 1984 major figures who had given hints of support for the rulers were confounded: Datuk Harun Idris disappeared from the political scene; Tan Sri Ghazali Shafie was dropped from the cabinet; Tunku Razaleigh was demoted from the Finance Ministry to that of Trade and Industry and failed in his bid for UMNO's deputy presidency. Meanwhile, those who had stood by the reforms – 'the magnificent seven' as Musa Hitam dubbed them[21] – rose in the party hierarchy. Furthermore, the government reinforced its control of the press; Datuk Seri Adib Adam, Minister of Information, accused the foreign journalists and local columnists who had commented critically on the government's conduct, of being 'anti-Mahathir'.[22] He was particularly hostile towards *The Star*, and it was surely no coincidence that in March 1984 the already strict censorship laws were tightened another twist by the Printing and Publications Act.[23] Finally, it should be noted that, despite predictions that the Parti Islam (PAS) would capitalise on the crisis to undermine UMNO's support in rural areas, UMNO had recovered any ground it may have lost by August 1986, when the elections severely embarrassed PAS at both state and federal levels.

HISTORICAL PERSPECTIVE

The 1983–4 constitutional crisis has been cited by various observers to illustrate not only the strengths and weaknesses of the Mahathir regime but also its novelty and singularity. Examined in a wider perspective, however, the affair loses many of its peculiarities, and appears to exemplify at least two major recurring themes in the recent history of Malaysia. One of these is the tension between central and state authorities that has characterised the administrative development of the peninsula since the 1890s. Ironically, in his desire to reduce the autonomy of the rulers, Mahathir, the radical and nationalist, was following in the footsteps of British proconsuls and agents of colonial centralisation from Swettenham to MacMichael. In 1895 the former persuaded the rulers of Perak, Selangor, Negri Sembilan and Pahang to accept a 'federal' arrangement which drastically curtailed their independence; fifty years later MacMichael concluded the treaties to which we have already referred and which, by shaming the sultans, provoked the formation of UMNO for the defence of the Malay community and its traditional leaders.

The marriage between princes and politicians has been the mainstay of Malay political hegemony ever since the Malayan Union crisis of

1946, yet this relationship has frequently suffered sour and tempestuous moments even when Mahathir's aristocratic predecessors had led UMNO. This is the second recurring theme in recent political history, of which the 1983–4 crisis is a manifestation. The founder-president of UMNO, Dato Onn bin Jaafar, was guilty of several acts of *lèse-majesté*. On 1 April 1946, at the height of the Malayan Union crisis, Onn physically barred Their Highnesses from attending the installation of the new British Governor, and propelled them onto the balcony of the Station Hotel, Kuala Lumpur, to acknowledge the loyal cheers of a crowd gathered below. Three years later, during a meeting of UMNO's general assembly, Onn incensed the Raja of Perlis, and the Sultan of Kedah in particular, by claiming that the rulers owed their thrones to UMNO, and urging the party 'to strive for a single independent sovereign state of Malaya',[24] thereby implying that the future lay in a Malaya without Sultans. These taunts stung Sultan Ibrahim of Johor into forcing Onn's resignation as Mentri Besar of Johor, a post which his two brothers, father and grandfather had occupied before him. His fall from royal favour was complete; Their Highnesses vetoed a proposal to create the post of Deputy High Commissioner because, suspecting that Onn would be nominated to it, they feared that the UMNO president would overtake them in the colonial order of precedence. Similarly, Tunku Abdul Rahman, Onn's successor as UMNO president, quarrelled with his half-brother, Badlishah, who served as Regent of Kedah after 1938 and reigned as Sultan from 1943 to 1959. In 1949 the Tunku wrote an article in the Malay newspaper *Utusan Melayu* bitterly criticising his Sultan-brother in particular, and warning the rulers as a whole of what could happen to them if they refused to back UMNO. The split between the brothers was not bridged until the Tunku became Chief Minister of the Federation in 1955, by which time Badlishah recognised that the Tunku possessed the greater power, while the latter realised the importance of rulers' support in the final phase of negotiating independence from Britain.[25]

Like Ibrahim of Johor, Badlishah of Kedah was heir to a proud tradition of state autonomy. Johor and Kedah Rulers were prominent in resisting any kind of all–Malayan union, be it controlled by colonialists or nationalists. Earlier in the twentieth century these states had erected Malay-manned administrations to withstand the intrusions of Kuala Lumpur or Singapore. As independence drew near, Malayan politicians replaced British officials as the major threat to the royal prerogative. The rulers feared ruin at the hands of UMNO, and, like the Indian princes in 1947, pleaded in vain for the continuation of their special relationship with the British. Ibrahim, for example, wanted the British Advisor to stay on in Johor after *merdeka* (independence), and charged Datuk Seth, his Mentri Besar, to stand firm at the independence negotiations in January 1956. During their leisurely journey to London for these constitutional talks, Tunku Abdul Rahman gently persuaded the rulers' representatives in the Malayan party to combine with the Alliance delegates in a joint approach to Britain. Datuk Seth abandoned Ibrahim's instructions with the remark: 'The Sultan could kick my buttocks on my return but I couldn't care less.'[26]

At the height of the 1983 crisis, the government recycled such anecdotes to add weight to the view that the rulers had been enemies of national independence. In fact, as we have seen, the rulers were not swept away by a wave of nationalist fervour in 1956–7 but were firmly anchored in the constitution of independent Malaya, and from the Agung's mast-head unfurled the twin flags of 'the special position of the Malays' and 'the legitimate interests of other communities.'

While Their Highnesses strove to protect state privileges in the 1950s, nationalist leaders looked forward to operating a strong central government and were active at the pan-Malayan level. Johor and Kedah Malays bulked large in both movements, because the apparatus of state administration and education, which in the past had enabled Ibrahim and Badlishah successfully to resist creeping centralism, had also heightened the aspirations of some of their subjects, and equipped them for the management of federal institutions and national organisations. The leadership of UMNO is a case in point: of the five presidents the party has had since its foundation, Dato Onn bin Jaafar and Tun Hussein Onn came from Johor while Tunku Abdul Rahman and Datuk Seri Mahathir are Kedah Malays.

The 1983 constitutional crisis was not at heart a clash between the people and the rulers, nor did it jangle that most sensitive nerve of Malaysian communalism. It was a dispute, or rather a series of disputes, between Malay elites; apart from contributions to the debate offered by Lim Kit Siang of the Democratic Action Party or Tan Sri Tan Chee Khoon, the former leader of the Gerakan party, non-Malays were not involved in the *imbroglio*, while the Malay public were pulled in only as and when it suited their principals to do so. The Prime Minister's confrontation with the Agung had, as we have seen, historical antecedents, both in the discord between central and local seats of authority generated at various stages during the century-old growth of the modern Malaysian state, and in the feuds between competitors for Malay loyalty provoked by the post-war development of modern politics. Though abrasive and obdurate by turns, the leaders who closed in constitutional combat in 1983 did not, however, break the mould of Malay politics, which for 40 years have been dominated by an unequal partnership of UMNO politicians and Malay princes fundamentally in agreement, though occasionally in spectacular contention, with each other.

Notes

1. See Tan Sri Mohamed Suffian bin Hashim, *An Introduction to the Constitution of Malaysia*, Kuala Lumpur, 1972, pp. 17–27, and Tun Mohamed Suffian, H. P. Lee and F. A. Trinidade ed., *The Constitution of Malaysia. Its Development: 1957–1977*, Kuala Lumpur, 1978, pp. 101–122.
2. A. C. Milner, 'Malay Kingship in a Burmese Perspective' in Ian Mabbett ed., *Patterns of Kingship and Authority in Traditional Asia*, London, Sydney etc., 1985, p. 178.
3. See J. de V. Allen, A. J. Stockwell and L. R. Wright ed., *A Collection of Treaties and other Documents affecting the States of Malaysia 1761–1963*, London, Rome, New York, 1981, vol. I, pp. 117–128, vol. II, p. 98 ff and p. 251 ff.
4. Colonial Office, *Report of the Federation of Malaya Constitutional Commission 1957*, London, HMSO, Colonial No. 330, 1957. See also *Constitutional Proposals for the Federation of Malaya*, Parliamentary Papers, Cmnd. 210, June 1957.
5. F. A. Trinidade, 'The Constitutional Position of the Yang di-Pertuan Agong' in Suffian, Lee and Trinidade, *op. cit.*, p. 101.
6. Michael Ong, 'Malaysia in 1983: On the Road to Greater Malaysia' in *Southeast Asian Affairs 1984*, Institute of Southeast Asian Studies, Singapore, 1984, p. 201 ff.
7. Tunku Abdul Rahman commented upon these events at the time in his regular column in *The Star*, Penang. His articles on the Malaysian Constitution and the role of the Sultans written between July 1975 and October 1984 have been reprinted in Tunku Abdul Rahman Putra, *Contemporary Issues in Malaysian Politics*, Petaling Jaya, Malaysia, 1984, pp. 21–157 and *Challenging Times*, Petaling Jaya, n.d., pp. 3–42.
8. 2 Oct 1981, reprinted in *Contemporary Issues*, p. 80.
9. *Far Eastern Economic Review*, Hong Kong, 14 July 1983, p. 16.
10. *New Straits Times*, Kuala Lumpur, 8 April 1982, p. 24.
11. Mahathir bin Mohamad, *The Malay Dilemma*, Kuala Lumpur, 1982 ed., pp. 116, 157, 170–1. First published in Singapore in 1970 this book was proscribed in Malaysia until after Mahathir became Prime Minister.
12. The narrative of events has been built up from the following sources: *Far Eastern Economic Review* particularly 25 Aug. 1983 pp. 21–2, 15 Sept., pp. 25–6, 13 Oct., pp. 17–8, 20 Oct., p. 20, 27 Oct., pp. 16–7, 3 Nov.,

pp. 16–7, 17 Nov., pp. 21–2, 24 Nov., pp. 18–20, 1 Dec., pp. 14–7, 8 Dec., pp. 27–31, 15 Dec., pp. 14–5, 22 Dec., pp. 16–8, 29 Dec., pp. 13–5, 19 Jan. 1984, pp. 36–8; M. G. G. Pillai's reports in *The Times* (London) and Chris Sherwell's reports in the *Financial Times* (London) over the same period; Jerry Bass, 'Malaysia in 1983: A Time of Troubles', *Asian Survey*, XXIV, 2 (Feb. 1984), pp. 167–77; Michael Ong, 'Malaysia in 1983: On the Road to Greater Malaysia', *loc. cit.*; Tunku Abdul Rahman, *op. cit.*

13. *Malaysia: Federal Constitution*, Kuala Lumpur, 1970, with amendments passed in 1971.
14. Cited by H. F. Rawlings, 'The Malaysian Constitutional Crisis of 1983', *International and Comparative Law Quarterly*, 35 (2), Apr. 1986, p. 249.
15. Michael Ong, *loc. cit.*, p. 202 ff. Lim Kit Siang's views were subsequently printed by the Democratic Action Party in *Constitutional Crisis in Malaysia*, Kuala Lumpur, 1983.
16. 17 Oct 1983, reprinted in *Contemporary Issues*, p. 88.
17. Tan Boon Kean, 'Orwell's year in the Malaysian Press', *Far Eastern Economic Review*, 20 Sept. 1984, pp. 40–1.
18. For example, the headline of a report in the *Financial Times*, 13 Dec. 1983, read 'Royal row threatens Mahathir's credibility'; another in *The Times*, 16 Dec., ran 'King has last laugh in Malaysia crisis', while Jerry Bass in 'Malaysia in 1983' (*loc. cit.*, p. 172) commented, 'In sum, the crisis lent further credence to perceptions of Mahathir as a leader with insufficient regard for established practice.'
19. Articles in the *FEER* on the aftermath of the crisis and the election of the Sultan of Johor as Agung include: 19 Jan. 1984, pp. 36–8, 9 Feb., p. 20, 16 Feb., pp. 10–11, 23 Feb., pp. 10–14.
20. Raja Azlan had reached the highest legal position in the land, Lord President of the Federal Court, and, it was said, had advised Their Highnesses wisely during the crisis.
21. The seven were: Adib Adam (Minister of Information), Anwar Ibrahim (Minister of Culture, Youth and Sport), Abdullah Ahmad Badawi (Minister in the PM's Department), Rais Yatim (Minister, Land and Regional Development), Rafidah Aziz (Minister, Public Enterprise), Sanusi Junid (Minister, National and Rural Development), and Sharir Samad (Minister, Federal Territory). *FEER*, 22 Dec. 1983, p. 17.
22. Tunku Abdul Rahman, *Contemporary Issues*, pp. 136–7. Mahathir attacked Malaysians who disagreed with him and wrote for the foreign press as 'pet poodles' providing 'twisted reports for their foreign masters', *The Times* (London), 14 Dec. 1983.
23. *The Times*, 29 Mar. 1984. David Watts began his report from Kuala Lumpur: 'George Orwell could scarcely have imagined a more awesome set of press controls than those passed by the Malaysian Parliament last night.'
24. Public Record Office, Kew, CO 537/4790 (file no. 52928/22), Gurney telegram to Colonial Office, 17 June 1949, and *passim*.
25. Harry Miller, *Prince and Premier. A Biography of Tunku Abdul Rahman Putra Al-Haj First Prime Minister of the Federation of Malaya*, London, 1959, p. 96.
26. Tunku Abdul Rahman, *Challenging Times*, p. 167.

12 The Double Role of the Indian Governors: Kashmir and Andhra Pradesh 1983–84

Douglas V. Verney

For Canadians, India's experience since Independence provides a fascinating study.[1] Issues and controversies that have occurred in Canada's long and eventful political history have had their counterpart in modern India.[2] Among these controversies has been the role of the Governors (in Canada Lieutenant-Governors) in affairs normally the responsibility of the state or provincial cabinet and legislative assembly. Once the British North American provinces were granted responsible government in 1848 the authority of the Lieutenant-Governors was circumscribed by convention. It is true that their reserve powers were retained in the British North America Act of 1867 and were still being occasionally used until the 1940s. It is also true that despite the Constitution Act of 1982 these powers have remained entrenched in the constitution. However, they are widely assumed to be obsolescent if not obsolete.[3]

India, like Canada in 1867, began in 1950 as a quasi-federal political system.[4] In India, too, the transition to a more federal system appears to be under way. There are signs that intervention by the Governor in a state's political activities may gradually be limited to genuine constitutional crises. Needless to say, the role of the Governors has long been a contentious issue, and remains so.

The Indian federal political system comprises not only two Houses of Parliament in Delhi but comparable parliamentary systems in 26 states. In their chambers over 4 000 Members of Legislative Assemblies (MLAs) meet and speak any of the country's 15 official languages – or English. The term 'head of state' therefore refers to 22 Governors as well as to the President of India.

Early on in the debates on the new Indian constitution, there was a proposal to have Governors elected, as in the United States. This was rejected, because the delegates feared friction between the Governors and popular ministries. Having adopted the principle of Governors being appointed by the centre, most members of the Constituent Assembly assumed that the conventions of the parliamentary form of government, with which many of them were already familiar, would apply in the states as well as in Delhi.

Indeed, the new Indian heads of state, whether President or Governors, were initially expected to play a largely formal role analogous to that of the British monarch.[5] As far as the President was concerned, there was much justification for the assumption. Whatever the constitution might suggest, by convention power in India lay, and still lies, with the Prime Minister (and the cabinet), not with the President.[6] At first it seemed that the Governors too would be governed by similar conventions: a proposal to have the Governors given written instructions by the centre was defeated.

THE GOVERNORS' DOUBLE ROLE

Even so, the office of Governor came to be treated differently from that of the President. As India's leaders gained experience of government between the grant of independence in 1947 and the adoption of the constitution of 1950 they came to the conclusion that a double role for the Governors was necessary. In normal times, to be sure, Governors, like the President, were to act as ceremonial heads of state, complete with *aides-de-camp* and elegant stationery, leaving to the Chief Ministers and their cabinets the responsibility for government.

But in critical situations, the Governors were to play a very different role, exercising a broad executive authority not exercised in Canada since 1848. The Indian Governors were entitled to recommend to the President that a situation had arisen 'in which the government of the state cannot be carried on in accordance with the provisions of this constitution.' At this point, when Article 356 was invoked, the President (that is, the government of India) could proclaim that he was assuming the functions of the state government, and could declare that the powers of the legislature were to be exercised by the Indian Parliament. The proclamation was to be laid before Parliament and was to be approved by both Houses within two months. Unless approved again, the proclamation would expire after six months. If approved again it could be extended to a maximum of one year.

In other words, in times of grave crisis, the constitution could be suspended, and Delhi could operate for a limited period after the manner of London in the days of the Raj. Federalism would be in abeyance, the state government dismissed, and the state legislature suspended or dissolved. Instead, the Governor would represent the centre, and be in charge as both head of state and the head of government, supported by the Indian Administrative Service, the various All-India Services including the police, and the state's own services. In normal times, the Governor acted like the head of state in contemporary London or Delhi: in times of crisis this was replaced by something approaching a 'surrogate Raj.'

By no means all members of the Constituent Assembly were agreeable to the insertion of this provision suspending the constitution. H. V. Kamath saw the possibility of a Hitler-like takeover by the union government. H. N. Kunzru asserted that the centre would have the power to intervene to protect the electors against themselves. However, there were other members who believed that the government and parliament of independent India (under Nehru) would exercise their responsibilities with due propriety. In any case they were only too well aware of the grave crises already facing the country after partition: terrorism in Bengal, communist guerrilla activity in Telegana, and the demand of the Dravidian Federation (DK) of Madras for an independent Dravidasthan.[7] Members were mollified by Dr B. R. Ambedkar's assurance on behalf of the government that the provision for what came to be popularly known as 'President's Rule' would be invoked only in exceptional circumstances.[8] For many this meant only in *constitutional* crises.

CONTROVERSY OVER THE GOVERNORS' DOUBLE ROLE

Despite Dr Ambedkar's assurances, President's Rule soon came to be used not only for constitutional crises but for governmental crises as well. Instead of letting the legislators in a state resolve crises resulting from, for example, squabbles within a ministry (especially when there was minority or coalition government), or waiting for the electorate to make a final decision on the matter, successive governments in Delhi, starting with Mr Nehru's interference in the Punjab as early as 1951, used Article 356 to dismiss ministries of which they no longer approved. By 1984, President's Rule had been invoked no fewer than 70 times, often for partisan purposes.

Not surprisingly, an increasing chorus of liberal and federal voices raised questions about the double role allotted to Governors. For many liberals, it smacked too much of the Raj. Indeed, Article 356 was modelled on the Government of India Act of 1935: no comparable provisions are to be found in the constitutions of Canada or Australia. As India became more federal in the actual operation of its government, state governments began to argue that Article 356 was incompatible with the federal principle. They asked that the powers of the Governor be curbed. Some governments, notably the government of Karnataka, went so far as to urge the abolition of the office of the Governor. It repeated this suggestion in a white paper prepared for the Sarkaria Commission on Centre-State relations early in 1985.[9]

FROM JAWAHARLAL NEHRU TO INDIRA GANDHI

It would be an exaggeration to say that despite the use of President's Rule from 1951 onwards there was much public concern about the 'surrogate Raj' in the Nehru years (1950–64). Even the serious implications of Nehru's acquiescence in the invocation of President's Rule to remove India's first communist state government (which had retained its majority in the legislature) in Kerala in 1959 was not treated with the attention it deserved. Granville Austin's brief, bland and inaccurate description is very different from more recent accounts.[10]

> Through 1964 there were, however, seven instances of President's Rule. In each case the Union entered the affair at the last moment, usually at the invitation of the Governor after other solutions had failed. In each case the intervention was made when parliamentary government temporarily failed, when fresh elections could not produce a majority for one party, or a coalition, and therefore no government could be formed. The Union government was quite evidently loathe to enter Kerala in 1960 (sic).[11]

Controversy over the use of President's Rule heated up after the 1967 elections in which the Congress Party, now led by Mrs Gandhi (1966–84), lost control over several state governments. Mrs Gandhi was accused of using President's Rule in a partisan manner. The role of defectors from one party to another became the object of scrutiny.[12] Opponents of Mrs Gandhi came to associate President's Rule with her political style and to long for the golden age of Mr Nehru.

Many observers were therefore surprised when the Janata Party, after it came into power in 1977, used President's Rule to dissolve nine

Congress-dominated legislative assemblies on the grounds that their membership no longer reflected public opinion. Clearly on this occasion there could be no pretence that each of nine state Governors reached an independent decision regarding the inability of the government of their states to be carried on in accordance with the terms of the constitution.

This unfortunate but useful precedent was duly noted by Mrs Gandhi, who also dissolved nine assemblies after her victory in 1980. Not surprisingly, constitutional authorities became even more disapproving of this almost casual use of Article 356.[13]

The climax of the 'surrogate Raj' came in 1984, a few months before Mrs Gandhi was assassinated. In Kashmir in July 1984 her new Governor, the loyal, skilful and determined (though perhaps controversial) Jagmohan, toppled the ministry of Farooq Abdullah which she as Prime Minister had come to distrust. This was followed in Andhra Pradesh in August 1984 , by a similar dismissal, that of the Telugu Desam government. However, partly because Mrs Gandhi's equally loyal Governor, Ram Lal, was less skilful and less scrupulous, she ultimately had to accept the return of the dismissed Chief Minister, N. T. Rama Rao, to power.

Of course in each instance it was not Mrs Gandhi but the Governors who exercised their discretionary power to replace a ministry. To all intents and purposes, they acted alone. At no point did Indira Gandhi take any responsibility for what happened. Indeed the Governors knew that in their exercise of discretionary powers they could not blame the centre. If they failed in their attempt to please the Party High Command in Delhi they could blame no one but themselves. By succeeding in Kashmir, Jagmohan was able to stay on as Governor. By failing in Andhra Pradesh, Ram Lal had no alternative but to disappear into ignominious retirement. We shall examine each of these crises in turn.

KASHMIR, 1984

There were indications that the Farooq ministry might be toppled long before July, 1984. Some months earlier the Governor of Kashmir, B. K. Nehru, an Indian Civil Service (ICS) officer of the old school, was transferred to Gujerat, to be replaced by Jagmohan, the young and dynamic former Lieutenant-Governor of Delhi. After this appointment, many observers expected a move against the Chief Minister, Farooq Abdullah. He had displeased Mrs Gandhi by participating in various conclaves of opposition Chief Ministers. In these conclaves, the Chief

Ministers were believed to be mapping a common strategy for the forthcoming parliamentary elections, and were seeking ways of having their own supporters elected to the Lok Sabha and in due course the upper house or Rajya Sabha.

In July, 1984, Jagmohan received a number of MLAs early one morning. They told him that Farooq's National Conference had split into two factions, and that Farooq had lost his legislative majority. Farooq had been in power since 1982, when his father Sheikh Abdullah (the Lion of Kashmir) died, pointing to Farooq as his heir. The Sheikh's daughter, Khalida, had hoped that her husband, G. M. Shah, a competent and less mercurial cabinet minister, would be selected as Chief Minister. Both Khalida and Shah were disappointed, but Shah accepted Farooq's invitation to be Finance Minister. Now, two years later, he was organising a party split, or, as Farooq's supporters insisted, leading a group of dissidents to the Governor's residence.

Jagmohan realised that he had an opportunity, and perhaps the obligation, to remove Farooq, and he did so at once. He informed the Chief Minister that he had lost many of his supporters and that as Governor he intended to nominate G. M. Shah instead. Having done so, he gave Shah a month's grace to put his new government in place before he had to test his majority on the floor of the House. It was widely understood that the month would be profitably spent in building up a majority for the new government through bribery and perhaps intimidation.[14] (Jagmohan drew a distinction between defection by dissidents, against which there were now rules in Kashmir, and a party split). There was nothing anyone in Srinagar or Delhi could do, except complain. In any case, it seemed to many outsiders that what had happened was an almost inevitable family feud following the death of Sheikh Abdullah.[15]

It is arguable that Kashmir is by no means typical of India's 26 states. For one thing, it has a relatively small population of little over six million, and for another, it is a border state. In addition its people are largely Muslim in religion. Most serious of all, Pakistan has refused to accept the integration of the predominantly Muslim state into the Indian Union. After three Indo-Pakistan wars, part of the state (called 'Azad Kashmir') remains in Pakistan's hands. Moreover, after the 1962 Indo-China border war, Aksai Chin in the North-east has been administered by China. Recently, Pakistan and China are believed to have held joint military manoeuvres in the area.

Situated as they are, the Kashmiris have been tempted to flirt with the notion of independence from all three neighbouring countries, since they are virtually cut off from all of them, even from India, by mountains.

Short of independence, some of the state's Muslims are thought to feel as much affinity with Pakistan as with India. However hard the government of India and the elected government of Kashmir may try, there is bound to be friction between them. The presence of an army in Kashmir to guard India's borders against Pakistan and China is essential, yet it can be perceived in periods of political crisis as an army of occupation, keeping Srinagar hostage to Delhi.

In early 1984, moreover, the government of India's nervousness increased as Sikh extremists in Punjab, suspected in Delhi of being trained in Pakistan, grew more militant in their demands for an independent State of Khalistan. Access from the rest of India to Kashmir lay through Punjab. After the storming of the Golden Temple in June, Punjab grew more tense and few Indian tourists were prepared to take holidays in Kashmir. There were fears that Kashmir might also experience a secessionist movement, aided and abetted by Pakistan and China – and that Farooq might not be able to contain this movement.

Unique though Kashmir is, in many ways it is treated politically like Indian States by the centre. The Congress Party does not like to lose power anywhere, including Kashmir, especially when the Opposition is divided or is a coalition of disgruntled (often ex-Congress) politicians. Under Mrs Gandhi, its strategy was to lure away Opposition MLAs by the promise of office. It was willing to bide its time while these politicians attempted to govern with its support. In due course the government fell, often to be followed by a period of President's (or in Kashmir) Governor's Rule preparatory to an election. During this period, there was a breathing space amid all the political excitement, corruption, violence and frustration which characterise Indian politics.[16] For a while civil servants governed alone, and some of the administrative efficiency associated by the older generation with the Raj temporarily returned. Then elections were announced and the Congress High Command planned a new strategy, perhaps with a new leader and with the offer of financial support. All being well, Congress hegemony, or the hegemony of a party in alliance with Congress, was restored.[17]

Objections to the 'surrogate Raj' in Kashmir

In *The Times of India*, 18 August 1984, a distinguished former home secretary and Governor of Assam, L. P. Singh, published an article entitled 'Governor's Rule in Crisis: Rights and Wrongs in Kashmir.' To L. P. Singh, and to enlightened liberal opinion generally, 'the whole affair has exemplified much of the evil and ugliness that have come to disfigure the working of our essentially sound constitutional system.'

Singh suggested that while Governors were legally empowered to dismiss ministers, there was also the matter of constitutional propriety and political wisdom, to say nothing of decency in the dealings of the head of state with the head of government.

Singh's argument was that the dismissal of a ministry should be the responsibility of the Legislative Assembly through a vote of no-confidence on the floor of the House (a view known in India as 'the floor theory'). He deplored the practice of defectors from a state's ruling party going to the Govenor and asking him or her to dismiss the ministry at once because it no longer had a majority. Governors appointed by the Congress government in Delhi had become only too willing to get rid of non-Congress state governments once they had calculated (and verified) that these governments had lost their majority. (This was called the 'verification theory'). Singh accused the Governor of improperly seeking advice from the acting Chief Justice of the state instead of consulting the Attorney-General of India through the President's Secretariat.[18]

Defence of the 'surrogate Raj'

A week after L. P. Singh's article appeared, Jagmohan published a spirited defence of his actions as Governor in a long letter to *The Times of India*.[19] He argued that Singh, by his own admission, was out of touch with recent events in Kashmir; that some of the facts of the case could not be divulged; and that Governors had to act with discretion because only they could fully assess the circumstances. Whatever the critics might say about the Governors' discretionary powers, he argued, neither the government nor Parliament of India had thought it appropriate to accept proposals which would have limited that discretion through written instructions or even guidelines. Nor was there any rule that the Legislative Assembly had to be called into session before a state government was dismissed. (In other words, in Jagmohan's eyes the 'verification theory' was as valid as the 'floor theory').

The Governor of Kashmir pointed out that the facts of the case were not in dispute: the Chief Minister, Farooq Abdullah, had admitted that he had lost his majority because of defections. Jagmohan went on to say that it would have been irresponsible for him as Governor to have allowed the minority government of Farooq Abdullah to continue even for a short while. He offered an explanation that showed how different parliamentary practice in Srinagar was from Westminster. Yet it was one that would have come naturally to a Governor during the Raj. Not to have dismissed Farooq

> would have implied turning a blind eye to the well-grounded apprehensions that 'instant' rallies would have been organised, communal and extremist exploited, public hysteria whipped up, administrative machinery misused, the 'traitors' dealt with appropriately, and the police made to say later on that, in view of the 'spontaneous' upsurge and understandable anger of the people, it could do nothing.

He went on to quote from a letter from his predecessor, Mr B. K. Nehru, to Farooq as Chief Minister. Nehru had written to Farooq in January 1984:

> Your opponents were afraid, firstly, that in the interval between their coming to me and the vote in the House, their houses would be burnt and their families attacked by the police under your orders. They were afraid, secondly, that the Rules of the House would be so bent as to preclude a fair and free debate and vote from taking place. I recognised the validity of these fears on both counts.

Jagmohan concluded that the dismissal

> was constitutionally valid, administratively justified, and in the overall national interest, as well as in the interest of public order and tranquillity.

As it happened. Farooq behaved more like the Leader of the Opposition-in-waiting than like a guerilla leader. His successor as Chief Minister was his brother-in-law, G. M. Shah. Shah, who had served in Farooq's ministry, had governed with the support of the other defectors from Farooq's National Conference Party – and with the acquiescence of the state Congress (I) Party.

G. M. Shah may have had administrative ability but he lacked the charisma so important in Kashmir. After about 18 months, when both the Congress Party and the Governor concluded that a change was needed (if only to lure back the tourists), the Congress Party withdrew its support, no doubt with New Delhi's connivance.

Once again the Governor did not wait for a vote of no-confidence. He appears to have dismissed G. M. Shah much as he had dismissed Farooq.[20] Armed with Governor's Rule, Jagmohan proceeded to do what he had earlier done in Delhi: he shook up the administrative structure of the State and announced a number of measures to restore the State's economy (and perhaps the fortunes of the Congress Party in Kashmir).[21]

THE 'SURROGATE RAJ' AND RESPONSIBLE GOVERNMENT

The 'surrogate Raj' as illustrated in the Kashmir case discussed here, allows a departure from both the norms of parliamentary (or responsible) government – and from the federal principle.

1. The Governor can dismiss the ministry. The Governor can even dismiss a ministry without waiting for a vote of no-confidence in the Legislative Assembly. This descretionary power, no longer used by the head of state in Britain or Canada, is incompatible with responsible government. In Canada it is now also considered to be inconsistent with federalism. For according to the federal principle, the provinces are not subordinate to the federal government but have powers co-ordinate with it.[22]
2. The Governor can select a new ministry from defectors. By appointing a new ministry of defectors, supported by the Congress Party opposition it is assumed that there will be a period without confrontation between the state government and Delhi. During the period it holds office, the Congress Party has time to regroup for the next election.
3. Later President's Rule can be introduced. As soon as the government led by defectors loses its legitimacy, support can be withdrawn. Since no party then has a majority, President's Rule can be introduced.
4. During President's Rule, new policies are not formulated. Instead, the civil service attempts to put into operation the programmes introduced by the previous government but not yet implemented. One useful term to describe this practice of Indian government is 'administrative federalism'. In other words, India is normally federal, but in time of crisis the states are administered from Delhi through the Governor and the Indian Administrative Service.
5. President's Rule is only temporary. It is dependent on the will of Parliament in Delhi.

Congress strategy has been based on a number of important assumptions which for a long time remained unquestioned, namely:

a) The reliability of Governors. These might or might not be selected for partisan reasons, in other words because they were willing to promote the interests of the Congress Party. But they *were* assumed to be competent.
b) Divided and undisciplined alternative parties. Other state parties

were assumed to be undisciplined and easily weakened if they attained office through the defection of their members to the Congress Party, because of the lure of office, or through bribery.

c) No alternative to Congress as governing party. Congress could assume that it was the governing party at both the national and state levels of government. It was confident in the knowledge that so divided were its opponents that no charismatic leader even at the state level, was likely to emerge offering a serious long-term challenge to Congress.

d) Law and order preserved. While there was always the possibility of popular unrest after defections, this could be contained by the forces of law and order at the disposal of the state and union governments. The political consciousness of state electorates were assumed to be low.

e) The image of the Congress Party: the only national party. As the governing party, Congress was disciplined. State leaders took their orders, when necessary, from Delhi. The Party High Command could replace them at will. Whatever the machinations of the Party High Command, the image of Congress as the only vehicle to promote the national interest was considered to be unchallenged.

HOW THE 'SURROGATE RAJ' CAME UNSTUCK: ANDHRA PRADESH – SUMMER 1984

The events of August–September 1984 in Andhra Pradesh were well-documented at the time, but for convenience are summarised here. On this occasion, everything went wrong for Delhi, and for the Governor, Ram Lal. The Governor tried to follow the example set by Jagmohan in Srinagar, but in very different circumstances.

For about 18 months, the government of Andhra Pradesh, with a population of over 60 million, had been in the hands of a new regional party, the Telugu Desam Party (TDP). Its leader, N. T. Rama Rao, was a popular film star who turned politician when nearing 60. Within a very short time he had built up his party into a formidable vote-gathering machine, winning 200 of the 294 seats in the Legislative Assembly.

Having been rushed to the United States for a serious operation, 'NTR' returned to Andhra in August 1984 to find himself being dismissed from office by the Governor, and replaced by his Finance Minister, Bhaskara Rao. The latter had informed Governor Ram Lal that he, Bhaskara Rao, and several dozen other TDP dissidents had come to the conclusion that NTR was not equipped to be Chief Minister.

Bhaskara Rao went to the Governor with the signatures of about 80 Telugu Desam legislators. These, he alleged, were MLAs who were dissatisfied with the performance of the government (which had been elected in January 1983 after over 30 years of continuous Congress rule). The Governor was also told that the Congress Party opposition of 57 MLAs, plus another 11 MLAs, would support these 80 dissidents in forming a government. These figures indicated that NTR's party had been reduced from 200 to about 120 MLAs, supported by perhaps 20 other MLAs. Between them the dissidents and Congress members numbered 149–a majority, though a bare one, of the 294 MLAs.

The Governor, Ram Lal, lost no time in satisfying himself that NTR had lost his majority. Likc Jagmohan hc adopted the verification theory. But in this instance there was misjudgment, and consequently faulty arithmetic. This midjudgment lay in informing NTR of his dismissal by a letter delivered just when the Chief Minister was meeting his legislative caucus in his film studio headquarters. Before any of the MLAs who had signed Bhaskara Rao's memorandum could defect to the new government, the doors were literally closed. Bhaskara Rao, the new Chief Minister, might claim to have obtained 91 signatures, but he was not able to produce more than 50 or 60 warm bodies. And contrary to custom, the Governor had not had the signatures verified!

Nevertheless, the Governor refused to accept NTR's contention that he still possessed a legislative majority. Ram Lal declined to meet the Telugu Desam party and to count heads. N. T. Rama Rao and his followers thereupon travelled to Delhi, with identification, and there paraded in front of the television cameras and the President, Zail Singh. For reasons of protocol the President refused to have his visitors counted or their credentials verified. (He thus made possible the assertion by the Bhaskara Rao faction that not all those who paraded in Delhi were in fact legislators).

How was it that *both* Telugu Desam leaders believed they had a majority? One explanation is that some MLAs wanted to be on both sides of the fence and offered support first to Bhaskara Rao and then to N. T. Rama Rao. Another, and plausible, explanation is that during Ramo Rao's month-long stay in the USA undergoing by-pass surgery, Bhaskara Rao had obtained the signatures of those members who were critical of the Chief Minister's delegation of all responsibility for government during his absence to the Chief Secretary instead of to his cabinet. However, not all of these critics were prepared to express their lack of confidence in the ministry once NTR had returned and was again in charge. Unwisely, the Governor transmitted to Delhi a report stating that 91 MLAs had signed a letter expressing no-confidence in Mr Rama Rao.[23]

In Andhra Pradesh, confusion reigned. The Governor had followed Jagmohan's precedent and allowed the new Chief Minister a month to put his government together before he met the Assembly. It was widely believed that even if Bhaskara Rao did not have a majority when he started in mid-August, he would certainly have one by mid-September, using the funds assumed to have been placed at his disposal by the Congress Party High Command, which was known to be anxious to see the Telugu Desam defeated. Bhaskara Rao merely needed to lure a dozen or more MLAs to give him a majority. But this was to underestimate NTR. The Telugu Desam leader kept a firm grip on his MLAs, taking them first to Delhi and then to Karnataka until the Assembly was due to meet. The discredited Governor Ram Lal thereupon resigned, to be replaced by an experienced Congress leader, Dr S. D. Sharma. The new Governor nevertheless allowed Bhaskara Rao to remain in office, where he proceeded to reverse many of NTR's policies.

With the month nearly up, the Governor summoned the Legislative Assembly for a vote of confidence in the new Chief Minister. But knowing their weakness, Bhaskara Rao and his supporters created such a commotion day after day that no vote of confidence could be taken. The Speaker resigned, and was promptly replaced by a partisan of Bhaskara Rao. The supporters of NTR sat quietly in their seats. It was obvious from the pandemonium created by Bhaskara Rao's supporters that he did not expect to win the vote. However, the Congress Party did not withdraw its support for the Telugu Desam dissidents, causing many people to draw the conclusion that the centre still supported Bhaskara Rao. Many observers now expected the Governor to declare that since government could not be carried on in accordance with the constitution, President's Rule would have to be introduced. Tension mounted.

The Governor sprang a surprise. Suddenly he announced that the 30 days were up, that Bhaskara Rao had been unable to obtain a vote of confidence in the time given him, and that he would be replaced by NTR. The former Chief Minister returned to office, and thanked the Governor, the President, Mrs Gandhi and the people of Andhra Pradesh. The tension subsided. The crisis of Andhra Pradesh was over, at least for the Telugu Desam party.

The crisis was not over for the state Congress Party, however, which had been in power from independence until the 1983 elections. Many of the assumptions noted earlier, and which had determined its strategy, had proved to be unsound. Chief among them were: the competence of Governors; a divided and undisciplined opposition; the absence of a credible alternative; the capacity of the police to preserve law and order; and the image of Congress as the only vehicle of the national interest.

Let us consider gubernatorial competence for example. The Governor, a former Chief Minister of Himachal Pradesh with a rather dubious record, proved to be far from competent. As for opposition indiscipline, the Telugu Desam party showed itself to be a disciplined party able to resist the inducements undoubtedly offered to its members (who in some instances were probably fearful of the reaction of their constituents). So cohesive was the party which NTR had forged, that later on it proved able to withstand the tide in Rajiv Gandhi's favour in the elections of December, 1984, and to return to power in the state elections of March, 1985. With regard to the capacity of the police to cope with the electorate's outrage over the politics of defection and the manipulation of the political process by Congress, so widespread was the unrest that the forces of law and order were unable to contain it.

The Lessons of Andhra Pradesh

A number of lessons can be drawn from the experience of Andhra Pradesh. One is that the era of a dominant Congress Party might be coming to an end. The second is that while political manipulation is possible when a party is divided, it is not possible when a party, or a majority of its members, are solidly united. A third lesson is that once the political consciousness of a language group is aroused, whether of Tamils, Bengalis or now Telugus, regional pride is a force to be reckoned with, and any policy which ignores the wishes of the voters in a state may backfire.[24]

It is tempting to draw a parallel between the fluid parliamentary party structure of India between 1950 and 1984 and a similar fluidity in Britain from 1832 to 1867, or in Canada from 1848 to 1867. But it is premature to argue that India is moving towards a two-party system at long last. Nevertheless, the era of organised mass parties, which began in Canada and Britain after 1867, may not be too far off, replacing the Congress system of factional alliances based on traditional patron-client ties. It is quite possible that Indians will opt for a novel party system, with a national party like Congress at the centre, and regional parties like Telugu Desam in many of the non-Hindi-speaking states.

We need to remind ourselves that Britain and Canada spent decades developing representative and responsible government. In India, too, responsible government evolved, not from revolution, but from the top downwards. Canada, which had enjoyed representative government since 1791 and responsible government since 1848, was still facing a national crisis of the constitution in 1926, and provincial crises in the 1930s, notably in Alberta. India, it will be recalled, has had a much shorter and more uneven experience. The provinces of British India enjoyed responsible government for only a couple of years or so before independence (mostly 1937–39). Many of the 562 princely states had been autocracies until the Republic of India was founded in 1950. The first national election (based on universal suffrage) was held in 1952, barely three decades ago. The year 1984, with its searing events in Kashmir, Andhra Pradesh, and above all Punjab, may prove as significant for India's political development as 1830 and 1848 were for England and 1837–38 for Canada.

CONCLUSION

We suggested at the beginning of this chapter that the role of the Indian Governor was in some ways reminiscent of that played by Canadian Lieutenant-Governors in an earlier era before the conventions associated with responsible government and federalism made the Lieutenant-Governor's powers obsolescent. The principle of responsible government conflicts with the notion of the Governor as both head of state and head of government. And as a country becomes more federal there is less willingness to permit the Governor to act as an agent of the centre, interfering in state or provincial affairs (for example, by dismissing a government).

Do recent events in India indicate that the political system is moving in a direction similar to Canada's, with the Governor's role being limited to that of head of state?

If the events in Andhra Pradesh are any guide, Governors are unlikely in the future to interfere in larger states where there is a developed state political consciousness and where there is either a strong regional party or a well-established two-party system. Governors are more likely to interfere where a state is weak and vulnerable to pressure. In Canada, too, interference was more probable in the weaker and more vulnerable western provinces than in, say, Ontario.[25]

Kashmir reminds us that where there are fears for national security, and especially if these fears are compounded by threats of secession, interference by the Governors is likely to continue. In 1986, once the Congress (I) party withdrew its support for the ministry headed by G. M. Shah, the Governor of Kashmir was still able to dismiss a ministry without first calling the Legislative Assembly into session and allowing a vote of no-confidence on the floor of the House.

Genuine constitutional crises are likely to remain more common in India than in Canada. They take three main forms. There are, first, long-term crises of national security. Until India's borders on the north-east and the north-west are secure, there will always be a special role for the Governor in border states. Second, there are secessionist crises. In a number of states there have been secessionist movements challenging the integrity of the country. Governors, working with the ruling party in Delhi, have done their best to wean the moderates away from the extremists in such states. They have been largely successful in Tamil Nadu and moderately successful in Kashmir. There is hope that the centre will also be successful in Punjab and the north-eastern States.

A third set of crises have arisen in the form of possible challenges to the liberal-democratic constitution following the rise to power of communist parties after state elections. India is the only federal liberal-democracy that has had to deal with elected communist governments at the sub-national level, and with the possibility of ideological confrontation. Initially the Governor played a vital role as a link between the centre and communist state governments. However, the communists in both Kerala and West Bengal appear to have accepted the norms of liberal-democracy. This type of constitutional crisis may be a thing of the past.

Canada has little to compare with the constitutional crisis in India arising from threats to national security from outside or the challenge to liberal-democracy from within. However, in the late 1970s there was the threat to the nation's integrity posed by the *Parti Québecois*. At that point the government of Canada had to face the possibility of secessionist action being taken by the government of Quebec. Had this occurred, the Lieutenant-Governor would have been placed in a very difficult position.

To return to India. Even if the ruling party in Delhi never again acts as it did in Andhra Pradesh, it does not follow that it will always confine its intervention in state affairs to constitutional crises. For the state Legislative Assemblies play such an important role in national politics that it may be tempting for Delhi to attempt to replace state governments through the Governor. There are two instances in which the Legislative Assemblies become significant.

The first of these involves the election of the President of India. This election is the responsibility of both Houses of Parliament – and the state legislatures. After a landslide victory in national elections, a new government in Delhi might be tempted to arrange elections in those states where it is not yet in power. Victory in the state elections would give it an advantage in securing the election of its own candidate for the office of President, since the state Legislative Assemblies as well as Parliament would have a voice.

The second instance is the role played by the state legislatures in the election of all except twelve of the 250 members of the upper house of parliament, the Rajya Sabha. While the Rajya Sabha is not a powerful body like the US Senate, its assent is necessary for legislation. A two-thirds vote in both Houses is required for the passage of the more important constitutional members.

Amendments to the constitution have on occasion been very important in India. 'Vested interests' have used the constitution and the courts to have such popular pieces of legislation as zamindari abolition, bank nationalisation and elimination of the princes' privy purses declared unconstitutional. In the past, the Congress Party was able to rely on its two-thirds majority in both houses to overturn the judgment of the Supreme Court by amending the constitution.

Much remains to be done to modernise India and make its economy more competitive. Many reforms are likely to affect vested interests of one sort or another. In the future, these interests may try to prevent reform not only through the courts but by obtaining control of enough state legislatures to block constitutional amendments. All it would take would be one-third (or 84 members) of the members of the Rajya Sabha from a number of key states. State elections could become crucial arenas where the battle over further modernisation occurred. Delhi might wish to invoke President's Rule to force elections – and once again the Governors would be expected to act as agents of the centre.

In sum, India may have passed through one stage in its transition towards a more federal society – the misuse of Governors by Delhi to manipulate the political process, as in Andhra Pradesh – but there remain a number of grey areas in which the 'surrogate Raj' might be invoked. One consists of constitutional crises (that is, threats to national security and challenges to the nation's integrity), a second presidential elections, and a third elections to the upper house of Parliament. The role of the Governor in each of these areas is open to various interpretations.

It is doubtful whether the office of Governor could be abolished, as some responsible Indians have suggested. It is difficult to see how parliamentary federalism could work in Canada or India without a Governor – and an appointed Governor at that. Although both countries are federal states, with sub-national governments enjoying a co-ordinate status denied to subordinate governments in unitary states, there are limits to the application of the principle of co-ordinate government. Sub-national governments must accept their responsibility to work within the constitution, and they must not challenge the nation's integrity.

Finally, one must not get too alarmist about events in either society. Neither Canada nor India has yet faced a proposal to secede on the part of any of their 36 elected sub-national governments. The political system they enjoy must get at least some of the credit for this.

Notes

1. This chapter is part of a larger study of governmental systems in which Canada and India are compared in the context of the tradition of British parliamentary institutions, the principles of American government, and the ideology associated with twentieth century socialism. I am indebted to the Social Sciences and Humanities Research Council of Canada, the Shastri Indo-Canadian Institute, and the South Asia: Ontario Consortium for assistance with this project.
2. During the Constituent Assembly debates, reference was made to the removal of Canadian Lieutenant-Governors on two occasions by the Government of Canada. This section of the debates was reproduced by the Government of Karnataka in its 1983 white paper *The Office of the Governor: Constitutional Position and Political Perversion*. This in turn was added to Karnataka's *Memorandum to the Commission on Centre-State Relations*.

   Curiously enough, there is no mention of the removal of Lieutenant-Governors in recent textbooks of constitutional law or political science. The removals occurred in Quebec (1879) and British Columbia (1900) after each Lieutenant-Governor had dismissed a ministry. 'These two cases of dismissal stand alone and as far as one can tell the federal government never again considered dismissing a Lieutenant-Governor.' John T. Saywell, *The Office of Lieutenant-Governor* (Toronto: University of Toronto Press, 1957), 255.
3. 'While a case can be made for the preservation of disallowance as the considered exercise of power in very exceptional circumstances by a careful and responsible federal government, no such case can be made for the reserve powers of the Lieutenant-Governor.' J. R. Mallory, *The Structure of Canadian Government* (Toronto: Gage, revised edition, 1984), 370.

4. The description of India as 'quasi-federal' appears to have originated with K. C. Wheare, *Federal Government* (London: Oxford University Press, 4th edition, 1964).
5. 'India was to have a President, indirectly elected for a term of five years, who would be a constitutional head of state in the manner of the monarch in England.' Granville Austin, *The Indian Constitution: cornerstone of a nation* (London: Oxford University Press, 1966), 116.
6. The state visits of the President of India are controlled by the Prime Minister's Office. See the article 'The President: a communication gap,' *India Today*, June 15, 1985, 30–31. The absence of the Canadian Governor General from the 'Shamrock Summit' of the Prime Minister, Brian Mulroney, with President Reagan in 1985 and from the opening of Expo 86, when the Prime Minister entertained the Prince and Princess of Wales, has been the occasion for comment in the press. See *The Globe and Mail*, 9, 10 & 11 June 1986.
7. See Austin, *The Indian Constitution*, 214–5, and B. Shiva Rao, *The Framing of India's Constitution* (New Delhi: Indian Institute of Public Administration, 1968), 802–823.
8. He asserted that before a State Constitution was suspended, the Central Government would give a warning. If that failed it would order an election. Only if both these remedies proved inadequate would Article 356 (then 278) be invoked. See B. Shiva Rao, *The Framing of India's Constitution*, 815 and *Constituent Assembly Debates*, IX, 176–177.
9. Government of Karnataka, *Memorandum to the Commission on Centre-State Relations*, January 1985, 19.
10. See, for example, T. J. Nossiter, *Communism in Kerala* (London: Oxford University Press, 1982), chapter 6 and Sarvepalli Gopal, *Jawaharlal Nehru: a biography* (London: Jonathan Cape, 1984), chapter 3.
11. Austin, *The Indian Constitution*, 216.
12. See, for example, S. C. Kashyap, *The Politics of Defection* (Delhi: National, 1969).
13. 'With the increasing use of this instrument, she was successful in her objectives, but she reduced provincial autonomy to a farce and made the Indian system a case of the pathology of federalism.' B. D. Dua, *President's Rule in India 1950–1974: a study in crisis politics* (New Delhi: Chand, 1979), 402.
14. 'In the 20 months of the G. M. Shah government, corruption has increased immensely, even by the standards set by successive governments in Jammu and Kashmir.' H. K. Dua, 'The Kashmir Imbroglio,' *Indian Express*, 8 March 1986.
15. Farooq complained that his sister 'never had much to do with me as she felt that I had taken the crown from her husband's head.' M. J. Akbar, *The Siege Within: challenges to a nation's unity* (Harmondsworth: Penguin, 1985), 278.
16. It was reported that after Governor's Rule was invoked in Kashmir in 1986 '. . . there is total support to Governor's Rule by the people of the State irrespective of their party affiliations.' S. S. Banyal, 'J & K parties worried at Governor's rule,' *Hindustan Times*, 16 April 1986.
17. The limits to this technique are described more fully in my 'The Limits to

Political Manipulation: the role of the Governors in India's administrative federalism, 1950–1984,' *Journal of Commonwealth and Comparative Politics*, XXIV, 2, 1986, 169–96.

18. In an interview in 1985, L. P. Singh suggested that the problem might have been that Jagmohan's interests were primarily in urban planning, not in constitutional niceties.
19. *Times of India*, 24 August 1984.
20. Curiously enough, the newspapers did not seem to notice that the Governor dismissed Shah. In an editorial entitled 'Good Riddance,' the *Indian Express* began 'No tears will be shed at the ignominious political exit of Mr G. M. Shah' (8 March 1986).
21. Within a few days of imposing Governor's Rule, Jagmohan had toured the State, transferred a third of the Indian Administrative Service officials, and sent a development plan to Delhi, which promised him an extra $10 million in the next few months. He planned to provide houses for the poor, boost electricity supply and redevelop Gulmarg and Pahalgam as two of the most attractive resorts in the country. *India Today*, 15 April 1986, 73.
22. The Task Force on Canadian Unity, set up by the Trudeau government, went so far as to recommend the principle of 'the equality of status of the central and provincial orders of government'. *A Future Together* (Hull, Quebec: Canadian Government Publishing Centre, 1979), 125. Note the use of the term 'orders' instead of 'levels'.
23. For a fascinating blow-by-blow account of events, see the cover story entitled 'Andhra Pradesh: Democracy Betrayed' in *India Today*, 15 September 1984.
24. At the time of writing, it was not certain whether Maharashtra would join those States which objected to a new Chief Minister being imposed by Delhi.
25. 'It was always easier to invoke the power against a distant or peripheral province.' Mallory, *Structure of Canadian Government*, 369–370.

13 The Crises that Didn't Happen: Canada 1945–1985

J. R. Mallory

There have been a number of constitutional episodes in Canada in the last 40 years that appeared to involve the discretionary role of the head of state, but on the whole they have been minor sources of temporary confusion and inconvenience – no more than that. In part this has been so because of what is probably a gradual change in Canadian political culture. In some cases the cause seems to have deep roots. Canadians have been conditioned to think that majority government is a natural consequence of democracy, and become uncomfortable when the electoral system is perverse enough to throw up minority governments. When the trauma of minority governments was combined with the almost-forgotten role of the head of state, the issue was seen in a particular light for a generation or so after the event. That episode was the constitutional crisis of 1926, and it is necessary to recall it here since it forms a backdrop to every consideration of the head of state role since.

In the general election of 1925 the Liberal government was reduced to minority status (it had been barely short of a majority before, but had no difficulty in remaining in office) with less seats than the Conservative Opposition. However, it hung on, faced Parliament and continued in office with third party support. That support was fragile because the Progressives, on doctrinal grounds, would not function as a disciplined party: they had even refused to become the 'official' Opposition in the previous Parliament.

Towards the end of June, in order to avoid the possibility of defeat in the House, Mackenzie King advised the Governor-General, Viscount Byng, to dissolve Parliament. To this the Governor-General refused, Mackenzie King resigned, and Lord Byng justified his action in his reply to the letter of resignation:

> In trying to condense all that has passed between us during the last week, it seems to my mind that there is really only one point at issue.

> You advise me 'that, as, in your opinion, Mr Meighen is unable to govern the country, there should be another election with the present machinery to enable the people to decide'. My contention is that Mr Meighen has not been given a chance to govern, or saying that he cannot do so, and that all reasonable expedients should be tried before resorting to another election.[1]

The Governor-General having committed himself, and brought about King's resignation, Arthur Meighen had no alternative but to attempt to form a government and carry on. For reasons which are too complex to recall here, he also found it difficult to carry on, and sought and obtained a dissolution after a defeat in the House on 2 July. Meighen's Conservatives were defeated in the subsequent election, Mackenzie King being returned with a majority. During the campaign King and his followers made much of the constitutional issue, which they presented as interference by a British Governor-General in a Canadian affair. From then on much of the conventional wisdom was that the discretionary prerogative in the dissolution of Parliament had become obsolete because it had been repudiated by the electorate. If that was the case, then clearly the dissolution of Parliament was to be at the uncontrolled whim of the Prime Minister.

As a result there have been various proposals to remove the power of dissolution from the head of state, and curb the capacity of the Prime Minister to abuse it by a variety of expedients such as a strict definition of votes of confidence to allow for more free votes in the House free of party discipline, and even to provide a fixed term for Parliament. These last two, in particular, reflect the overwhelming cultural influence of US institutions on Canadians. One example will suffice. The 1972 Joint House–Senate Committee on the constitution was presented by the New Democratic Party with the proposal that dissolution should only take place if the government were defeated on a motion of want of confidence or on a measure which it itself had decided in advance to be a vote of confidence. This would prevent elections without good reasons of public policy. Furthermore, the House could – by resolution – vote for a dissolution.

There is a difficulty here, as that staunch defender of the royal power of dissolution, Eugene Forsey, pointed out. An election might produce a tie, so that it would not be possible to elect a Speaker. If there is no Speaker, there can be no vote or any other business in the House. As he said, 'It's very unlikely to happen. But it could, and you don't want to find yourselves, for four solid years, with a government getting its money by Governor-General's special warrants, and totally incapable of bringing in any legislation whatever'.[2]

The 1970s were a time when Canadians had an irresistible urge to tinker with the constitution. Inevitably the government of Canada was drawn into the game. In June, 1978, it tabled a Constitutional Amendment Bill in the Commons, which sought to tidy up a number of matters which – in its view – fell wholly within the constitutional amending power of Parliament under Section 91(1) of the British North America Act. Among the proposals was an attempt to give constitutional definition to the cabinet and to reduce the conventions governing votes of confidence and the rules governing the dissolution of Parliament to specific constitutional rules. In the event of a defeat on a vote of confidence the Prime Minister was required 'as soon as possible' to advise the Governor-General whether Parliament should be dissolved, and if this advice was tendered and refused (in which case the Prime Minister was apparently deemed to have resigned) the Governor-General was to decide whether to ask the Prime Minister to form another administration, or to send for someone else.

As set out, these rules do not seem any clearer than the present conventions. Furthermore, it was provided that in any dispute as to whether the cabinet was able to command the confidence of the House, the 'conclusive' decision on this matter was to be made by the House. These provisions, of course, are open to the same objections in the event of a 'hung' election as the one adduced by Senator Forsey. By placing the rules in the constitution, it could well have been that the whole matter in the end might have been subject to judicial review, the consequences of which seem not to have been considered. In the event the Supreme Court found that the part of the Bill which sought to reconstitute the Senate to be beyond the powers of Parliament[3] and the Bill was allowed to die on the order paper.

So, for 60 years public attention has shifted away from the head of state powers, which were mistakenly thought to have been a relic of imperial interference in Canadian affairs, which had been swept aside by the Imperial Conference of 1926 and the Statute of Westminster. Such is the power of myth. Meanwhile attention shifted to ameliorating the awesome power of the political executive, which might be tempered by electoral reform, or by changing the habits of elected legislators by freeing them from the iron grip of party discipline. From this no results have as yet flowed, but the popular conception that constitutional evolution has changed the head of government into an automaton remains.

Before dealing with such crises as existed in this unpromising – from the point of view of the head of state – environment, it is probably necessary to explain a little about Canadian heads of state. There is no ambiguity about the Governor-General. He is appointed by the Queen on the advice of the Prime Minister and possesses the powers of the executive, to be exercised with the advice, or with the advice and consent, of the Queen's Privy Council for Canada, or in his discretion. What this means in practice is that cabinet government is defined by the conventions of the constitution, for Canada has, as the preamble to the British North America Act says, 'a constitution similar in principle to that of the United Kingdom.'

The Governor-General's counterpart in the provinces is termed the Lieutenant-Governor, but there are significant differences between the two offices. Not only is the Lieutenant-Governor appointed by the Governor-General on the advice of the Prime Minister of Canada, he also still possesses – as the Governor-General does not – the power to reserve a Bill for the assent of the Governor-General (which means in practice the Governor-General-in-council, that is, the federal government), but also the power to withhold assent. All this has been spelled out in Sections 55 and 90 of the constitution, and led Sir Kenneth Wheare to conclude that the Canadian consitution was only quasi-federal.[4] The fact is that most of the time these powers of the Lieutenant-Governor (in his role as what used to be called a 'Dominion Officer') are of no consequence, and every serious discussion of constitutional reform for 60 years has taken for granted that they should be abolished. They remain, a tiny bargaining chip in the hands of the federal government in recurring negotiations with the provinces on constitutional reform.

In spite of my mandate, I propose to begin with a major crisis of the 1930s which was handled so smoothly that practically no one knew about it until it surfaced with the release of Mackenzie King's *Diaries* 30 years later. In 1938 the relations between the Social Credit government of Alberta and the federal government were seriously strained. The Alberta legislature had passed legislation, inspired by agrarian discontent and infused with Social Credit ideas, which seriously invaded the federal government's exclusive jurisdiction over banking and monetary policy. Some of this legislation had been reserved by the Lieutenant-Governor, some had been disallowed by the federal government, and some had been challenged in the courts. In this atmosphere of conflict and high tension between Alberta and Ottawa, Mackenzie King learned that a constitutional *coup* was being planned to dismiss the Alberta government and replace it with a combination of opposition parties which then planned a dissolution and a general election in which they expected to be vindicated by the electorate. Mackenzie King was horrified. Not only would chaos ensue in Alberta and the plotters would fail, but the plotters were relying on an exercise of the royal prerogative, the defeat of which was one of King's most cherished triumphs. His diary entry tells it all:

> Mr Gardiner and Mr MacKinnon [the senior ministers of Saskatchewan and Alberta] came to the office to talk over the Alberta situation before going to Council. The present Lieutenant-Governor wants to dismiss the Alberta Ministry, and has asked Gray [the Alberta Liberal Leader] to form a Ministry which is to be composed of the different political parties of the Province. It is sheer madness. Action of this kind would almost certainly have repercussions in Saskatchewan which would cause [*sic*] the Liberals the election there, and might bring on a sort of civil war in Alberta. I had Gardiner phone Gray and MacKinnon phoned the Governor, and later tonight I phoned Gray myself and dictating a letter which I had thought of sending him and which I am binding into the diary.[5]

The letter recalls the position of Arthur Meighen (his Conservative opponent) in 1926, and stresses the political consequences of the proposed Alberta *coup* to the Liberal Party. King was insufferably moralising and sometimes mean-spirited, but he was a master politician. He acted swiftly and effectively to squelch the manoeuver, and was so successful that the whole affair was unknown to the public until the King Papers were opened.

King's own view of the head of state functions as essentially rubber stamp became so much an accepted part of standard discourse about the constitution that when a political crisis did occur few people realised that the head of state did have a role to play in the matter at all. The crises that did occur during the years 1945–1985 usually centred on a change of government as a result of an ambiguous electoral result, although three arose out of the unexpected death of a first minister. Two others came about through the exercise, in unusual circumstances, of a Lieutenant-Governor's reserve powers in relation to legislation. These, as Sir John A. Macdonald had made clear in a minute of council in 1882, should generally be exercised only on instruction from Ottawa. The facility of communication brought about by the electric telegraph, he thought, made it generally unnecessary for a Lieutenant-Governor to act in the light of his own unguided reason.[6]

The first case to arise involved three elements worth noting: the

Lieutenant-Governor rejected the advice of his ministers on grounds of conscience, the ministers sought to rectify the situation by unconstitutional means, and the courts found the right answer but failed to perceive the correct constitutional grounds for doing so. The matter arose in the tiny province of Prince Edward Island, which at that time was the last part of Canada to prohibit the sale of alcoholic beverages. In 1945 the government of Prince Edward Island introduced a modest amendment to the Prohibition Act. When the Lieutenant-Governor prorogued the legislature on 19 April, 1945 he withheld assent to that particular Bill, which appeared to have offended his prohibitionist principles. His five-year term in the office had already expired and in the following month a successor was appointed. In September the cabinet advised the new Lieutenant-Governor to sign the Bill, which he did on 28 September, and on the following day a proclamation issued asserting that the Bill had passed the necessary three readings in the legislature and that royal assent had been withheld but that 'by this proclamation' assent was given. Subsequently litigation arose when a person arrested under the Act for unlawful possession raised the question of the validity of the amended Act. The Supreme Court of Prince Edward Island found that royal assent in these circumstances was invalid.[7]

Another matter arose in 1961 which involved the discretionary powers of a Lieutenant-Governor, when the Lieutenant-Governor of Saskatchewan reserved a Bill in the course of proroguing the legislature on the grounds that the Bill was against the public interest and that there were doubts as to whether it was within the powers of the legislature.[8] As with the withholding of assent, the reservation of a Bill for the pleasure of the Governor-General-in-council is not expected to be undertaken by a Lieutenant-Governor on his own. His actions came as a nasty shock to the federal government, which subsequently advised the Governor-General to give royal assent. The Prime Minister, Mr Diefenbaker, promised in the House to issue clarifying instructions to Lieutenant-Governors to prevent such embarrassments in the future, but nothing seems to have been done. The most authoritative view of the matter was given by Mr Justice Kerwin in the Supreme Court of Canada in an earlier case. He said, 'the power of reservation is to be exercised by the Lieutenant-Governor "according to his discretion", but subject to the Provisions of this Act and to the Governor-General's Instructions'.[9]

The instances that have been cited above are examples of perverse exercises of reserve powers by Lieutenant-Governors in relation to policy issues which they did not approve on grounds that were perhaps more personal than political. More than anything else they indicate that one of the attributes expected of the head of state – political neutrality – had not been inculcated into the various provincial Lieutenant-Governors, who were in many cases appointed by the federal government for reasons of political patronage.

The one with which I now propose to deal hinges on the more traditional head of state function of designating a first minister in periods of political uncertainty and crisis. In the twentieth century political parties choose their leaders through one system of internal party election or another. Thus it is taken for granted that it is the party that designates the leader, not the Crown, and that the reins of government go automatically to the party which possesses a majority of seats in the legislature. The role of head of state thus becomes quite automatic in designating as prime minister the party leader chosen by the party which has a majority in the legislature.

This rubber stamp role becomes suddenly dauntingly real in the event of the death in office of a prime minister, or of an election from which no party appears as a clear winner. The general election in British Columbia in 1952 resulted in a great deal of confusion because no one seems to have known what to do in the light of the result. In the words of H. F. Angus, 'The election of the summer of 1952 in British Columbia has shown how little the public knows or cares about constitutional principles'.[10]

The Liberal government which had brought about the dissolution of the legislature was the survivor of a wartime coalition of Liberals and Conservatives. The break-up of the coalition left the Liberals and the Conservative opposition with, as Angus put it, 'a certain community of interest' since they both perceived the socialist party – the Co-operative Commonwealth Federation or CCF – as a major threat. Accordingly it was provided that the next election would be fought on the basis of the single alternative vote. It should be noted parenthetically that this system in Alberta had led to the extinction of the CCF, since a Liberal or a Conservative voter would automatically give his second preference to the dominant Social Credit (and anti-socialist) Party. In the upshot of the 1952 election it was to be the Social Credit Party (newly established and attractive to many disillusioned supporters of the older right-wing parties) which was to be the principal beneficiary of the new system. When the first choices were counted Social Credit had elected three and the CCF one. Including these victories the CCF held or was leading in 21, Social Credit in 14, Liberals in nine, Conservatives in three, and an Independent Labour candidate in one. Three weeks were to elapse before the second ballot results were to be declared, a process complicated by a large number of three- and two-member constituencies. It was further complicated by the fact that in one constituency electorial irregularities led to a court order for a recount which turned out to be impossible since the ballots had been removed from their envelopes to facilitate counting the second choices. It was clear that the Liberal government had lost, that no party had a majority, and it suddenly became important to know which party in the end had the largest number of seats. This latter consideration became a matter of doctrine which 'was pressed to the extreme limit by the CCF which contended that no government should be formed until the last recount had been made; and even that a government once formed, should resign if it lost its plurality. Underlying the doctrine there seemed to be an implicit feeling, foreign to parliamentary government, that the people elect not only the legislature but an administration as well'.[11]

Furthermore, Angus added, it was argued that 'if it is the leader of the largest party who should be summoned, the Lieutenant-Governor has no choice to make except in the event of a tie. It was suggested that if there were a tie the preference should be given, as a matter of fact, to the party which had constituted the official Opposition in the previous legislature. The Lieutenant-Governor, therefore, even on the rubber stamp theory of his functions, stands in no need of advice'.[12] In the end the crisis sorted itself out without much overt intervention by the Lieutenant-Governor. Social Credit emerged with 19 seats to 18 for the CCF (the others were Liberal six, Conservative four, and the Independent Labour candidate one). The Premier resigned, and the Lieutenant-Governor sent for the leader of the Social Credit Party. It is not known on what basis (or possibly advice) he acted.

In the end, the Lieutenant-Governor seems to have played a passive role in the whole affair, and one consequence of that, curiously enough, was to strengthen the general conviction that constitutional convention had – one way or another – left him with no discretion in the matter. Angus ruefully concludes:

> There has been some popular discussion of the possibility of dissolving the new Legislative Assembly without allowing it to meet. Some say that if the Premier were to advise a dissolution the Lieutenant-Governor would be bound by constitutional usage to act on his advice; others that the Lieutenant-Governor would be constitutionally bound to reject the advice and allow the leader of the CCF party, Mr Winch, to attempt to form a government. The significant point in this discussion is the unanimity of opinion that the

> Lieutenant-Governor has no constitutional discretion in the matter. The rubber stamp theory is universal and is, no doubt, the result of colonial tradition.[13]

The 1952 British Columbia election seemed at the time to be almost a freak of nature, brought about by the coincidence of a major party realignment in the province and a new electoral law which had brought about the bizarre result. The new government, with probably heartfelt support from all parties, soon amended the law to return to the traditional voting system. This, however, was not to be the end of minority governments in Canada, for they were to recur again with some frequency for the next 30 years and each time, the issue was largely perceived in the terms of the rubber stamp theory as adumbrated by Professor Angus.

The next notable episode followed the federal election of 10 June 1957. It was a stunning defeat of a Liberal government, which, under Mackenzie King and later Louis St Laurent, had been in office for 22 years. It was not clear what else it was, for the party standings (Progressive Conservative 112, Liberal 106, CCF 25 and Social Credit 19) made it clear that neither of the major parties could form a stable government without support from both minor parties. The Conservatives were indeed the largest party (recall that this argument had been used in British Columbia) but there is no persuasive constitutional argument that this is decisive. In fact in 1925 Mackenzie King, with fewer seats than the Conservatives, had remained in office and was sustained in the House with third party support. This no doubt was an important consideration to many Liberals. Thus Paul Martin, who was even then a minister of some consequence:

> St Laurent immediately called his cabinet to Ottawa for a conclave. From the outset, my view was that the government should not resign. Instead, we should meet parliament. This is what Mackenzie King had done in somewhat similar circumstances in 1925. If we had followed this course, my friend Vincent Massey the governor-general would have passed several sleepness nights, but no constitutional expert would argue with parliament's right to decide who should form the government. And, after all, we had received more votes than the Tories – 42 per cent to 39 per cent.[14]

Note the essentially irrelevant reference to the proportions of the total vote, accounted for by largely wasted majorities in St Laurent's home province of Quebec, then and for many years thereafter a Liberal stronghold. Note also the casual reference to the discomfort of the Governor-General, who would presumably have to ratify whatever Parliament decided. But what if the Liberals could not even elect a Speaker? Would there be another dissolution crisis similar to 1926, or would the party leaders sort it all out behind the scenes? Clearly the public was puzzled, but St Laurent was not. He had been stunned by the result of the election and was determined to resign. He may have been comforted by being reminded of Stanley Baldwin's remark in 1929 that whether or not the public wanted the honourable gentleman opposite, they had made it plain that they did not want him. Paul Martin continues his account of the cabinet deliberation at that time:

> St Laurent wanted to quit and would not agree to leave the decision to the party caucus. The choice, he said, was his alone. He did not wish to give Canadians the impression that he was hanging on to power for its own sake. If his health, age and strength had permitted, the prime minister might have taken a different course, but he believed that his choice was honourable – and indeed it was. Yet, although St Laurent's high-minded view was understandable, I think he had made the wrong decision. Diefenbaker could not count on the CCF's support. Jimmy Gardiner [the Minister of Agriculture] and I urged St Laurent not to resign, but the rest of the cabinet backed the prime minister, even though half of them would not be in their usual places when parliament met.[15]

Paul Martin makes the point that 'no constitutional expert would argue with Parliament's right to decide who should form the government.' True, although the modern practice whenever the result of the election is clear is not to await the ceremonial *coup de grace* of a defeat on a vote of confidence but to resign fairly quickly. In general the Canadian practice is to have an interval of about ten days, both for an incoming Prime Minister to undertake the complex calculus involved in cabinet-making and to allow an outgoing government time to clear up routine business. 1957 incidentally was the first occasion when ministers were in most cases persuaded to entrust their official papers to the Public Archives, thus avoiding what had often been in the past systematic destruction to avoid political embarrassment.

But what if Mr St Laurent had hung on? At the best of times it takes a little while to summon the House, partly because members' election expenses have to be filed before they can take the oath, but there would have been little enthusiasm for a Parliament that was required to meet in the sticky heat of an Ottawa summer. After a while Mr Massey may well have had another round of sleepless nights if the session did not get under way fairly soon. And what could a government, many of whose members had fallen in the election, do in the meantime? Unless it could negotiate fairly firm support from the lesser opposition parties it would be bound to risk defeat at the outset of the session. Should Mr Massey be forced to consider refusing ministerial advice (for example involving secure tenured appointments such as those to the bench or the Senate) as happened in 1896, and leading either to the resignation of the government or its dismissal? Clearly Mr St Laurent was right to reject the advice of those of his ministers who wanted to hang on, since it would very likely have led to a messy constitutional crisis.

A rather similar crisis threatened in 1972, although it was closer in its main lines to that of 1926. It was clear that the Liberals had lost their majority, but the Conservatives had failed to make sufficient headway to be winners either. Again Martin gives the inside account:

> Election night was not a happy one. For two days, Robert Stanfield held a one-seat lead, but when the dust finally settled, it was we who had a single seat advantage . . . As in 1957, the cabinet hurriedly met to discuss courses of action, but ministers were undecided on what to do. Once the Tories' one-seat edge had disappeared, we decided to meet parliament and not resign. I had no doubt that this was the right course to take. St Laurent had erred in not doing the same 15 years before.[16]

So conscious is Martin of the rightness of his own preferred tactic in 1957 that he fails to make clear the important difference between the two dates. In 1957 there was no real prospect of the Liberals carrying on with minor party support. In 1972 it was very different. There was only one party to deal with, the New Democratic Party (which had been created out of the old CCF in 1961), and it was possible to arrange a tacit deal for support on the promise of certain legislative measures. And again he harps needlessly on the significance of the one-seat margin over the Conservatives which had been so persuasive in British Columbia in 1952. In the upshot it may as well be noted that the Liberals survived for two years until it became expedient to contrive a defeat in the House,a dissolution, and a restored majority in the subsequent election. The significant thing is that there was no crisis, no anxious moments for the Governor-General, and therefore no head of state role in the matter.

In the same year occurred a more perplexing crisis in Newfoundland. The election left a Liberal government, which had been in power since that Province had entered the Union in 1949, virtually neck-and-neck with the Conservative opposition, while one seat was won by the New Labrador Party. In addition, the results were so close that recounts had been demanded in several seats, and in one of them – St Barbe – this proved to be impossible since one Deputy Returning Officer had (as was her custom) burned the ballots after they had been counted. A good deal of unseemly manoeuvring took place to tempt some elected members to change sides, but in the end the Liberals resigned. The Conservatives took office, but it is clear that they would have lost their majority once they had elected a Speaker. The problem was solved by the new Conservative leader seeking a dissolution on the evening of the first day that the House met. It was granted, and they went on to win the subsequent election.[17] Was the Lieutenant-Governor right to grant the dissolution in these circumstances? It is submitted that he had no choice, for the initial election result seemed to suggest that no stable government, by either party, would have been possible – even for a day.

The most recent constitutional near-crisis was brought about by a provincial general election in Ontario on 2 May 1985. In that province the Conservative Party had been in office for over 40 years. The results were a nasty shock to the party. It elected only 52 members, while the Liberals were close behind with 48, and the NDP clearly held the balance of power with 25. The Conservatives had recently replaced their highly popular leader, William Davis, who had combined emphasis on his small-town origins with an ability to sense which way the wind was blowing and blandly adapt to it. He had a notoriously efficient political machine and had retained support by running a sophisticated and apparently non-political government. His successor lacked both the charm and the political senstitivity of his predecessor, and appeared to represent a swing to the right in the party. His political ineptitude lent a certain air of unpredictability to his actions after the defeat, and added to the general uncertainty.

The NDP had, in its recent history, a peculiarly third-party problem. Twice in the early 1970s – once in Ontario and once in Ottawa – it had held the balance of power. One of the consequences of this kind of stalemate is that a second election shortly after the first is far riskier to third parties, since the reaction of the electorate is to prefer to break the stalemate by voting strongly for what they hope will be a majority party. A minority government which is in control of the timing of the election can create the most favourable political situation and then go to the people. The third party supports the government because it is afraid of an early election, may exact a few legislative concessions, but invariably is massacred in the next election. There was a further difficulty. In

Ottawa in 1972 the NDP had supported the Liberals. In the situation in Ontario in 1985 it would be very difficult to justify supporting the right-leaning Conservatives. In policy terms the Liberals were a better hope. But how to avoid the risk of being badly burned in a quick election?

Naturally speculation was rife, particularly among the media who seem to have learned nothing and remembered nothing from previous situations of this sort. Thus there was much talk of a coalition. But coalitions have a bad name in Canadian political history. One of the most memorable – the Union Government of 1917–1920 – brought deep cleavages in the Liberal Party which took Mackenzie King many years to heal, and was even more damaging to the Conservatives, who even today are having trouble re-establishing a stable base in Quebec as a result of the conscription crisis during the First World War, which also continued to haunt them in the Second. Wartime coalitions in British Columbia and Manitoba did almost irreparable harm to almost all of the participants. No Canadian politician with a knowledge of Canadian history would dream of entering a coalition. The problem for the NDP was to avoid the risks of previous minority situations by finding a way to put off as long as possible the next election and avoid publicly swallowing their principles by supporting an offensive government policy to stave off an election, the date of which was out of their control in any event.

What emerged after some complex and difficult negotiations was a written agreement with the Liberals involving certain policy issues, and an agreement to avoid a government defeat on a vote of confidence for a period of two years. This, however, did not particularly simplify the problem for the Lieutenant-Governor, who was understood to be a very worried man. He was near the end of his normal term of office, which would expire in September 1985, and hitherto his tenure had been a pleasant and uncomplicated one, unclouded by crises or embarrassments.

The affair must have been particularly poignant for John Aird, a lifelong Liberal who had been translated from the comparative peace of the Senate to the Lieutenant-Governship of Ontario – a fitting end to the career of one who had essentially been a backroom politician. What if the worst happened? The unpredictable Frank Miller, the Conservative Premier, might choose to hang on to office, meet the legislature, suffer immediate defeat and then seek a dissolution. This was 1926 all over again. The only difference from 1926 was that that time the Opposition professed to be a government-in-waiting, although they realized that Byng's refusal of a dissolution (which had led to King's resignation) had put them in an awkward tactical situation. In the circumstances the Conservatives had felt that they had a duty to support the Governor-General. In 1985 there was known to be a written agreement between the Liberals and the NDP, so that there was in fact a stable alternative government-in-waiting. However if Aird refused Miller his dissolution, he would be doing to a Conservative Premier what Byng had done to Mackenzie King, and every Liberal had been taught that Mackenzie King was constitutionally correct in arguing that Byng had no such discretion. Any Liberal would be in agony at such a dilemma.

He might have been further dismayed by the argument, put forward in some letters to the editor, that the Liberal–NDP deal was unconstitutional because it fettered the royal prerogative! This rather bizarre argument must have been based on the fallacious belief that the Lieutenant-Governor possessed the power to dissolve the legislature on his own with no ministerial advice needed. Such a belief is nonsense. And the agreement would in no way have prevented a Lieutenant-Governor from dismissing a government if there were grounds for doing so. It will be recalled that Sir John Kerr (wrongly, I think) did dismiss Gough Whitlam on the ground that illegalities would occur in the future if he did not, and then dissolved Parliament on the advice of his newly-commissioned Prime Minister.

As it turned out, none of these terrible things happened. Miller was persuaded (probably by the wiser counsel of some of his advisors) to resign, David Peterson assumed office, and so far at least the agreement seems to hold. Nevertheless, the issues for once were widely discussed, and it is to be hoped that the press has successfully passed a crash-course on this aspect of the Westminster-style constitution. Next time around the politicians and the media will at least know what they are talking about, and that will be a good thing.[18]

Nevertheless, it must be said that the head of state role in the constitution in Canada has suffered considerable attrition since 1926. Nowhere is this more evident than in the once-important role of choosing a Prime Minister. In the last century the only path to legitimacy for a party leader was through the machinery of intra-party democracy. We are a long way from the days when the most legitimate way for a party leader to emerge was through the exercise of the royal prerogative, so that the leader was anointed by something approaching divine grace.

Since the historic Liberal Leadership Convention in 1919, the preferred method of anointing the leader has been by voting delegates in convention, most of whom are elected representatives of constituency parties.[19] Even selection by the parliamentary caucus, either by formal vote or by some mysterious process of 'sounding the caucus', is now out of fashion. The demise of that method is best illustrated in Canada by the last surviving examples of it.

Normally, the selection of a leader by either the caucus or convention method comes about relatively simply when a leader resigns, in most cases at a time convenient for the party to arrange the succession in an orderly manner. This is not the case when a leader dies in office and a vacuum is created at the centre of government which must be filled without delay. This difficult situation arose in Quebec on no less than three occasions in the ten years between 1959 and 1968. All of them happened to the Union Nationale, a nationalist and right-wing party founded by Maurice Duplessis which flourished in Quebec for 35 years, occupying the electoral space previously occupied by the provincial Conservative party.

Duplessis's last term as premier lasted from 1944 until 1959. While touring mining developments in the north of the province he suddenly suffered a stroke which left him paralysed and without the power of speech. Further seizures followed and he finally died on 7 September.[20] Characteristically, he had carefully avoided indicating his choice as successor. Nevertheless, there was an obvious successor in Paul Sauvé, an experienced and successful minister who had the further advantage of comparative youth in what was by that time an ageing ministry. There was widespread speculation that it would be the duty of the cabinet to choose a successor. This was clearly a misapprehension, since the cabinet according to constitutional doctrine ceased to exist with the death of the premier. Nevertheless, it was equally true that individual ministers continued in office and as members of the Executive Council. There were several informal meetings of ministers to consider the situation and to plan funeral arrangements. The last was on the evening of 10 September when the ministers signed a petition to the Lieutenant-Governor asking him to call upon Mr Sauvé to form a government. This was subsequently approved by the Union Nationale caucus and formally presented to the Lieutenant-Governor, who then sent for Mr Sauvé. The whole process had the appearance of denying the prerogative altogether.

Paul Sauvé, whose premiership seemed to herald a rejuvenation of the party and the government, lasted in office for about a hundred days, when he too succumbed to a heart attack on 2 January, 1960. This time ministers knew what to do, but there was an important difference. There was no agreement on an obvious successor. At least four ministers were rumoured to be candidates. To avoid disunity there were suggestions for an interim premier and a caretaker government pending a party convention. In the end all of the candidates save one, Antonio Barette, withdrew so that the ministers presented an unanimous recommendation to caucus. There was more difficulty, but finally caucus agreed. However unhappy they might have been, there was no way of forcing a leadership contest if the contestants refused to remain in the field. In the event, Mr Barette's tenure was brief and he led the party to defeat in the next election.

However the party was not free of problems in managing its leadership succession. The party recovered from its defeat and returned to office in 1966 under the leadership of Daniel Johnson. For all his skill, Johnson was not in office long enough to complete the restoration and modernisation of the party. He too died of a heart attack in 1968, and the party proceeded to choose a successor by a process with which they had now become all too familiar. But there was a difference. The new Premier, Jean-Jacques Bertrand, moved swiftly to arrange a party leadership convention to confirm his leadership. Thus the North American style of leadership convention finally came to embrace the last significant adherent to an older style of leadership selection.

One can conclude therefore that even in the case of the most significant symbolic role of the head of state – the designation and legitimation of the party leader – the spread of twentieth century democratic values had tended to erode at least the public perception of the role. In all of the various episodes above there was at least a symbolic, and in some cases possibly a constructive role for the head of state in Canada. However the public perception of matters was so managed that it was hardly noticed and made to appear automatic. What that implies if a genuine and serious constitutional crisis should arise in the future is not easy to predict.

Notes

1. Quoted in Roger Graham, *Arthur Meighen. Vol. 2. And Fortune Fled* (Toronto, 1963), p. 415. This is a sympathetic, but full and careful biography of Meighen. The best and most authoritative account of the crisis is still Eugene Forsey, *The Royal Power of Dissolution of Parliament in the British Commonwealth* (Toronto, 1943).
2. Eugene Forsey, 'Parliamentary Reform is More than Mechanics' in John C. Courtney (ed.), *The Canadian House of Commons: Essays in Honour of Norman Ward* (Calgary: The University of Calgary Press, 1985), p. 197.

3. *Reference re Legislative Authority of Parliament to Alter or Replace the Senate*. [1980] 1 S.C.R. 54.
4. K. C. Wheare, *Federal Government*, Third Edition (London, 1953), p. 20.
5. Public Archives of Canada, *King Diary* (May 18, 1938), pp. 471–4.
6. G. V. LaForest, *Disallowance and Reservation of Provincial Legislation* (Department of Justice, Ottawa, 1955), p. 46.
7. An account of the episode is in Frank MacKinnon, *The Government of Prince Edward Island* (Toronto: University of Toronto Press, 1951), pp. 155 ff. The case is *Gallangt* v. *the King* (1949) 2 D.L.R. 425.
8. This episode is dealt with in J. R. Mallory, 'The Lieutenant-Governor's Discretionary Powers,' *Canadian Journal of Economics and Political Science* XXVII:4 (Nov. 1961), p. 518.
9. *Reference re Dissalowance and Reservation* (1938) S.C.R. 71 at p. 95.
10. H. F. Angus, 'The British Columbia Election, June, 1952,' *Canadian Journal of Economics and Political Science* XVIII:4 (Nov. 1952), p. 518.
11. Angus, op. cit., p. 521.
12. *Ibid.*
13. *Ibid.*, p. 524.
14. Paul Martin, *A Very Public Life. Volume II: So Many Worlds*. (Toronto, 1985), p. 305.
15. *Ibid.*
16. *Ibid.*, pp. 674–5.
17. The whole affair is fully described in Peter Neary, 'Changing Government: The 1971–72 Newfoundland Example,' *Dalhousie Law Journal* V:3 (Nov. 1979), pp. 631–57.
18. A briefer account of this episode is contained in J. R. Mallory, 'An Affair of Discretion,' *Queen's Quarterly* 92/4 (Winter, 1985), p. 758. The two-year negotiated truce did last. Shortly thereafter Premier Peterson sought a dissolution of the legislature, and the results of the general election of 10 September produced the following result in a slightly enlarged House: Liberal 95, NDP 19, Progressive Conservative 16 – total 130. The Liberals thus obtained an overwhelming majority, the NDP suffered the inevitable post-minority loss but gained the position of 'official' opposition. The devastated Conservatives fell to third place.
19. John C. Courtney, *The Selection of National Party Leaders in Canada* (Toronto, 1973).
20. Some of these matters are described more fully in J. R. Mallory, 'The Royal Prerogative in Canada: The Selection of Successors to Mr Duplessis and Mr Sauvé,' *Canadian Journal of Economics and Political Science* XXVI:2 (May, 1960), p. 314.

Appendix: A List of Episodes

The following is an outline list of occasions since the Second World War when a constitutional head in the Commonwealth has been involved in decision-making or when a constitutional head's position has been in issue. For earlier occasions reference may be made to A. Todd, *Parliamentary Government in the Colonies* (2nd. ed. London 1984), A. B. Keith, *Responsible Government in the Dominions* (2nd. ed. London 1928), H. V. Evatt, *The King and his Dominion Governors* (London 1936), W. I. Jennings, *Cabinet Government* (Cambridge 1936), and E. A. Forsey, *The Royal Power of Dissolution of Parliament in the British Commonwealth* (Toronto 1943). The list does not include the many occasions when President's rule has been declared at state level in India, nor the no less frequent occasions there when a Governor's discretion has been politically important or called in question, especially when a state has had a 'hung parliament': for these many additional Indian instances see for example, B. D. Dua, *Presidential Rule in India 1950–1974*, Delhi 1979, J. R. Siwach, *The Office of Governor*, Delhi 1977, M. S. Dahiya, *Office of the Governor in India*, Delhi 1979. More generally the list does not include those occasions when constitutional change or *coup d'etat* have led to the supersession of constitutional headship and the establishment of an executive presidency; nor those occasions when Governments or their heads have changed without the head of state's discretion being called upon; nor the many dissolutions of Parliament granted without significant public controversy:

1945 Australia (Prime Minister's death in office).
1945 Victoria, Australia (Hung Parliament and eventual Dissolution).
1945 Prince Edward Island, Canada (Withholding of consent to Bill).
1951 Australia (Disputed request for 'Double' Dissolution)
1952 Ceylon (now Sri Lanka) (Prime Ministers' death in office)
1952 British Columbia, Canada (Hung Parliament and further Dissolution)
1952 Victoria, Australia (Supersession of short-term Premier and Dissolution)
1953 Pakistan (Dismissal of Prime Minister)
1954 East Pakistan (Dismissal of Chief Minister)
1954 Pakistan (Dissolution of Constitutional Assembly–Legislature)
1957 Britain (Choice of Prime Minister)
1958 East Pakistan (Dismissal of Governor)
1958 South Africa (Prime Minister's death in office)
1959 Quebec, Canada (Premier's death in office)
1959–60 Ceylon (now Sri Lanka) (Prime Minister's death in office and two disputed Dissolutions)
1960 Quebec, Canada (Premier's death in office)
1961 Saskatchewan, Canada (Reservation of Bill for Federal decision)
1962 Ceylon (Replacement of Governor-General following abortive *coup*)
1962 Western Nigeria (Dismissal of Premier)

1963 Britain (Choice of Prime Minister)
1963 Perak, Malaysia (Dispute with State Government)
1963 Selangor, Malaysia (Dispute with State Government)
1964 India (Prime Minister's death in office)
1965 Rhodesia (Unilateral Declaration of Independence)
1966 Sarawak, Malaysia (Dismissal of Chief Minister)
1966 India (Prime Minister's death in office)
1967 Jamaica, West Indies (Prime Minister's death in office)
1967 Australia (Prime Minster's death in office)
1967 Grenada, West Indies (Governor pressured to resign)
1968 Canada (Special vote of confidence following Government's Budget defeat)
1968 Quebec, Canada (Premier's death in office)
1969 Malaysia (State of Emergency)
1969 St Kitts/Nevis/Anguilla, West Indies (Governor's resignation after unwillingness to accept tendered advice)
1971–72 Newfoundland, Canada (Hung Parliament and disputed second Dissolution)
1974 Australia ('Double' Dissolution)
1974 Grenada, West Indies (Removal of Governor-General on Independence)
1975 Queensland, Australia (Withdrawal of Governor's Commission to act for Governor-General)
1975 Australia (Dismissal of Prime Minister and 'Double' Dissolution)
1975 Western Samoa, South West Pacific (Prime Minister's death in office)
1977 Kelantan, Malaysia (Refusal of Dissolution)
1977 Fiji, South West Pacific (Reinstallation of defeated Prime Minister)
1977 Australia (Governor-General's premature resignation)
1977 Papua New Guinea, South West Pacific (Governor-General's premature resignation)
1978 Grenada, West Indies (Governor's premature retirement)
1978 Cook Islands, South West Pacific (Replacement of Prime Minister following judicial decision against him)
1978 Pahang, Malaysia (Choice of Chief Minister)
1978 Johore, Malaysia (Removal of Chief Minister)
1978 Perak, Malaysia (Removal of Chief Minister)
1979 St Lucia, West Indies (Governor-General pressured to resign)
1979 India (Installation of Prime Minister without parliamentary vote)
1979–81 Pahang, Malaysia (Refusal to sign money bills)
1981 St Kitts/Nevis, West Indies (Dismissal of Governor)
1982 Canada (Governor-General's reference to 'causing an election')
1982 St Lucia, West Indies (Dismissal of Governor-General)
1982 Selangor, Malaysia (Uncertainty over Chief Minister's appointment)
1982 Western Samoa, South West Pacific (Election petition against Prime Minister and replacement by Opposition Leader)
1983 Grenada, West Indies (Murder of Prime Minister and US invasion)
1983 Bermuda, West Indies (Governor's resignation following alleged financial indiscretions)
1983 Queensland, Australia (Refusal of Ministerial resignations)

1983–84 Malaysia (Refusal to sign legislation)
1984 Solomon Islands, South West Pacific (Retrospective validation of Government)
1984 Turks and Caicos Islands, West Indies (Dismissal of Chief Minister following arrest on drug charges)
1984 India (Prime Minster's death in office)
1985 Sabah, Malaysia (Two installations of Chief Ministers in 24 hours)
1985 Canada (Dispute over reception of U.S. President)
1985 Victoria, Australia (Governor's resignation following alleged financial indiscretions)
1985 Western Samoa, South West Pacific (two refusals of Dissolution)
1986 Britain (Queen's alleged concern about Commonwealth divisions over South African sanctions)
1986 Turks and Caicos Islands, West Indies (Chief Minister's resignation and suspension of Constitution)
1987 India (Public disagreements between President and Prime Minister)
1987 Fiji (Governor General's intervention in military *coup*, and Queen's involvement)

Index*

*Compiled by Richard Wright.